Why
We're
EQUAL

Also by Val Webb,
published by Chalice Press

In Defense of Doubt:
An Invitation to Adventure

Why We're EQUAL

Introducing Feminist Theology

VAL WEBB

Chalice Press
St. Louis, Missouri

All scripture quotations, unless otherwise indicated, are from the *New Revised Standard Version Bible,* copyright 1989, Division of Christian Education of the National Council of Churches of Christ in the USA. Used by permission.

Cover design: Elizabeth Wright
Art direction: Michael Domínguez
Interior design: Elizabeth Wright

This book is printed on acid-free, recycled paper.

Visit Chalice Press on the World Wide Web at
www.chalicepress.com

10   9   8   7   6   5   4   3   2   1   99   00   01   02   03   04

Library of Congress Cataloging–in–Publication Data

Webb, Val.

    Why we're equal : introducing feminist theology / by Val Webb.

    p.   cm.

    Includes bibliographical references.

    ISBN 0-8272-4240-9

    1. Feminist theology.   I. Title   II. Title: Why we are equal

BT83.55.W43   1999   98–43562

230'.082–dc21   CIP

Printed in the United States of America

CONTENTS

PREFACE

The worst part about writing the preface to a book—which ironically is done *after* the book is finished to explain what you did and didn't do—is realizing how much you left out. Why I ever imagined I could "introduce feminist theology" and explain "why we're equal" in one slim volume amazes me! I have therefore made choices, geared around the initial idea of providing a "user-friendly" glimpse at what women have brought to theology and the church over the last thirty-some years—not just theologians and clergy, but lay women as well who have claimed their voice as wise women of God. As I sit in church pews and participate in discussion groups, however, I am still appalled at how little of this liberating breath of fresh air has infiltrated many local worshiping communities. Lay folk still struggle with conflicting messages about women from biblical texts and outdated theologies, with little help from anyone to see things from a new perspective. The snippets about feminist theology they do hear or read more often than not create fear rather than inspiration, because no one has taken the time to expose the deep roots of women's subordination in church and life!

While this book was percolating in my mind, I had a phone call from a woman lawyer, a member of a congregation that did not encourage women to preach or take leadership roles in worship. She had made one presentation from the pulpit, but this had been carefully billed as *not* a sermon. Her professional background rejected such arbitrary differentiation between sexes, yet she had to abide by such interpretations of scripture—or leave. Seeing inconsistencies in the use of biblical texts, she battled ambivalence within herself because her life experiences of women's abilities and worth did not agree with how a "Christian woman" was being described. She asked me to recommend a book on feminism to share with folk in her church, a book that would explain the issues without antagonizing defensive members into automatic resistance. I could not find one that met *her* practical need, despite many texts on feminist theology, so I decided to put my own thoughts on paper. I'm not sure if I have succeeded, but certainly my intent has been not to alienate Christian women and men but to encourage them to make an honest journey with me. *My* responsibility along the way is to present as much helpful scholarship as will fit into one volume, not to tell you how you *should* think, but to persuade you to think *seriously,* with an openness to new directions and challenges. The study questions can be used in private reading, or in a discussion group, to invite further reflection.

As I was nearing the end of the book, having been immersed up to my ears in the arguments for months, I began to wonder how people could even *contemplate* that women were subordinate on the threshold of the twenty-first century. I had certainly convinced *myself* all over again of the scandal of it all! Two things happened to reconfirm the timely relevance of this book. The Southern Baptist Convention overwhelmingly voted to add to their official statement of beliefs that "a wife should submit graciously to the servant leadership of her husband"; and two of the bright young women students at the University of Minnesota became quite defensive in my seminar on feminist theology because their "litmus test" for the "truth" of anything I said was that it fitted with the "divine rule" that women should submit to their husbands. The time is ripe to take a serious look at the verses under which these promising young women are about to spend their adult lives!

Much of the writing about women's equality in the church has been in connection with women's ordination. I have only mentioned that in passing, since there are already many books that deal with that issue. I also have a concern that, when church women think about feminist theology or women and the church, they *assume* it applies to women clergy and not them, thus denying them once again new ways to think about themselves and their role. And they are perhaps right in many cases, given the way things are played out in congregations. Since the ordained ministry is one of the most patriarchal systems remaining in our society, many women who finally *enter* the ranks feel the victory has been won. However, torn between what is expected of them as clergy loyal to the system and what they believe as advocates for women, the institution that controls their hard-won career often wins. Many traditional doctrines that feminist theologians challenge are still central to denominational statements of faith that women clergy must uphold, and many biblical arguments used for the "difference" between clergy and laity are ones that have also perpetuated divisions between men and women. I am convinced, along with many other feminist theologians, that it is *ordination* as an institution, not just women's ordination, that needs a closer, critical look—but that is another book! For now, my concern is that women—and men—*in the pews* become equipped with arguments that help them articulate feelings they already intuitively have—that we are *all* equal in the sight of God and no amount of theological justification to the contrary can change this fact. It is the very *heart* of the Christian tradition proclaiming liberty to the captives, freedom to the oppressed, and inclusion of the weakest and most downtrodden.

One of the difficulties of talking about feminism is that, because it suggests women can make life choices and *also* be mothers—as men have careers and *also* are fathers—it "smells" of antimotherhood. Although I do not talk much about "feminist" motherhood in this book—that is a *third* book—I will don my "mother" hat for a few moments. My personal challenge as a Christian woman has always been to "live abundantly," to relish all that God offers, and desires, in this good creation. One of the greatest experiences of "abundant living" has been a long marriage that has transformed the lives of both of us and allowed both our spirits to soar. Our three children, and now their spouses and children, teach us something new each day about what it means to love and be loved. My careers in science, art, business, and theology, and our family passion for peace and justice that has taken us around the world and also inspired us to work locally, have enriched *their* lives as well as ours. Being a mother is not just about food and shelter, but about inspiring those you love to live lives that constantly transform them and others. Mothers who love their children as *unique* human beings, not just extensions of themselves through whom they live vicariously, need to model this, especially to daughters, by taking *themselves* seriously as unique human beings with gifts from God not *limited* to the still necessary tasks of laundering clothes and carpooling. If we want our children to believe they can be all they are called to be, our personal demonstration of that truth as *our* way of life will speak louder than words!

Speaking of those who support and enrich my life, my thanks go to all those who allowed this book to happen:

To my mother Joan Skerman, who raised two feminist daughters, before she or we realized it, by living creatively through everything she did; and to my father Perce (who died as this book was being completed), who demonstrated the value of women by encouraging our education to the highest levels.

To my "Theology for the Nineties" class at Christ United Methodist Church, Rochester, Minnesota, a group of inspiring, stimulating, rebellious women—and men—from many walks of life and with loads of wisdom, on whom I test my ideas each Friday and who continually nurture my spirit.

To my editor David Polk and his colleagues at Chalice Press, who believed I had *another* book in me after *In Defense of Doubt: An Invitation to Adventure* and who cheerfully prompted me until it was done.

To my children, Helen, Paul, and Karen and their families, who phone, write, call, visit, and love me from many parts of the world, assuring me that they didn't suffer *too* much when I read a book while changing their diapers or continued a theological argument through three courses of dinner!

To my first granddaughter Rhys, whose presence in my life, with all the enthusiasm, joy, trust, and wonder that shines out of her beautiful one year old eyes, has made me even more determined that the world we leave for her as a woman will be just, fulfilling, and peaceful.

To my husband Maurice, who somehow maintains his enthusiasm and affirmation for everything I try to do even after more than thirty years of my evolving feminism—probably because he is one of the greatest feminists, and humans, I have ever met! Thanks for filling my life with joy and being my best friend!

And now to you, my readers. You have honored me by committing this time to read my musings. I have tried not to give a one-argument, surefire set of "proof texts" to convince you of the blessings of feminist theology, but rather to surround you with many, many women who believed in their heritage as God's creatures enough to act, whatever their limitations. I hope their combined voices will urge you to find your place amongst them and change our world, so that never again will our daughters and granddaughters want for strong women role models. Hang in there when my arguments get a little more difficult! Doctrines that have managed to convince women for centuries that their voice is less legitimate than men's have been woven very tightly and need much unraveling to tease out all the knots. When you are done, and you see yourself as a bead on that string of beads called feminism, encourage a friend to read the book as well, so the string becomes longer and longer and reaches around the world!

CHAPTER 1

I'm Not a Feminist But . . .

A few weeks after I was awarded my Ph.D. degree, my husband and I climbed into a taxi in Denver to go to the famous Tattered Cover Bookstore. The taxi driver addressed my husband as if I was not present: "That's a great bookstore. Get her in there, and she'll get lost. You won't have to give her money to go shopping in the mall across the road!"

Feminism is a dirty word in many circles. I have often titled workshops on feminism "the dreaded F word." When audiences realize I'm not going to mention *that* word, "feminism" is a considerable relief! This way I gain a toehold into the lecture before the defensive bristles and negative mental images form about "feminism." There are those who will immediately assume I am antimen and scramble for their programs for indications of my marital state. It helps hold the audience if I mention my husband in the first few minutes!

Antifeminist feeling comes in many forms. Some young career women see "feminists" as a pathetic, aging breed clinging to the past. I remember biting my often unruly lip at a dinner party. A thirty-something woman with two children, a Ph.D., and a well-established career, held forth in a disparaging voice about "feminism," as if it was some highly contagious disease. *She* had never had a problem in her career, and those who did created their own problems. I longed to remind her that if women of the sixties, her mother's generation, had not put themselves on the line, demanded childcare, sought entry to exclusively male professions, and fought for places in graduate school, she could not have established an academic career by her late twenties and raised two children as well. It's like a nose-ringed teenager telling Rosa Parks it's not such a big deal to sit in the front of a bus!

1

Others respond with a hesitant phrase, "I'm not a feminist, but…" They believe in the issues of women and promote them in their own way, yet don't want to be associated with "bra-burning, angry radicals" and other feminist images the media and others cleverly construct to make ordinary people feel uncomfortable. I'm not saying such feminists don't exist. They do. But that is not the only breed of feminist. There are also many people who claim to be "Christian" and promote their ideas on TV with whom *I* am uncomfortable sharing a label! Feminists come in many colors and styles—like Christians! The "I'm not a feminist, but…" group think we should have a new word for feminism, but why should a noble movement in history be disguised because some defame its label? Methodists could have abandoned that derogatory nickname which John Wesley and his friends earned at Oxford University for their "methodical" study of the Bible before dawn and stringent discipline throughout the day, yet they embraced it for their movement.

Negativity toward "feminism," in whatever form it takes, has to do with our habit of naming the "other"—the opposition or enemy—as bad. We do it all the time. As a child, the food I loved more than anything else was pickled relish. (I love you, Mom!—She tires of examples from my childhood that involve her!) I exasperated my mother because, rather than spreading a thin layer over the meat in a sandwich, I ate the relish straight from the bottle, or at least made it the leading act of the sandwich. Store-bought relish was a luxury in those days. I remember my mother warning me that too much pickled relish would give me an ulcer, or worse. It was effective. I began to see pickles as the enemy, even though I craved them. I envisaged a massive rotting process in my stomach, each spoonful threatening to perforate my intestine. Of course, being from a good Calvinist home, I was able to understand that things I liked most were usually sinful, so went lightly on pickles as a religious exercise as well! My mother has no recollection of all this. Like most crises children remember, it probably happened once, on a day when the relish jar was empty before dinner. However, I still have vaguely ambivalent feelings in the presence of pickled relish.

The issue of negative naming is larger than pickles. Naming the "other" as bad or the enemy destroys people and nations. When indigenous cultures are called "primitive," teenagers with green spiked hair labeled "problems," and nations other than our own dismissed as "undemocratic," they are being negatively classified against those with the power to classify, who, of course, epitomize the good, the correct, the norm. Collectively naming the "other" as bad makes it easier to justify aggression toward them. I remember being jolted into reality during Desert Storm when the TV briefly showed the Baghdad Symphony Orchestra, handsome, talented people in tuxedos playing *our* classical music with great sensitivity and skill just like us! Yet "Iraqis" as a race had become the metaphor for evil, "the enemy," and therefore not capable of such beauty and culture in our perception. I am not denying problematic aspects of

Iraqi international politics, but to portray a nation as "evil" does not account for people themselves—a mix of good and bad, appropriate and inappropriate, creative and fanatic, brash and gentle, sensible and silly.

Feminism has been named "bad" by many, as if it is a collective, homogenous whole exemplified by disquieting stereotypes of certain women or behavior. As a result, the label makes some folk uncomfortable, others down-right defensive, others vitriolic, as if any who associate with the label are automatically evil. Some of you will have dragged your stereotypes into place as you read. Yet changing the word is not the solution. Any word for any movement that challenges the status quo will soon be trashed by those it threatens. New names simply divert opposition for a while until these also come under attack.

The goal of this book is to look at the diversity of the feminist movement and show how limited and inaccurate negative stereotyping is. I want to introduce you to an infinite variety of "feminists" and a plethora of feminist issues, some even in conflict with each other. The feminist movement is broader than a label and older than a recent trend. It spans history and involves people like our mothers, our aunts, our cousins, our heroes and heroines, and our best friends, even though they might balk at being called feminist! I hope in the following chapters to develop a "user-friendly" feminism for both men and women, so it can be redeemed and celebrated in our history and churches, allowing even closet feminists to proudly declare who they are.

I have moderated a local theology class for many years, mostly pre–Baby Boomer, college-trained women who, for the most part, have been traditional wives and mothers. At the first session, I suggested we talk about feminism. Some shuffled uncomfortably, some were suspicious, and others politely expressed frustration that they had been enticed into a "feminist trap" under the guise of "Bible study." To diffuse the uneasiness, I asked them to brainstorm about what they thought feminism was. The usual images emerged—aggressive women, bitches, angry antimale troublemakers—even though few personally knew anyone thus described. The media had done its task of negative naming well!

As we talked in the following weeks, the mood changed. For starters, these women knew me well in other settings and realized the stereotypes didn't fit me—well, not all of them! They knew my husband well enough to know he was not a whimpering, idiotic mess as a result of living with me. At first, some sheltered their inner feelings behind the "I'm not a feminist, but…" line. Then, as we talked of injustices to women and their exclusion throughout history, how systems of male privilege had worked against them, and how the remnants of these systems—assumptions of different behavioral standards for men and women—still color our contemporary language, Pandora's box opened. We had to take numbers to speak! Frustration and anger surfaced about artificially created codes that controlled their lives as they realized how subtle and complex the rules had been and their innocent complicity in their situation. Predictable guilt followed every confession, the guilt of "disloyalty." Questioning the system had been equated with criticism of husbands with whom they lived good lives and accepted society's rules for "good" marriages and "family values." The realization that they had been trapped in a system that demanded a restricted role of them in the relationship dawned slowly—or rather, emerged at last from the deep soul prison in which the rebellious feelings were incarcerated. It is this ambivalence, these mixed messages with which such women—and their men—have been assigned to live, that feminism challenges.

Unfortunately, many of these mixed messages come from Bible stories, absorbed since childhood on the assumption that biblical culture can simply be transposed into today's society as "rules" for living. We do not do this with other stories. While Shakespeare had an uncanny ability to describe human nature, we appreciate his insights without adopting the social mores of Olde England or the difficult language patterns, which have to be interpreted for us. The difference, of course, is that we believe biblical stories incorporate the wisdom of *God,* and so we uncritically apply ancient Hebrew social codes and purity laws along with the "good news." Many women realize these biblically prescribed "God-given" roles have not always matched their inner yearnings for fulfillment, yet they have learned to accept them, conforming their wills in Christian duty regardless of the fit. The notion of rebellion as "sinful" has assisted this process. Often they cannot quite put a finger on the discrepancy between the external and internal messages, but they know it is there.

Last year I was booked months ahead to speak at a church women's event on women. The program committee selected a "generic" title about women for their advance publicity. Not surprisingly, it was "Mary and Martha." Although this Bible story (Lk. 10:38–42), where Jesus brings his followers to Martha's home, produces ambivalent feelings in women, it is the one clergy most often use for Women's Sunday, with stereotypical contrasts between good and bad women, right and wrong actions. Mary traditionally is the "good" one who chose the better way—sitting and listening at Jesus' feet. She embodies the Catholic contemplative woman "religious" as opposed to the "non religious" Marthas who are mothers, wives, housekeepers, and caregivers. Mary's concerns are "spiritual" rather than "mundane," the eternal dualism that grades one experience better than the other. Martha by default is the domestic one, the one that did *not* choose "the better way." The usual message is for Marthas to stop fussing over trivial things when the opportunity for spiritual "food" is present.

Yet this message flies in the face of reality for most church women over fifty. Their designated roles from time immemorial have been running the church kitchen, staffing the nursery, cleaning and decorating the sanctuary, and generally being "wife and mother" to church, pastor, and male committees.

Often they do not get to worship, answering phones, minding children, preparing refreshments so others can. Yet this story chides them for not sitting at Jesus' feet. It suggests they should not do dishes during the sermon, even though women know what will happen if the kitchen is not cleaned when everyone wants to leave, and the custodian needs to lock the building! As one "backbone" of the church described her feelings, the domestic "Martha" role is relegated to her gender whether she prefers it or not, and if she doesn't accept it, the job won't get done, and she will be blamed for aspiring to the other! Christian women are assigned caretaking roles as "natural" for them, but scolded for choosing them when the opposite is better!

Feminist biblical scholars, realizing the tension between how this story is interpreted and how women feel, have looked more closely at this story and the society in which it is set, discovering features ignored for centuries that suggest other ways to "read" it. The house was *Martha's* house—unusual, because her brother Lazarus also lived there. As *head* of the household, she was host to her visitors, who probably were there, not just for a snack, but accommodation as well. Her "many tasks"—organizing servants to prepare food and rooms—were far greater than "rattling pots and pans in the kitchen," as one pastor of mine always caricatured Martha. She had good reason to be annoyed at Mary's lack of help.

The bigger question is why this story was included in the Bible. It is *only* in Luke's Gospel. What was happening in the community to which this Gospel was addressed that might give us clues about how to read this story? The Gospel of Luke was written toward the end of the first century, when a debate was raging over women leaders in house-churches. It will only be a few decades before women are totally removed from the church leadership they enjoyed since the early days. The Greek word *diakonia* used to describe Martha's busyness means "service or ministration," the *same* word used by the early church for the house-church leader's role—presiding over the supper and preaching. Luke tells the story, carefully distinguishing between Martha's role of serving—*diakonia*—and Mary's role of listening. Mary's choice is praised and defended over Martha's distracted and anxious serving. The readers of this Gospel, knowing the pressure to remove women from leadership, would catch the drift of the story. Listening was the *better* way for women, as opposed to a leadership role Martha had assumed in her house.

To see the story in *this* context puts an entirely different slant on it and offers a bigger canvas than two squabbling women! Martha, as a symbol of women resisting subtle exclusion from leadership, is a model for women today, who protest *whatever* excludes, harms, or disadvantages them. Martha will not be silenced by the institution or powers that be, despite darkening clouds of opposition forming around her and against her legitimacy. When we see her anger in this larger setting, we can return to the house where Mary still sits silent and look at these women in a new light. The ambivalence women have felt in this story is that *Martha* is the one with whom they identify—a practical woman with a justifiable complaint that should have gained Jesus' support. She is angry. Who wouldn't be! Yet *Mary* is usually praised as the "good woman." We can now read the story as a struggle for justice and equality wrongly being taken away. Women *must* become angry in the face of injustice, and not sit silent and obediently still. The task of biblical scholars is to dig like this behind traditional interpretations of biblical stories that reinforce certain roles for women in society, in order to determine what was *really* meant by the new way of Jesus.

One thing needs to be clarified from the start. There is a difference between biology and gender. Biology is the observable, physical fact that women and men are different. We learn this early, much to parental consternation when the discovery is made with loud comment in public places. I remember hastily leaving a tour in an Athens museum when our small children insisted on touching, inspecting closely, and discussing at the top of their voices certain appendages—or absence thereof—on ancient marble statues. But there is something we also learn early that is more subtle. We learn there are characteristics that are "nice" in little girls and others only "proper" in little boys, the gendered rules society has created about how we should behave.

This gendering of roles and behavior is at last being challenged, thanks to "angry feminists." No matter how much we want to believe changes in cultural myths happen by themselves "in good time," it is historical fact that significant change emerges only through overt, often radical rebellion. The civil rights movement did not happen because nice white folk realized one morning over cornflakes that they had behaved horrendously toward half of America despite a Constitution declaring that all people were created equal. It happened when Rosa Parks *applied* the Constitution's claims to *herself* and sat in the front of the bus. Many had to go to prison and die before nice white church folk did anything.

The problem with gendering society—naming what men and women can acceptably do—is that those with authority to name can assign roles other than their own as subordinate, a "natural law" written in permanent ink in the universe. Take the quality of virtue. We think of a virtuous man as a powerful, single-minded, courageous person, the hero image of literature who rides off to save the world before returning home to a wife waiting for him. Now, let's apply that same image to a woman. Is a virtuous woman a powerful, independent heroine who leaves home to save the world while her husband awaits her return? I imagine the local diner crowd would have a different slant on that woman's "virtue"! Virtue for women is described in *opposite* terms to men in a society where men lead and women support. Women's "virtue" is defined in relation to the *man*—sexually pure, faithful, and modest, with qualities of submissiveness or "servanthood"—meekness, gentleness, patience, soft-spokenness, others before self. Male "virtue," on the other hand, praises independence and individuality without reference to wife or family, and often over such attachments, like wandering Greek heroes, American cowboys, and workaholic CEOs.

During my late-blooming evolution into feminism many years ago, I visited Australia, my country of origin, and dined with old friends. During the evening, the husband did most of the talking, using negative Australian stereotypes about blacks, foreigners, and women and expecting the usual laughs. After a while, I challenged these assumptions, not in a confrontational way, but as a contribution to the conversation. My host said, "What's happened to you, Val? You've become an angry radical. You used to be such a nice, quiet, happy little thing." I had upset the rules by daring to shrug off the feminine virtues assigned to me.

Anger is a major problem for women. They have been taught that female anger is not "nice." For example, a congressman rolls the text of his speech into a baton and bangs it on the podium for emphasis, raising his voice in passionate anger about something he perceives is wrong with the world. Listener response is good. This strong man is committed to challenging the evils of the world, and thus worth voting for. If a congresswoman used the same body language, we would feel uncomfortable—*we*, because women feel embarrassed when other women break "nice woman" rules. Such body language in men denotes strength and passion, but in women it is considered brash, aggressive, bitchy, angry—certainly "not nice." Angry men are heroes who change the world; angry women are "radical feminists." Such gendering of behavior disadvantages women who must compete for votes in an open forum, yet avoid tactics proven to be vote winners in a male-oriented system. Only one type of anger is condoned in women—the animal fury of a mother whose offspring is threatened or wronged. This anger is acceptable and noble because it lies within the role society has approved for women—the good mother.

Negative press about feminism, especially in the church, plays on the "angry woman" image. Feminists are billed as women who hate men and want to destroy the family by reneging on motherhood as their "natural" lifework. Somehow, women questioning a society that defines them *exclusively* as mothers, but does not define men *exclusively* as fathers, are seen as opposing motherhood *and* men! What is going on? Feminism is not *against* motherhood. The vast majority of feminists *are* mothers and see that role as one of the most rewarding and important in their life, but not their *only* role. Feminist mothers *and* fathers seek the wholeness of *each* human, male and female, and think of women as both mothers *and* people who contribute varied gifts to society, just as men are both fathers *and* people who contribute varied gifts to society. This leads to wholeness for men as well, encouraging them to value their parental role as much as their career role. It also allows women to be viewed as full human beings if they choose not to, or cannot, reproduce, rather than something less than complete. Feminism is not simply about changing "him" and "his" to "them" and "their," and "man" to "people" or "human beings." That is the tip of the iceberg. Rather, it challenges the *whole* iceberg of assumptions that include and exclude men and women by naming acceptable, limited roles for each.

Men who realize feminism also liberates them to live as whole people, free of defining roles, are great feminists. Take my husband—figuratively, I mean! He was raised by a widowed mother and survived my feminism. As a gynecologist, he spends his professional time caring for women. However, he *first* named his inherent belief in the equal value and abilities of men and women "feminist" as his daughters approached adulthood. When he saw these beautiful, talented women whom he has adored since birth and put through college and graduate school suddenly hindered by subtle male and female codes, the injustice became "outrageous." He, like many others, recognized that when women are excluded from all-male professional clubs, or treated marginally if they join, the issue is not militant women invading the sacred space of poor, hen-pecked males. Such "good old boys" clubs have long been places where business deals, networking, and positioning for professional success happen, and the exclusion of women denies women this essential professional advantage in the workplace.

What then is feminism, and why is it a problem? My *Webster's New Universal Unabridged Dictionary* says feminism is:

(a) The theory that women should have political, economic and social rights equal to those of men
(b) The movement to win such rights for women
(c) Feminine qualities.[1]

A "feminist," male or female, is "an advocate or supporter of feminism." There seems little to argue with here! *The Encyclopedia of Feminism* says feminism is not a homogeneous movement, but includes in its "widest possible definition" all that is now, and has been, called feminism:

> We may call feminist anyone who recognizes women's subordination and seeks to end it, by whatever means and on whatever grounds. This includes every shade of political thought along the scale from liberal feminists who believe their demands for equality can be met without otherwise changing the structure of society, to those lesbian feminists who propose that all power be put into the hands of women and men reduced to no more than ten percent of the population. Anti-sexist men are included herein, revolutionaries, reactionaries, scholars, artists, activists, and even women who say "I'm not a feminist, but…"[2]

This "I'm not a feminist, but…" Syndrome earned a separate entry defining it as follows:

> Mental state of women who have become aware that sexism exists, that they suffer from it, and that feminism—or something exactly like it but

preferably with a different name—must be necessary, yet are afraid of being mistaken for one of the ugly, humorless, dogmatic, man-hating lesbians who are labeled feminists.[3]

One point I wish to make loudly and clearly through this book is that feminism covers a multitude of actions and ideas that work toward women's being fully recognized as part of the history of the human race, and against assumptions that exclude women or recognize the male as the norm for humanity. Feminism is the plethora of movements throughout history that have advocated the belief that women should have rights equal to men's, not just those assigned to them over against men. If the claim that women have been excluded from history sounds dramatic, think about it! We gaze uncritically at "Old Masters" dominating art museums around the world, never questioning the unspoken message that great women painters were nonexistent before the twentieth century. We measure the progress of nationhood by the achievements of founding fathers and military heroes, as if male pursuits *alone* accounted for the shape and continuity of society. The courage, pain, suffering, uncertainty, and death of women in childbirth alone—that essential act of replenishing rather than destroying the human race—must surely have equaled, if not exceeded, the trauma encountered by men in war, yet this chronicle of women's courage has never been recorded, even in a small volume, despite tomes of war history lining library shelves around the world. And what of women writers? The church fathers forbade women to write, in case their writings might be used to instruct men, an activity supposedly forbidden in the New Testament. Thus, our knowledge of what people did and thought throughout history is mostly limited to what men did and thought. From the remnants and hints about women that have survived, we realize we have lost "her story."

Those who are reluctant to admit the lost history of women readily produce names of famous women—Cleopatra, Helen of Troy, Elizabeth I. Interestingly, when the list is analyzed, *most* who made it into the history books were (a) wives, mothers, daughters, or mistresses of famous (and infamous) men; (b) women who inherited public power for a time from husband, father, or son; (c) women who did something wrong or caused their man to be led astray; (d) women who stepped out of proper "female" roles, for good or bad, usually forgoing marriage to take on a man's role; (e) a few women whose exemplary actions would be newsworthy in *any* human! These "exceptions" give little view of how half the world—women—lived their lives. To uncover this silent history, feminist historians dig among the deeds of great men for casual asides about a wife, mother, daughter, or adversary.

While many church folk cast a disinterested eye at such women's history, they take notice when the retrieval of women is directed at biblical texts! Outrage surfaces at feminist theologians who mess with the Bible, reading it differently from church school classes—you can't do that! Why not? Theologians have done it for years! If theology—talking about God and the human condition—had not continuously undergone revision and reconstruction over the last two thousand years, seminary training would take a couple of weeks and one good textbook. Feminist theologians do what other theologians have always done, reexamine the way stories have been traditionally interpreted, to separate ancient cultural beliefs from essential meaning. For example, was it of divine importance that women cover their heads in public, as the first letter to the Corinthians advised, or was this an accommodation to ancient cultural rules of modesty and womanly conduct? Should we use Hebrew tribal warfare over territory and ethnic purity to justify conflict in Bosnia or Ireland today, or dismiss it as a method we have moved beyond for conflict resolution? Can the story of Sarah ordering her servant Hagar to sleep with Abraham to produce an heir be used as a biblical solution for infertile couples, or are there contemporary ethical values that discourage this?

Of particular interest to women theologians is the reality that the Bible was written in a culture where women were male property, like land or cattle, to be used at their owners' discretion. They get suspicious when these ancient cultural ideas of male dominance are simply transposed into contemporary biblical arguments to justify male dominance as divinely decreed. Feminist theologians argue that such interpreters have not done the homework of separating the biblical message from Hebrew and Greco-Roman cultural baggage, and support their claim by pointing to overlooked biblical stories that advocate the equality of men and women and the radical call of Jesus to a discipleship of *equals*. They also appeal to the common sense experience of life. Do we *really* believe only men can lead a household or church, when in reality women outnumber and outwork men in mainline churches today and have organized families for centuries? Does the possession of a certain appendage automatically bestow a talent, or have we been playing a game, acquiescing to first century societal ideas of male headship as some "natural order of creation," while all the time knowing this is not how it works in everyday experience? Why have we been willing to abolish slavery, even though it was a household custom among early Christians, yet argue we cannot abandon male authority "because it is in the scriptures"?

Church women have always challenged in subversive ways their exclusion—based on biblical teachings—from leadership and full involvement, even while giving nodding agreement to male leadership. When I speak to church groups, I often ask women to raise their hands if they belong to a Women's Guild or Mission Society. While these groups are disappearing as women find other ways to use their gifts in the church, they were for years the backbone of both church and missions. I see a room full of hands and call them sister feminists! These groups intrigue me because they were once the only place church women could have leadership, and the leadership was *all* women! Despite the supposedly exclusive possession of leadership gifts by males, these women's groups were usually the *healthiest* organizations in the church, raising incredible amounts of money and achieving incredible goals. Yet the Bible is used to say women must be silent and let men lead!

Also, the money raised by these women's groups did *not* go through church budgets or to men on finance committees! Why? Because the women designated it for *missions*, the only legitimate cause *outside* of male administrative control! Women with no income of their own and excluded from decision-making on church boards had created their own subversive domain of discipleship and women-power. They knitted, sewed, and baked up a storm, turning skills to cash that went across the sea, mostly to female missionaries—their hands and feet on the "mission field." Men who have served on Finance Committees know what I'm talking about. No one could touch this money, even if the general church budget was short, without a formal request to the women for financial assistance, preferably accompanied by begging! The women conferred in private. Because their money was for "missions," no one could fault or override their cause. Women had found a way to claim their power, even in the midst of their own powerlessness. A parallel story occurs in Judges 11 in the Hebrew Bible.[4] When Jephthah, a mighty military leader, sacrificed his only daughter to settle his private bargain with God, her women friends, although unable to stop her death, instigated an annual memorial day to honor the powerless, nameless girl, recording their protest against women's powerlessness in that society.

If women have subversively resisted their subordination for centuries without a label or an "-ism," why do we need one now? The results speak for themselves. Despite countless challenges throughout history, which will be described in the following pages, the *system* that legitimized rule of men over women persisted, aided and abetted by biblical interpretations of passages about women. Only now has this *system* begun to crumble under the concerted public protest called the feminist movement, challenging the deeper assumptions of society rather than the individual consequences of it. Earlier protests were isolated, localized in one area over one issue, and thus died under opposition or disbanded when the issue was resolved. If women think their problem is unique—that they are alone in their search for justice—their resistance is easier to overcome, but when women discover many others struggling against the same system, even though their fight may express itself in different issues in different areas, the solidarity of a *named* common experience—feminism—gives strength to continue with the resistance.

This happened in the '60s, not with one event, but with many slow realizations of inconsistencies rising like steam through "manholes" in the winding streets of women's lives. Women began to voice a nagging suspicion something was wrong. One wrote about it…then another…and another. Soon women were talking together about a forbidden subject—"women's place"—in almost every arena of life. Whispered sighs incorporated enough voices to become a roar, an "Aha!" of common experience as women discovered they were not weird, strange, or sick for questioning their situation.

The word "feminism" was not a new word. It had been used in the women's rights movement at the turn of the century. By reclaiming the word, no doubt also stamped on and muddied then by opponents of women's suffrage, Sixties women found their roots in a *history* of rebellion, adding their bead to a silenced string of beads throughout history. The movement spread, gaining new shapes as it encountered women in different places and circumstances across the world. African American women broadened the challenge to include oppression of *all* blacks by whites. Asian feminists focused on abuse of women as playthings, reproductive machines, and victims of dowry deaths. Professional women sought inclusion in the "old boys network." Women in the church demanded ordination and representation on church boards. Poor single mothers pursued legislation ensuring financial support from delinquent fathers. Feminism became "feminisms," encompassing a variety of causes, people, and challenges, the common *word* offering solidarity, cohesion, and strength.

But many voices threaten. A tremendous backlash has tried to divide, and thus conquer, women, picking them off as they cross the pass separating male and female privilege. The negative naming of "feminisms" is a very powerful weapon in the backlash—the promotion of only disturbing examples of feminist activity in media, literature, and the church, while ignoring strong, charitable women who continually change the world for both men and women by feminist principles. Negative naming works particularly well on other women—especially church women—when feminist ideas are demonized as anti-Christian, and biblical texts are offered as "proof."

In the following pages, I will argue that feminism is not about negatives, angry women out to destroy the family and the "natural" order of things, which is how those whose authority and lifestyle are threatened by the changes feminism seeks, portray it. Rather, it has been around for centuries, wherever women and men have seen injustice, inequality, and pain, and fought for liberation, freedom, power, and life for *everyone*. As such, it is very *Christian*. Galatians 3:28 contains an early baptismal formula recited when converts joined the Jesus Way. It highlights what was *different* about this new movement from the rest of Judaism (Gal. 3:25–28):

> But now that faith has come, we are no longer subject to a disciplinarian, for in Christ Jesus you are all children of God through faith. As many of you as were baptized into Christ have clothed yourselves with Christ. There is no longer Jew or Greek, there is no longer slave or free, there is no longer male and female; for all of you are one in Christ Jesus. And if you belong to Christ, then you are Abraham's offspring, heirs according to the promise.

According to Galatians, "being clothed with Christ Jesus" was about breaking down cultural and social systems of inclusion and exclusion in first century society—Jew and Greek, slave and free, male and female—declaring all "one in Christ Jesus."

Feminism recovers this way of Jesus. A feminist is "someone who struggles for the full development and equality of both men and women, and accepts no particular barriers on the basis of sexual identity." Sounds like Galatians 3:28 to me! A feminist is "a person who seeks the full humanity of women, so that they be a contributing part of every conversation." Sounds like Galatians 3:28 to me! Feminism is not *against* anyone, but *for* everyone, a *reaffirmation* of the baptismal promise to reject systems that disadvantage some by exclusion, denying life at its fullest. Those who attack feminism do so for the same reason Jesus was attacked in his day—they benefit from a system with some "naturally" above others in a "divine" order, and feminist ideas of shared power and radical equality threaten this status quo. If "traditional" roles of women supporting men change, their privileged way of life will also have to change.

When feminism is seen as a commitment to Galatians 3:28—that baptism makes everyone equal and demands a community where this equality is preserved—to be a Christian *is* to be a feminist! Feminism is a *specific* example of this radical idea, more revolutionary than simply burning bras. The message of the early church as a discipleship of equals *prefigured* the feminist movement, and if Christianity calls itself the Way of Jesus Christ, feminism is not in opposition, but *central* to it. My hope for this book is that readers will examine their negative or ambivalent feelings about feminism; listen afresh to the long history of women who have sought change, in and outside the Church; and begin to see feminism as the *continuation* of the commitment to radical discipleship of the early Galatian community.

CHAPTER 2

Ever Since Eve

"I wish Adam had died with all his ribs in his body!"

Dion Boucicault, Irish playwright[1]

"Let's start at the very beginning," the song says. With feminism, the beginning is easy to find—it started with Eve! The difference between men and women is the oldest pleasure—and problem—in the world. *Biological* differences are not the problem. We can look in a medical textbook for that. The problem is what else is included with differences in body parts! Because women breast-feed, does this make them "naturally" superior to men as nurturers, and thus confined to lifelong caregiving? Does the ability to give birth go with "natural" weakness, irrationality, and need for male rule, as is often argued for women? Why does having a uterus mean it is not nice to be angry or sound aggressive, but that same behavior is okay for men? Somehow, along the road of history, extra characteristics were added as "natural" qualities to being a woman; since it was *men* doing the teaching, writing, and public decision-making about how society was to be, we need to be a bit suspicious when these "extras" also served to put women in a position subordinate to men.

In the following chapters, we will walk through Christian history to see how "natural" differences between women and men, far beyond biological ones, were decided upon. With this background, we can evaluate whether these differences are real, or whether they were constructed by the social and cultural ideas of the times. Since much of the description about women has come from religious beliefs, we need to investigate these origins as well to see if the arguments still hold for the twenty-first century. Many women have spent their lives imprisoned by what the Bible or the church said about women, not realizing the basis on which the theory was built has long since been

14

debunked. It is like the story of the new husband who asked his wife why she chopped the ends off French baguettes. She said her mother always did this. When he asked the mother, she said *her* mother did as well. Fortunately grandmother was still around to inform her new grandson-in-law that *she* did it because her bread box was too short!

Like it or not, when the Roman Empire took on Christianity in the fourth century, Western thinking and Christian thinking were linked together, first under an emperor, then under the pope. Greek philosophy, Jewish law, and the writings of the early church fathers shaped how the Bible was assembled and later interpreted. All these traditions—Jewish, Greek and Christian—operated under a patriarchal world view. *Patriarchy* means "rule of the father," a societal system where all legal, social, economic, and political activities assumed the rule of the male over dependent persons in the household and/or public arena—wives, unmarried daughters, dependent sons, male and female slaves.[2] While sons eventually became heads themselves and male slaves could be freed to establish households, daughters, wives, widows, and female slaves remained dependent on the male head of the household in which they lived *because* they were women.

In general, women under patriarchy had no legal status in their own right. They could not vote or hold office. The lineage of children passed through the father, and male children were preferred to female. A wife's body belonged to her husband, and he could beat her, restrict her movements, or sell her into bondage if he so desired. Her education was usually limited to household skills and basic literacy. Her right to inherit property was restricted and, if permitted, administered by a male. This was not simply a set of rules but part of some grand cosmic order of "how things were." Jewish philosopher Philo from the time of Jesus puts it in perspective:

> For the nature of communities is twofold, the greater and the smaller, the greater we call cities and the smaller households. As to the management of both forms, men have obtained that of the greater, which bears the name of statesmanship, whereas women have obtained that of the smaller, which goes under the name of household management.[3]

With women confined to the household, men in the public arena interpreted events, wrote history, and determined society's roles, including those of men over women. Patriarchy shaped our early European legal codes excluding women from public voice. This was not challenged until the late-nineteenth century women's movement in various parts of the world, when women finally won legal status as citizens, the right to vote, hold public office, make property transactions in their own name, and access higher education and professional careers. Christian doctrine was also shaped by the language of patriarchy, which took for granted male superiority. God was therefore described in metaphors from this world view, as was the relationship between men and women. The "natural" rule of men over women that was articulated by Greek philosophers became in biblical language the "natural, divine order of creation"—the "will of God." When this is challenged today as part of a patriarchal system of women's exclusion now legislated against, people become nervous thinking it is *God, not the system, that is being questioned.* Criticism of patriarchy is *not* antimale or a criticism of men or God, but a critique of an ancient *system* shared by a number of early societies that basically gave all rights to free males, and made everyone else, including women, dependent on them. Any such critique has to include religious teachings from such a system claiming to be "natural" or part of a "divine" order, to see if they were divinely commanded or simply part of the ancient culture.

Patriarchy exhibits itself in different ways in different societies at different times. In some societies, the better word is patrilineality, emphasizing not male rule but how the line of heredity is passed down through the father. In other societies, while males may hold legal authority, females have created an important place for themselves *within* the system—a mutuality between men and women that looks different in different situations. Patriarchy is a *system* with the potential for dominance of men over women, and what we will look for in the patriarchal societies that influenced Christian traditions is how that is played out and affects women.

In Judaism, the patriarch was head of the clan. Jewish men were part of God's covenant, doing acts of piety that subordinate and economically dependent women did not do. Women were included in the covenant under husbands, fathers, or sons. Through marriage, a man acquired a wife, sometimes two, and could end that marriage simply by writing a bill of divorce. The woman could not divorce the man. Since the Torah stressed the importance of children, a childless man's widow was obliged to marry his brother to produce offspring for her dead husband. This concept of "ownership" of women emerges in the Ten Commandments where male readers are told not to covet anything of their neighbor's—ox, ass, wife, manservant. Bible stories of male affront over a woman's rape are not only about *her,* but about theft and desecration of *his* property, especially since a resulting child might not be his "seed." Hebrew women were further excluded by bodily cycles. Purity laws declared them ritually "unclean" during menstruation and after childbirth. Men could control their purity by ritual acts of bathing and sacrificing; women were *controlled by* their "impure" bodies and excluded from "pure" places. Any Hebrew Bible story about women must be interpreted *within* the rules of this social system to see if and how the story can be applied today.

Greek and Roman patriarchal ideas also influenced Christianity. The New Testament letters are full of debates as to how much "pagan" influence should be allowed into Jewish Christianity. Should Jewish Christians eat with Gentile Christians? Should Gentile followers be circumcised? By the end of the first century however, Christianity had become "Hellenized"—influenced by Greek culture—and Greek philosophical ideas became the backbone of Christian theology. For the Greeks, all knowledge—philosophy, religion, physiology—fitted an umbrella theory of the cosmos as a universal graded order. Biological laws were not arrived at from anatomical investigation, but described by philosophers to fit this overall scheme of things. Not surprisingly in a graded cosmic order described by males, men were ranked above women. While both possessed spirit (mind) and body (matter), spirit was superior, and men had three quarters spirit and one quarter body, while women had one quarter spirit and three quarters body! Women's excessive bodiliness was demonstrated by their functions of menstruation, childbirth, and lactation, and, because women were "naturally" deficient in spirit, they were weak, gullible, and frail of mind.

This graded cosmic order was also used to explain the origins of a person. Fourth-century B.C.E. [4] philosopher Aristotle said male semen was the sole contributor to the fetus because, in the cosmic hierarchy, males were superior. The female "semen" (menstrual fluid containing embryos) was simply a "passive" nutrient for the seed, mirroring the cosmic order of dominant, generative, male sun and receptive, female mother earth. Men produced only male sperm, which, under perfect conditions, produced male offspring. However, if the woman's womb failed to nurture the seed correctly, a "defect not of nature's intention" occurred, resulting in a "misbegotten male"—a female.

Aristotle's philosophical biology became law. Second-century C.E. physician Galen illustrated this theory by drawing women's reproductive organs the same as men's but inverted *into* their bodies—misbegotten—not outside like *properly* developed male organs. The defect nevertheless was fortuitous, according to Galen, since females made great "flowerpots for the seed." Aristotle's biology still prevailed in 1572, when a Spanish anatomist was concerned that his chapter on ovaries (female testicles) in *History of the Composition of the Human Body* might make women more arrogant knowing they, like men, had testicles! Even in 1677, when sperm was first examined under a microscope, it was called "animalcules," human babies in minuscule form complete in themselves, ready to simply be nurtured in the womb.

Surely we can ignore Aristotle's biology with our enlightened knowledge of anatomy and physiology. Not so. Thomas Aquinas, the great church father of the Middle Ages, used Aristotle's *biology* to form his *theology* about men and women, a theology that still shapes Catholic ideas about women and reproduction even though its *biological* base has been disproven. Copying Aristotle, Aquinas described women as defective and misbegotten by nature, a hiccup in the development of a perfect male from a male sperm. This *biological truth* from Greek philosophy indicated that women were not "nature's first intention" but "second intention," and was backed up biblically by the story of Eve as God's afterthought, formed from Adam's rib and thus inferior and subordinate. This biological theology was further embellished in *Malleus Maleficarum*, the 1486 Inquisition guide to identifying witches:

> There was a defect in the formation of the first woman since she was
> formed from a bent rib, that is, the rib of the breast, which is bent as it
> were in a contrary direction to a man. And since through this defect she
> is an imperfect animal, she always deceives.[5]

You see what I mean? Women and men might be *biologically* different, but it
depends on how this is interpreted in practice, and what *other* conclusions
about women deduced from speculation have been claimed as the unques-
tionable will of God.

This cumulative evidence as to women's inferiority—God's afterthought,
Adam's defective rib, subordinate in patriarchal society, misbegotten male—
caused Aquinas to insist that women be excluded as witnesses in law courts,
and that fathers be loved and honored as the determinative principal more
than mothers. Divorce was discouraged because man's higher reason would
be denied the children, and anyway, good order demanded weak women be
governed by someone wiser than themselves. Actually, Aquinas saw little use
for women in a marriage other than for reproduction:

> We are told that woman was made to help a man (Gen 2:18,20). But she
> would not be fitted to help man except in generation, because another
> man would have proved a more effective help in anything else.[6]

The depreciation of women and marriage from Aristotle to Aquinas parallels the rise of another Greek idea in Christianity, sexual abstinence (celibacy). Greek philosophers believed mental energy was lost with semen at
intercourse; thus abstinence was preferred by philosophers and athletes as the
control of mind over body. Women did not need to abstain since they had no
semen to lose and little mental energy to protect! Stoic philosophers rejected
sex for pleasure altogether, seeing marriage as only for those who could not
abstain. Such abstinence in the Greeks was not revulsion at sexuality or the
female body as it would become with later Christian fathers, but rather the
triumph of the disciplined mind. Stoic Seneca warned against too much pleasure, not because sex was sinful, but because succumbing to passion signified
being out of control:

> It is also shameful to love one's own wife immoderately. In loving his wife
> the wise man takes reason for his guide, not emotion. He resists the as-
> sault of passions, and does not allow himself to be impetuously swept
> away into the marital act. Nothing is more depraved than to love one's
> spouse as if she were an adulteress.[7]

It would only take a few centuries for Greek ideas on abstinence as fitness
of body and mind to become the Christian idea of celibacy—abstinence as
rejection of sinful sexual desire, with woman the enemy. Marriage became the
downside for virginity. Fourth-century church father Jerome, whom we will
discuss from time to time, wrote to the celibate Eustochium:

It is not disparaging wedlock to prefer virginity. No one can make a comparison between two things, if one is good and the other evil. Let married women take their pride in coming next after virgins… I praise wedlock, I praise marriage; but it is because they produce me virgins. I gather the rose from the thorn, the gold from the earth, the pearl from the oyster.[8]

Given these diverse influences from the patriarchal societies, which would shape Christian relationships between men and women, perhaps the best way to trace this transformation of women's biology into a theology of women as subordinate and inferior, excluded from many areas of society, is to watch how three women in Jewish and Christian history were "shaped" into models of womanhood.

Let's start with the story of Adam and Eve—and Lilith. Lilith? Before you scour Genesis for Lilith, let me remind you there are *two* creation stories in Genesis, coming from different oral traditions into the written scriptures. Genesis 1 says God created man and woman together in the image of God, naming neither of them but giving both dominion (stewardship) over the created world (Gen. 1:27–28a):

So God created humankind in his image, in the image of God he created them; male and female he created them. God blessed them, and God said to them, "Be fruitful and multiply…"

They are told to eat of *every* tree without restrictions (Gen. 1:29):

God said, "See, I have given you…every tree with seed in its fruit; you shall have them for food."

Genesis 2, on the other hand, tells of the creation of Adam who, unable to find companionship among the animals, becomes lonely. God then creates Eve out of Adam's rib as his "helper."

Eve will become the "bad woman" in Christian tradition, but not in Judaism probably because *another* woman took that title—Lilith. In Jewish midrash (Rabbinical writings that expand and explain the Torah), Lilith, first wife of Adam, created with him and equal, fits the Genesis 1 story. There was apparently trouble in Paradise over male-female relationships prior to the apple:

Adam and Lilith never found peace together. She refused to lie beneath him in sexual intercourse, basing her claim for equality on the fact that each had been created from earth. When Lilith saw that Adam would overpower her, she uttered the ineffable name of God and flew up into the air of the World. [9]

It would seem Lilith had a good argument, but remember, this story is a patriarchal story of beginnings told to "legitimate" the rule of men over women. Lilith loses, first to Adam, who attempts to overpower her, then to God, who tries to return her to Adam's side—or underneath him, as the story goes! There are many symbols at play here. Since procreation represents sexual difference, the relative positions of the couple symbolize the male–female order in patriarchal society. Interestingly, the two patriarchal religions coming out of Judaism—Islam and Christianity—*also* declared this sexual position the correct one.[10]

Lilith's utters the name of God before flying off into "the World," thus compounding her unpardonable behavior. According to Jewish tradition, God's name was not to be uttered. God sends angels to retrieve Lilith, but she ignores them, refusing to be subordinate rather than equal as created. She settles near the Red (Reed) Sea, becoming the "mother" of agrarian tribes there. Lilith's refusal to obey sets the stage for her "fall" from grace. In Jewish tradition, she becomes the symbol of unbridled promiscuity, coupling with demons and giving birth to hundreds of demonic baby "lilims" daily. So, the Jewish story continues, God produced Eve out of Adam's rib as Lilith's docile replacement, the creation story of Genesis 2. While early Christian Fathers ignored the differences in these accounts, Jewish midrash interpreted them as successive women for Adam, the "bad" one insisting on equality, the "good" one accepting her subordinate position. Male authority could thus be sanctioned by God.

The Lilith story serves a further purpose for Hebrew "beginnings." Lilith's name was linked with Sumerian and Babylonian goddesses from the area where Abraham grew up, and also the Canaanite deity Baalat, the promised land where Abraham's descendents settled. Thus, she became for the Hebrew people a symbol of the many gods and goddesses (polytheism) that Abraham rejected for the one God (monotheism). Lilith's mating with demons to produce the agrarian tribes of the Red Sea also accounts for those tribes worshiping fertility and earth goddesses who resisted invasion by nomadic herdsmen such as Abraham. But more of this later. It is not surprising then that Lilith looms into demonic proportions in Judaism as the smoke beneath the door of old fertility goddesses, becoming the symbol of rebellion, rage, and untamed female sexuality as opposed to good, docile Eve. Jewish kabbalist teachers claimed Lilith adorned herself like a "harlot" with poisonous wine to seduce innocent male victims.[11] Her infamy continued in her demon daughters "lilims." Into the Middle Ages, Jewish men wore amulets to fend off these lustful females given to teasing sleeping men into wet dreams.

Lilith was still notorious in Jewish and Gnostic texts in Jesus' day, and, in Greek stories, lilims became "daughters of Hecate," also known to wander at night. Although Lilith is not mentioned by name in the Bible, lilims are featured in Christian tradition. Called "incubi" and "succubi," they could reverse their sex at will, begetting "changeling" babies with humans—the medieval interpretation of deformed children and those of doubtful paternity. These demonic beings, also called "harlots of hell" or "night-hags,"[12] provoked great discussion among medieval church fathers, including Aquinas, since they could carry seed from a sleeping, innocent man to a woman, making him (perhaps a priest) "both virgin and father." Monks slept with their hands clutching crucifixes across their genitals. If male babies smiled in their sleep, lilims were fondling them. Parents drew circles around boys' cradles, calling on the angels sent to return Lilith to Adam for protection, although these angels proved incapable of dealing with *her*.[13] While this seems unbelievable for serious theological debate, the Inquisition witch-hunts of the Middle Ages were based on these ideas. Thousands of women were charged with having sexual encounters with demonic beings and were killed as witches. Suffice to say, free and independent Lilith, whose crime was to claim her God-given equality, became a symbol for female evil. Jewish feminist scholars have restored Lilith, naming their journal after her to celebrate her insistence on her rightful place.

What about Eve? In the creation story of Genesis 2, Eve was an after-thought created from Adam's rib. *Before* Eve is even around, God tells Adam not to eat the fruit of one tree in the garden. When a serpent later encourages Eve—with Adam at her side—to eat, telling her they will not die but gain godlike knowledge, Eve eats and gives some to Adam. They realize they are naked and make fig-leaf covers. God appears, curses the serpent, and says Eve and her descendants will bear increased pain in childbirth, together with a desire for husbands who rule over them. Adam is assigned to a life of working the land for food, since they will now be outside Paradise's garden. From this story, Eve, like Lilith, will emerge the bad one. Adam disobeyed, but *Eve* has been accused throughout history of treachery, willful evil, and the transmission of original sin to all humanity. How does this happen? How is Eve also recruited, like Lilith, for patriarchal purposes to "divinely" sanction the natural superiority of man over weak, even wicked, woman?

The story of Adam and Eve was never central to Judaism. Although there were some Jewish stories around about Eve in Jesus' day, it was Paul's outline of the scheme of salvation linked to Adam that led church fathers to focus on the apple as the introduction of sin into the world.[14] Jewish theologians saw it differently. Some described the Garden simply as the place where Adam and Eve acquired wisdom, not sexual or moral but *technological*, in other words, the arts for civilization. There was no evil suggested with this acquisition. Only later, in the third century, did Jewish texts talk about Eve's sin. The Adam and Eve story was also used around Jesus' time in discussions about marriage and divorce, affirming the purpose of marriage as procreation, and thus the possibility of divorcing a barren wife. One debate raged between different Pharisee schools on "grounds for divorce"—whether a wife's adultery was the only legitimate cause, or whether less serious causes such as burning the soup qualified.[15]

Jesus was caught in the divorce argument when the Pharisees asked him if it was lawful for a man to divorce his wife for *any* cause (Matt. 19:3–15; Mk. 10:1–12). For his answer, Jesus goes back to creation:

> "But from the beginning of creation 'God made them male and female.'
> 'For this reason a man shall leave his father and mother and be joined to

his wife, and the two shall become one flesh' So they are no longer two, but one flesh. Therefore what God has joined together, let no one separate" (Mark 10:6–9).

Forget the nit-picking rules and exceptions. Marriage is not a convenient arrangement with easy escape clauses for male whim, but a divinely intended mutual relationship—one flesh. The important issue is not how many' loopholes can be found, but security and respect in the relationship, especially for women who were cast off by such loopholes. This is the *only* time Jesus mentioned Adam and Eve, and then not by name. He made no mention of Eve's sin, or any evil in the Garden; nor did he describe himself as the new Adam, sent as restorer of the "fall." He did not even argue the superiority of man over woman. Yet the story becomes central to Christianity. We have to keep asking why.

As we shall see later, Paul introduced the first couple into the footlights of Christianity by calling Jesus the New Adam. This set in motion a frenzy among the church fathers describing exactly what happened in the garden. Different camps developed over Adam and Eve, the meaning of the fall, and their exclusion from the garden. Although we are not told why the serpent talked with *Eve,* it did not take long for Adam's disobedience to become Eve's fault. Greek philosophy had declared women weaker and more gullible than men, thus more susceptible to temptation. 1 Timothy 2:14, written well into the second century, argued that Adam was not deceived, but Eve was. The Greek legend of Pandora was well known to church fathers, and, by the Middle Ages, an Eve–Pandora caricature of "woman" had developed with a childlike curiosity lacking moral sense. Dante's *Paradise Lost* declared Eve's weakness greed— she had to have it! Stories from prehistory of the association between snakes and goddesses, together with the Latin Bible rendering the snake feminine, led to charges that Eve was in cahoots with the devil-as-female-snake. Eve would become a symbol of evil, eliciting the male fears of women in the Middle Ages that would lead to the witch-hunts.

But we have jumped ahead. Clement of Alexandria (150–215 C.E.) did not think the Adam and Eve story was a sinister story about the beginning of sin, but about human disobedience in the face of moral freedom to choose and moral responsibility to act. Adam and Eve chose to disobey, and the rule of man over woman was the consequence for Eve. The majority of second- and third-century fathers, like their Jewish predecessors, agreed that the first couple's misuse of freedom brought pain, labor, and death into an originally perfect world, and from their disobedience, we draw practical lessons, but they did *not* believe Adam's transgression affected the free will of everyone forever. Each person chose good or evil as Adam did. That was the ability they acquired from eating the fruit and becoming responsible for their own fate.

Other church fathers however, argued that the "sin" of Adam and Eve was not disobedience but sexual awareness. The forbidden tree of knowledge was knowledge about sexual desire because, when they heard God's voice, "they knew they were naked." Theologians Tatian and Cyprian further insisted that Adam and Eve were *virgins* in Paradise, and the human race was poised to multiply asexually "like the angels." Their "sin" was to eat, become sexually aware, engage in sexual intercourse, and thus "invent" the institution of marriage. For this, they were expelled from Paradise.[16] "Undoing" the sin of Adam and Eve, therefore, meant celibacy, with marital sex only for procreation and followed by celibacy once reproduction was over.

Why did sexual abstinence become important in Christianity when Judaism advocated marriage so strongly, and why did it become linked with Adam and Eve? We have to go back to Jesus' statement about divorce. In Matthew 19:9–12, a later gospel than Mark's, Jesus' comments about divorce have been linked with a follow-up discussion not found in any other gospel:

> "And I say to you, whoever divorces his wife, except for unchastity, and marries another commits adultery." …His disciples…said to him, "If such is the case of a man with his wife, it is better not to marry." But he said to them, "Not everyone can accept this teaching, but only those to whom it is given. For there are eunuchs who have been so from birth, and there are eunuchs who have been made eunuchs by others, and there are eunuchs who have made themselves eunuchs for the sake of the kingdom of heaven. Let anyone accept this who can."

The disciples would have been familiar with eunuchs (castrated males) in Roman society. Some were castrated as punishment or as spoils of war, others for use in imperial courts to guard royal harems (see Esth. 2:3, 14; Acts 8:27). Since castrated men could not procreate, they were excluded from the Jewish Assembly (Deut. 23:1) and assigned literally to a no-man's land between male and female in Greek culture.

Matthew's passage, however, introduces eunuchs who "made themselves eunuchs for the sake of the kingdom of heaven," a metaphor for those choosing not to marry in order to further the gospel. This was not the celibacy of later church fathers, which negated sexuality and the body, nor the celibacy of Jewish Essenes, who avoided marriage to battle the forces of darkness, but a choice against time-consuming household responsibilities. Given the "problems" with marriage and divorce, the disciples' question as to whether it is better not to marry introduces the possibility of a legitimate state of singleness *some* people might espouse "for the sake of the kingdom."

Since early Christianity preached freedom from Jewish law and Roman social codes as the subversive message of Jesus, singleness came to be seen as freedom from the onerous bonds of marriage for *both* men and women, as Greek philosophers long recognized. "Selling all you have" to follow Jesus was *also* about dismantling the edifice of social and familial responsibilities. Gregory of Nyssa understood:

He whose life is contained in himself either escapes (sufferings) altogether, or can bear them easily, having a collected mind which is not distracted from himself; while he who shares himself with wife and child often has not a moment to give even to regretting his own condition, because anxiety for those he loves fills his heart.[17]

Paul's ambivalent comments about marriage also fueled this thinking, as did the popular story of Thecla that circulated in the first century. Thecla, a young woman whose marriage had been arranged for her, heard Paul preach about freedom in Christ and ran off to join him. Despite opposition from family, and an encounter in the arena with wild beasts, she escaped martyrdom and became a revered teacher, encouraging her sisters to choose celibacy over arranged marriages, the benefits being

[a] masculine and voluntary mind, one free from necessity, in order to choose, like masters, the things which please us, not being enslaved to fate nor fortune.[18]

The Matthew passage encouraged *further* speculation, however, since "eunuch" implied not just deferring marriage, but permanent celibacy. Could this passage mean celibacy was a *higher* calling than marriage? This was an alien idea for Judaism, where the body and sexuality were to be enjoyed and used well, yet the Gospel of Matthew was written in 80–90 C.E. when Christianity was becoming more Gentile than Jewish. The author was addressing a community recently excluded from the synagogue and finding its way outside of Judaism. We have already seen the Greek emphasis on sexual abstinence as superior. It is only a small step from singleness as useful for the spread of the gospel to celibacy as superior—the rejection of sinful sexual expression; a small step from Adam and Eve and marriage as the norm for male–female relations to Adam and Eve and marriage as succumbing to sinful sexual desire. This small step will be lethal, especially for Eve.

As celibacy rose in honor, overcoming sexual *desire* became the paramount virtue for celibate church fathers, and women became the enemy, objects of desire and temptresses of virtue. In the fourth century, Saint Jerome elevated the superior mental anguish of self-imposed celibacy to new heights:

How often, when I was living in the desolate, lonely desert, parched by the burning sun, how often I imagined myself among the pleasures of Rome! [H]e who, in fear of hell, had banished himself to this prison, found himself again and again surrounded by dancing girls! My face grew pale with hunger, yet in my cold body the passions of my inner being continued to glow. This human being was more dead than alive; only his burning lust continued to boil.[19]

As celibacy soared, marriage fell by default—a lesser state. Jerome's revulsion at his past sexual conduct led him to change the order of things in Genesis 2, placing Adam and Eve's marriage *after* the fall, thus making it part of God's judgment on sin:

> As for Adam and Eve, we must maintain that before the fall they were virgins in Paradise; but after they sinned, and were cast out of Paradise, they were immediately married. *Then* we have the passage, "For this cause a man shall leave his father and mother, and cleave to his wife, and they shall become one flesh."[20]

Jerome incorporated Paul's comments in 1 Corinthians 7 about remaining unmarried and claimed that *all* sexual intercourse, in view of the purity of the body of Christ, was unclean, and marriage was inferior to perpetual chastity. Thus married couples should be celibate after bearing children, living in holy, pure love. When Jerome's colleague Jovinian argued that celibate Christians were no holier than his married brothers and sisters, Jerome, Ambrose, and Augustine condemned him for "heresy." For the record, Jerome was no small player in church history. He was responsible for translating the Bible into the Latin Vulgate, still the official translation for Catholics!

Fourth-century church father Augustine would finalize the elevation of celibacy over marriage, theologizing it and implicating Adam and Eve firmly in the drama. Augustine had struggled, like Jerome, to control his sexual desire. After his conversion, he had renounced his concubine of fourteen years and an impending marriage, to embrace celibacy. Later in life, he decided the battle against sexual desire was unwinnable, even for the most saintly. Taking his experience as the norm for all humans, he denied that humans had moral freedom or free will to choose good or evil—the idea earlier church fathers had read from Adam and Eve—and declared *all* humanity doomed to sin from birth because of "original" sin inherited from their mother's womb. While Jesus mentioned Adam and Eve only once and not as sinners, Augustine made their story central to Christianity, the beginning of inescapable sinfulness for *everyone.* Augustine's predecessors, Jewish and Christian, had not seen Adam's choice as removing all human choice, yet Augustine interpreted Adam as a corporate personality, bringing on *all* humanity not only death, but universal, inevitable sin.

Acording to Augustine, Adam's seed from which *all* are propagated was contaminated by Adam's sin, tainting everyone in the womb. (It is hard to see why, if tainted *seed* is the problem, Eve was blamed as the transmitter!) Jesus was the exception, since his conception did not involve human seed. Augustine went further to identify *sexual desire* as the "original sin" acquired in the womb. His *proof* that sexual desire was the "original sin" came from his own personal experience of sexual arousal despite his willing against it—his "parts of shame" acting as their own master. Even in marriage, he believed that the "diabolical excitement of the genitals" was hideously out of control, creating "boundless sloughs of lust and damnable craving." Such uncontrollable sexual desire must not have existed in Paradise before Adam's sin:

The members of a man's body could have been the servants of man's will, without any lust, for the procreation of children...because he did not obey God, [man] could not obey himself.[21]

Augustine's theology of original sin triumphed over his opponents, clouding both the goodness of God's creation and the freedom of the human will and dominating the church with a pessimistic attitude to human nature and sexuality. Not surprisingly, Eve acquired major blame. *She* was from Adam's rib, thus the "weaker" of the two. The serpent approached *her,* supposing Adam less gullible and her more malleable. *She* tempted Adam with the fruit, causing the fall into sin. Adam slides away from blame:

We cannot believe that the man was led astray...he fell in with her suggestions because they were so closely bound in partnership...Eve accepted the serpent's statement as the truth, while Adam refused to be separated from his only companion, even if it involved sharing her sin.[22]

Furthermore, if sexual desire was the original sin, Eve as temptress was evil, not in herself, but because of her effect on male self-control. Original sin was *also* Eve's fault, since it is transferred to her offspring through *her* womb! According to Augustine, the *consequences* of her culpability was God's rule of male authority over her, which also divinely sanctioned for Augustine the social, legal, political, and economic machinery of male domination in his world.[23]

Adam emerged merely disobedient. The medieval church declared him forgiven by God, a chivalrous, besotted man so inflamed with love he would do anything for Eve. But for Eve and her daughters, there was no forgiveness. Through this woman, the race was condemned, and stays condemned through every woman since. Female evil ultimately caused the death of Jesus, according to Tertullian:

And do you not know that you are each an Eve? The sentence of God on this sex of yours lives in this age; the guilt must of necessity live too. You are the devil's gateway...the first deserter of the divine law; you are she who persuaded him whom the devil was not valiant enough to attack. You destroyed so easily God's image, man. On account of your desert— that is, death, even the son of God had to die.[24]

This linking of sexual desire with sin struck a blow to sexual expression. Sexual intercourse was permitted only for propagation. Even Clement, who supported marriage against many of his contemporaries, condemned marital intercourse for reasons of passion alone, and also contraception, which acknowledged the intent of sexual pleasure without procreation. Virginity became *the* virtue that Christianity perfected. Married people were encouraged to live in "holy love," although Augustine doubted the purpose of "celibate" marriage:

I don't see what sort of help woman was created to provide man with, if one excludes the purpose of procreation. If woman is not given to man for help in bearing children, for what help could she be? To till the earth together? If help were needed for that, man would have been a better help for man. The same goes for comfort in solitude. How much more pleasure is it for life and conversation when two friends live together than when a man and a woman cohabitate.[25]

Although celibacy for priests was not fixed by law until 1139, as early as the fourth century, married priests were advised to abstain from sex if serving at the altar. Augustine's contemporary Pope Siricus called priests who had sex with their wives a "shame on honorable religion, masters of sin enslaved to lust." By the sixth century, priests were advised to live with their wives as brother and sister. Peter Damian (died 1072) justified priestly celibacy because Christ was born of a virgin, and thus must be served by virginal hands in the mass. The argument that Peter, the first Pope, was married was dismissed since Peter washed away the filth of marriage with the blood of martyrdom. At the Second Lateran Council of 1139, marriages contracted after ordination became invalid. Priests' wives were called whores by Pope Alexander III (died 1181) and adultresses by Pope Innocent III (died 1216). Some were even denied church burial.[26]

This elevation of celibacy over marriage is crucial to our discussion of women, since women's purpose, value, and nature was being described *theologically* by men whose celibate honor was secured against women as the *enemy*. John Chrysostom (died 407) voiced his fears:

There are in the world a great many situations that weaken the conscientiousness of the soul. First and foremost of these is dealings with women. In his concern for the male sex, the superior may not forget the females, who need greater care precisely because of their ready inclination to sin. In this situation the evil enemy can find many ways to creep in secretly. For the eye of woman touches and disturbs our soul, and not only the eye of the unbridled woman, but that of the decent one as well.[27]

How can women be described as whole human beings and halfway decent people when those doing the describing fear them so? In prehistory, women were "taboo" because their dangerous bodily powers could harm men in contact with them. In church history they remained "taboo"—dangerous "others" to be controlled in order to protect celibate males. Sexual activity in marriage, although necessary for procreation, had to be carefully controlled against sinful sexual desire. Scholars of the Middle Ages described women's usefulness in marriage as medicine for male fornication, "hospitals" for weak men who could not handle virginity. Stephen Langton, Archbishop of Canterbury (died 1228), went so far as to say, "the wife must rather let herself be killed than her husband sin."[28] Eve has been well and truly condemned!

CHAPTER 3

The Plot Thickens

The female sex is forbidden on apostolic authority to teach in public, that is either by word or by writing…All women's teaching, particularly formal teaching by word and writing, is to be held suspect unless it has been diligently examined, and much more fully than men's. The reason is clear: common law—and not any kind of common law, but that which comes from on high—forbids them. And why? Because they are easily seduced and determined seducers; and because it is not proved that they are witnesses to divine grace.[1]

John Gerson (d. 1429)

The scene is the Middle Ages, with its climate of antiwomen, antisexuality theology brewing from the fourth century. The plot revolves around mixed messages about men and women, celibacy and marriage, sex and sin. Enter the doomed lovers Heloise and Abelard, and listen as their story unfolds!

Peter Abelard (1079–1142), a brilliant Parisian scholar, fell in love in his thirties. So what? we might ask. It is not that simple. As a scholar, his only career was in the church. Celibacy was the preferred state, both as a single-minded philosopher of the Greek ideal, and for a theologian resisting the dastardly sin of sexual desire. Heloise, a brilliant seventeen-year-old with "a gift for letters so rare in women that it added greatly to her charm and had won her renown throughout the realm," was his student, living, as did Abelard, in her uncle and guardian's house. Let Peter tell you about it himself:

> We were united, first under one roof, then in heart; and so with our lessons as a pretext we abandoned ourselves entirely to love…with our books open before us, more words of love than of our reading passed between us, and more kissing than teaching. My hands strayed oftener to her bosom than to the pages; love drew our eyes to look on each other

more than reading kept them on our texts…our desires left no stage of lovemaking untried, and if love could devise something new, we welcomed it.[2]

The couple were caught together a few months before Heloise discovered she was pregnant. Her uncle was away, so Abelard sent her to his sister's house until she gave birth. On the uncle's return, Abelard confessed the "deceit" love had made him commit, bemoaning that women since the beginning of the human race had brought the noblest men to ruin! He offered to marry Heloise, so long as it was kept secret and did not damage his reputation and career.

Heloise's uncle agreed, but *Heloise* objected, arguing that it would not satisfy her uncle, which proved true, and that the church would lose Abelard's brilliance, chained in marriage to one woman. She also argued that Paul advised against marital responsibility, as did the philosophers and the church fathers. Heloise shared the philosophical ideal that marriage only legitimated weak flesh, arguing she would rather be mistress than wife, held by love, not a marriage tie. Perhaps she also had dreams that would be dashed by the restraints of marriage. She was unable to convince him, however, and cried prophetically, "We shall both be destroyed. All that is left us is suffering as great as our love has been."[3] Heloise's uncle did reveal their marriage, heaping abuse on them, so Abelard sent Heloise to a convent for safekeeping. Her uncle misunderstood, thinking Abelard had rid himself of her, so, in revenge, had Abelard castrated! Abelard was overcome with shame—as well as other feelings—reading it as a judgment on the parts of his body that had weakened through pride.

> Hitherto I had been entirely continent, but now the further I advanced in philosophy and theology, the further I fell behind the philosophers and holy fathers in the impurity of my life. It is well known that the philosophers, and still more the Fathers…were especially glorified by their chastity.[4]

Abelard and Heloise then took holy vows, not seeing each other for ten years when Heloise, now a prioress, accepted accommodation for her order in a center under Abelard's spiritual care.

Heloise's early convent life had been filled, not with Christian hope and vocation, but with despair, especially since Abelard made no effort to keep in contact. When they did make contact again, she made no bones about her feelings. It was not vocation, but love for him that made her obey his command to join a convent and destroy herself.

> [I]mmediately at your bidding, I changed my clothing along with my mind, in order to prove you the sole possessor of my body and my will alike. God knows I never sought anything in you except yourself; I wanted simply you, nothing of yours…I believed that the more I humbled myself

on your account, the more gratitude I should win from you, and also the less damage I should do to the brightness of your reputation.[5]

Abelard defended his silence, assuming she no longer needed him. Heloise became more explicit. While Abelard might have changed spiritually and physically, she had not, and was now without a vocation and tormented by frustrated sexual love:

In my case, the pleasures of lovers which we shared have been too sweet— they can never displease me, and scarcely be banished from my thoughts. Wherever I turn they are always there before my eyes, bringing with them awakened longings and fantasies which will not even let me sleep.[6]

Her vows, taken for Abelard, not God, made her a hypocrite. She was envious that Abelard's mutilation turned *him* to God but only intensified her desire. She could not repent her "sin" of longing, nor fathom a divine logic that forbade her deepest feelings and experience:

How can it be called repentance for sins, however great the mortification of the flesh, if the mind still retains the will to sin and is on fire with its old desires?[7]

Abelard didn't get it. He coolly reminded her of the events that justified God's punishment—making forbidden love during Easter observance in a monastery, and dressing in a nun's disguise. *Fortuitously,* God's mercy had freed them "from the flesh," that barrier to *divine* love. He urged her now to seek *Christ's* love, a happy transfer from marriage to a mere mortal to the bed of the King of Kings. Earthly suffering gave the chance of a martyr's crown, and, though parted in life, they would be united in heaven. Heloise's reply marked the turning point in her life. She would cease troubling him with heart-searchings. Instead, she sought his help in occupying her mind with constructive thoughts, and her intellect and energy flowed into the administration of her nuns, teaching them Greek, Hebrew, and Latin. We will never know what happened deep within her heart. Abelard went on to clash with the church authorities and be charged with heresy, and was confined to a monastery in perpetual silence. When he died at sixty-three, his body was brought back to Heloise. Twenty-one years later, she was laid to rest beside him.

Abelard and Heloise are examples of women and men caught in the quagmire of negative theology over sex. Both intellectually brilliant and delighted by scholarly pursuits, *neither* sought marriage and its responsibilities, but love betrayed them, condemned by a theology that negated sexual desire and marriage as weakness and sin. The pregnant Heloise was prepared to remain Abelard's mistress to keep his career options open, so long as it had to be either/or, but Abelard would not ask that of her. His guilt made him see his castration as punishment fitting the "sin" of succumbing to sexual desire, and his solution was monastic orders for them both—literally and figuratively "eunuchs for the Kingdom of Heaven." Heloise, victim of a society that dictated her options, would not allow it to dictate her feelings. To repent the "sin" of enjoying physical love and delighting in its memory did not fit her experience as a woman!

The theology that prevailed in Abelard's time would be gathered together and recorded in many volumes by Thomas Aquinas (1225–74), the most famous theologian since Augustine. Aquinas would accelerate the downward spiral of marriage, sex, and women, combining Augustine's ideas of women as temptresses and transmitters of original sin with Aristotle's biology of their natural inferiority and "misbegotten" nature into a theology of women as weak, fickle, promiscuous, and dangerous to "pure" men. Perhaps it is clearer now why Aquinas and his colleagues spent so much time discussing the dangerous activities of Lilith's daughters and their effect on sleeping men! These beliefs about women led to a disastrous era for women in church history—the witch-hunts. More than a million people, primarily women, were put to death, convicted by the Church Inquisition led by the Dominicans, Aquinas' order.

The majority of victims were midwives—poor women, often widows with no means of support, who combined midwifery tasks with herbal treatments from plants gathered in the forest. Fueled by a hatred of women and their sexual power over men, the church believed that the devil, in cooperation with such "feeble" women, could interfere with male sexuality through these potions:

> Since women are feebler both in mind and body, it is not surprising that they should come under the spell of witchcraft. For as regard intellect, or the understanding of spiritual things, they seem to be of a different nature from men.[8]

In 1484, Pope Innocent VIII appointed two Dominicans inquisitors to identify, search out, and destroy women found dabbling in sorcery. Their infamous encyclopedia of demonology became the authoritative guide to identification, with its section on witches, *Malleus Mallificarum* (Hammer of Witches).

One German widow-midwife was tried in 1587 for killing one child at birth and poisoning another with salve, obviously difficult deliveries gone wrong. She lived alone; thus her sexual behavior was suspect. And she possessed the power of healing, believed also to be the power to kill. Under torture, she "confessed" the devil made love to her at night, leaving a devil's mark on her shoulder. Though she had been the town midwife for years, she became the scapegoat for people's fears and superstitions. At her public execution, her breasts and arms were mutilated with red-hot irons, her right hand cut off, her body burned, and her ashes thrown in the river. All her goods and estate went to the bishop's treasury.

Older women were accused of attracting younger women to witchcraft as a feminine conspiracy against men. Their activities would normally not have concerned men, except for special powers witches had over male sexual performance. The witch-hunt manual declared:

> Such hatred is aroused by witchcraft between those joined in the sacra-
> ment of matrimony, and such freezing up of the generative forces, that
> men are unable to perform the necessary action of begetting offspring.[9]

Apart from dampening and removing sexual potency, witches also caused
abortions in cattle and humans and did things unmentionable to men. One
innocent young man found himself horribly bewitched:

> Many heard him tell that he had often wished to refuse the woman, and
> take flight to other lands; but that hitherto he had been compelled to rise
> up in the night and to come very quickly back, sometimes over land, and
> sometimes through the air as if he were flying.[10]

If that was not enough, witches also collected male organs, according to the
handbook,

> …in great numbers, as many as twenty or thirty members together, and
> put them in a bird's nest, or shut them up in a box, where they move
> themselves like living members, and eat oats and corn, as has been seen
> by many and is a matter of common report. A certain man tells that,
> when he lost his member, he approached a known witch and asked her
> to restore it to him. She told the afflicted man to climb a tree and that he
> might take which he liked out of a nest in which there were several
> members. And when he tried to take a big one, the witch said, "You must
> not take that one, adding, because it belonged to a parish priest." [11]

Witch-hunts became a sport, with victims stripped naked in public courts
as men searched them for devil's marks. In Cologne, between 1627 and 1630,
nearly all the midwives were killed. A common charge was killing unbaptized
infants. Since some ancient theologians had taught that God condemned unbaptized infants to hell, this was evidence they worked hand in hand with the
devil. They were also accused of distributing contraception information. As to
why there were more witches than warlocks, the *Malleus Malleficarum* concluded:

> Everything happens because of carnal desire, which is insatiable in them
> [women]…they have dealings even with the demons, so as to quiet their
> desires…Logically, therefore, the heresy to be named is that of female
> witches, not male…praised be the Most High, who has to this day so
> preserved the male sex from such shamefulness; It was in this sex that he
> [God] wished to be born and to suffer for us, and hence he has thus
> shown his preference for it.[12]

Witch-hunts were not confined to Europe or to the Catholic Inquisition. Reformation Europe continued the slaughter of independent women who stepped
out of place. The Salem witch-hunts in Massachusetts remind us that Puritans
also transported it to America.

Protestant ignorance or arrogance has long assumed that everything was reversed from bad to good with the Reformation, but what did it do to improve the lot of women, marriage, and sex? Luther is credited with allowing monks and priests to marry, but he was himself still a monk trained in the footsteps of Augustine, the proponent of original sin as sexual desire. While refuting celibacy as the better way and arguing that all should fulfill God's command to "reproduce and multiply," he still shared Augustine's ambivalence about sin and sex:

> It is a great favor that God has preserved woman for us...both for procreation and also as a medicine against the sin of fornication. In Paradise woman would have been a help for a duty only. But now she is also, and for the greater part at that, an antidote and a medicine; we can hardly speak of her without a feeling of shame, and surely we cannot make use of her without shame. The reason is sin. In Paradise that union would have taken place without any bashfulness, as an activity created and blessed by God...Now alas, it is so hideous and frightful a pleasure that physicians compare it with epilepsy or falling sickness. Thus an actual disease is linked with the very activity of procreation...[W]e cannot make use of woman without the horrible passion of lust.[13]

Following Paul, Luther rejected the theory that Eve's innate weakness and flaw caused the fall, but Adam still had the better press:

> Because Satan sees that Adam is more excellent, he does not dare to assail him; for he fears that his attempts may turn out to be useless. And I, too, believe that if he had tempted Adam first, the victory would have been Adam's. He would have crushed the serpent with his foot and would have said: "Shut up! The Lord's command was different!"[14]

Adam is at fault for allowing the order to be disrupted, but guilt hovers over Eve as instigator. Because of her disobedience, she is tied more stringently to Adam's rule and her own desire for him, and consequently to fulltime childbearing. Luther thought her punishment fair:

> If the woman had not been deceived by the serpent and had not sinned, she would have been the equal of Adam in all respects. For the punishment, that she is now subjected to man, was imposed on her after sin and because of sin, just as the other hardships and dangers were: travail, pain and countless other vexations.[15]

While Jesus made no use of the story to outline male–female roles, Luther built his whole case for the place of men and women on it. Because of Eve,

> [T]he rule remains with the husband, and the wife is compelled to obey him, by God's command. He rules the home and the state, wages wars, defends his possessions, tills the soil, builds, plants, etc. The woman, on the other hand, is like a nail driven into the wall. She sits at home...for just as the snail carried its house with it, so the wife should stay at home

and look after the affairs of the household, as one who has been deprived of the ability of administering those affairs that are outside and that concern the state. She does not go beyond her most personal duties.[16]

While Adam's specific assignment of working the soil for a living has expanded into every domain—ruling home and state, waging war, defending his possessions, building, planting, and tilling, Eve's "punishment," pain in childbirth and her husband's rule, restricts her to a single role in the private domain. Luther sees no problem:

> Women are generally disinclined to put up with this burden, and they naturally seek to gain what they have lost through sin. If they are unable to do more, they at least indicate their impatience by grumbling. However, they cannot perform the function of men, teach, rule, etc. In procreation and in feeding and nurturing their offspring they are masters. In this way Eve is punished; but, as I said in the beginning, it is a gladsome punishment if you consider the hope of eternal life and the honor of motherhood which have been left her.[17]

Luther even made a case from Eve for women taking their husband's name. God gave Adam power to name the animals, and, since Adam was also lord over Eve, it was in his power to name Eve.

> It would be unnatural if a husband wanted to be called by his wife's name. This is an indication and a confirmation of the punishment or subjection which the woman incurred through her sin.[18]

At the beginning of this chapter, I said feminists oppose not biological differences between men and women but the layers of "extras" packaged with those difference as "natural." Luther presents a full package!

Humanist scholar John Calvin, founder of the Reformed Church tradition, held to the secular belief of the day that the universe, state, and individual were part of some grand orderly scheme, and that disruption in one sphere caused disruption in every sphere. In this natural order where everything had a place "ordained" by God from the beginning, women were subservient to men. For Calvin, *Adam* was responsible for the fall, not Eve. His sin was not sexual desire but unfaithfulness. Adam's disobedience upset the created order, and its original excellence was lost. While Calvin acknowledged that there was no difference between male and female in the image of God, for him this applied to the *spiritual* kingdom. Until the world passed away, the order of creation with man created first and woman created from man's flesh, thus making her subservient, remained the legacy of the fall, the way society must be organized to avoid disorder. If women were unhappy with this *natural* order, it was a small yoke to bear until the restoration of God's Kingdom. Calvin released Eve from blame for the state of the world, but retained the patriarchal implications of her curse—that she should bear children in pain, and submit to the rule of her husband.[19]

It would take three hundred years for someone to ask the obvious question—why was Adam given the ruling power in the wake of the apple-eating fiasco? Elizabeth Cady Stanton, leader of the nineteenth-century women's movement, challenged this traditional "order of creation" in *The Women's Bible* of 1895, *praising* the superior conduct of Eve in her discussion with the serpent, who promised her not jewels and riches, but wisdom and knowledge. Elizabeth[20] questioned why Adam's *reward* for not taking the lead, and not resisting, was to rule *over* Eve:

> Then the woman, fearless of death if she can gain wisdom, takes of the fruit; and all the time Adam standing beside her interposes no word of objection...Had he been the representative of the divinely appointed head in married life, he assuredly would have taken upon himself the burden of the discussion with the serpent, but no, he is silent in this crisis of their fate. Having had the command from God himself he interposes no word of warning or remonstrance, but takes the fruit from the hand of his wife without a protest...The subsequent conduct of Adam was to the last degree dastardly. When the awful time of reckoning comes, and the Jehovah God appears to demand why his command has been disobeyed, Adam endeavors to shield himself behind the gentle being he has declared to be so dear. "The woman thou gavest to be with me, she gave me and I did eat," he whines—trying to shield himself at his wife's expense! Again, we are amazed that upon such a story men have built up a theory of their superiority![21]

As we shall see, *The Women's Bible* was swiftly discredited, and tucked under the rug for almost a century by Elizabeth's *women* colleagues, who saw her theological challenge as jeopardizing the Suffrage movement. Women could not afford to challenge the status quo *too* quickly!

But back to the 1700s! New rumblings were afoot as theology was challenged by scientific thought during the Enlightenment. This liberation of thinking for Enlightenment era men did not liberate women, however. Frenchman Jean-Jacques Rousseau (1712–78) epitomized Enlightenment thinking with his vision of the intellectually and morally self-sufficient man living in an ordered society modeled on the patriarchal family, where the ruler corresponded to the father and the people to wife and children. While all were born free and equal, subordinates surrendered liberty "for their own advantage." For Rousseau, egalitarianism destroyed sexual differences, class and national distinctions, and everything that threatened ordered society. Maleness and femaleness were "natural" qualities, not changeable roles, and the survival of the family depended on women's being wives and mothers, with no idea they could play roles that men played in the great theater of life. To say men and women were similar beings produced competitive tension, a clash of wills and struggle for mastery by which each exploited the other. They were different and complementary, each imperfect and requiring the other to be whole—two forming one single whole being. Woman "ruled" man by submitting to his will, knowing how to make him will what she needed to submit to! Thus, man's freedom of will was preserved and woman's will not denied—a mutual domination of each other.

While this all sounds mutual, we need to look further. Rousseau allowed women's power and equality *only* in the domestic arena, where they were assigned by *nature* to preserve the race. Women were equal *only* as wives and mothers, not as workers or citizens. The noble and free male walked in an ordered public world; the noble and free woman circled an enclosed space. Given their "inevitable" state of affairs, women compensated for their "slavery" by enslaving men with their modesty. Thus, Rousseau successfully projected that monstrous view of women as manipulative beings in the home, working on and through their men, which would carry European male thinking through the Victorian era and into this century. While promoting married mutual enslavement, Rousseau himself chose the asexual or nonheterosexual existence of the aristocratic few. [22] It was Rousseau's theories that would invite the first sustained feminist argument for equal rights for women—Mary Wollstonecraft's 1792 treatise *The Vindication of the Rights of Women*—setting the pace for the women's movements of the last two centuries.

Lots of water has flowed under the bridge, damming up into a deep ocean of reasons why women *must* be subordinate. It would be nice to report that in this century, Eve could lay her burden of blame down. But no. Let's hear from two heavyweights of the first half of this century from each side of the theological fence—Pope Pius XI and his 1930 *Casti Connubii,* an encyclical letter on marriage, and Karl Barth, the most influential Protestant theologian of this century.

The encyclical letter was a response to the women's rights movement, which gained the vote for many women around the world at the turn of this century, and also the 1930 Anglican Church's Lambeth Conference endorsement of contraception. The Pope's letter claimed the "illustrious Doctor of the Church" Augustine as its "authority" on women's place and role in marriage:

> Domestic society being confirmed, therefore, by this (marriage) bond of love, there should flourish in it that "order of love," as St. Augustine calls it. This order includes both the primacy of the husband with regard to the wife and children, the ready subjection of the wife and her willing obedience, which the Apostle commanded in these words: "Let women be subject to their husbands as to the Lord, because the husband is the head of the wife, as Christ is the head of the Church."[23]

Women's primary role within this "order of love" was reproduction, thus contraception other than "virtuous continence" agreed to by both parties was forbidden as frustrating the marriage act. For those who wished to justify such "criminal" activity—couples, weary of children, wishing to gratify desires without the consequent burden, couples who cannot remain continent, yet put the mother at risk with pregnancy, or couples who cannot afford more children—the encyclical says:

> No reason, however grave, may be put forward by which anything intrinsically against nature may become comfortable to nature and morally good. Since, therefore, the conjugal act is destined primarily by nature for the begetting of children, those who in exercising it deliberately frustrate its natural power and purpose sin against nature and commit a deed which is shameful and intrinsically vicious.[24]

There is no acknowledgment that celibacy also frustrates the natural course of things!

The authority for forcing women into constant pregnancy, or fear of pregnancy, as the expression of their whole being and purpose, was Augustine:

> As St. Augustine notes: "Intercourse, even with one's legitimate wife, is unlawful and wicked where the conception of the offspring is prevented. Onan, the son of Judah, did this and the Lord killed him for it."[25]

The antennae shoot up. Who was Onan, and what did he do (Gen. 38: 4–10, Deut. 25: 5–10)? Onan as an argument against contemporary contraception takes the cake! It's like comparing apples and oranges—no, not even that close. This is the type of argument that feminist theologians challenge, arguments that have crippled women's lives without their even knowing the flimsy structures on which they stand. In Hebrew tribal law, if a man died childless, his brother was obliged to father a child for him by his widow. Onan's father, Judah, insisted Onan marry his dead brother's wife. During intercourse, Onan withdrew prior to ejaculation, because the baby would not be for his line but his brother's. The *offense* for which Onan was killed was neither masturbation (onanism) nor birth control—sex without risk of pregnancy. The *offense* was refusing to fulfill his legal and family obligations to his brother's wife, hardly an issue in our society!

While Augustine and his successor, Pope Pius XI, used Onan's "divine" punishment to extract some moral and ethical rules against conception "from the Bible," they *conveniently* ignore other "family values" in the rest of the story! At Onan's death, his father, Judah, promised his twice-widowed daughter-in-law his next son. He failed to follow through, so the daughter-in-law, determined to produce a child, as Hebrew women must do, disguised herself as a prostitute in a neighboring city and slept with Judah, her unsuspecting father-in-law, who was there on business! When her pregnancy was discovered, her father-in-law accused her of whoredom and ordered her burned, but she had planned well and produced tangible evidence of Judah's night with her, saving her skin and ensuring her child a legitimate inheritance.

Why is God's judgment on Onan used as God's "no" to contraception in twentieth-century marriages, when the rest of the story flies in the face of marriage ideals today? Why not also argue that God commands men to marry their brother's widow, that God wills childless, single women to prostitute themselves to have a baby, that God approves of consorting with prostitutes on business trips, or that God orders the burning of women caught in sin? Over and over in this book I ask that we dig more deeply into the context when a verse of scripture is used to validate God's divinely ordained will for women. This is not subversive or heretical. It is common sense and justice, the way any *responsible* theological conclusions have been drawn for centuries!

The 1930 encyclical's response to contraception when a mother's life was in danger put the priority on procreation (my italics):

> Holy Mother Church very well understands and clearly appreciates all that is said regarding the health of the mother and the danger to her life. And who will not grieve to think of these things? Who is not filled with the greatest admiration when he sees a mother risking her life with heroic fortitude, that she may preserve the life of the offspring which she has conceived? God alone, all bountiful and all merciful as He is, can reward her for the fulfillment of the *office allotted to her by nature*, and will assuredly repay her in a measure full to overflowing.[26]

There is a reason why the mother's distress is not a priority—Eve's punishment, legitimating women's suffering in childbirth. In 1853, theologians brought charges against Queen Victoria's physician when he used anesthesia on her during childbirth, saying it was a violation of the "natural" curse on Eve and thus all women—"In pain you shall bring forth children."[27] There is an underlying vindictiveness toward women in these attitudes that I find abhorrent as a woman and a theologian. It is telling when we realize that no such righteous indignation surfaced from male theologians when the plow and the tractor eased the burden of man's natural "curse" of laboring in the fields!

The encyclical reaffirmed Adam and Eve as God's model for marriage and the subordination and obedience a wife owes her man. It still promoted Augustine's idea of sin as sexual desire, condemning sex and contraception for "impure gratification" rather than "honest wedlock"—meaning procreation. It claimed the suffrage movement's demand for women's vote, equal status as citizens, and ownership of property was a *crime,* not the true emancipation of women or the "rational and exalted liberty which belongs to the noble office of a Christian woman and wife."

> It is rather the debasing of the womanly character and the dignity of motherhood, and indeed of the whole family, as a result of which the husband suffers the loss of his wife, the children of their mother, and the home and the whole family of an ever watchful guardian. More than this, this detriment of the woman herself, for if the woman descends from her true regal throne to which she has been raised within the walls of the home by means of the Gospel, she will soon be reduced to the old state of slavery (if not in appearance, certainly in reality) and become, amongst the pagans, the mere instrument of man.[28]

On the other side of the ecclesiastical fence at this time, Protestant theologian Karl Barth was also developing his theology about women in response to writings by French feminists like Simone de Bouvoir. He began his argument not from the Fall, but from the creation story where man and woman are created for each other because it was not good for man to be alone. Woman's creation was the *pinnacle* of creation, since it gave Adam his "helpmeet." At this point, man and woman were fully equal before God, standing or falling together. Sounds good, but not for long. Barth, like Luther and Calvin, must reconcile this with the hierarchical order they "read" into Eden from the New Testament letters as the model for all relationships—God to Christ, Christ to Church, preacher to congregation, man to woman—the divine order in creation.

Reacting to feminist moves to break down designated role differences between men and women, Barth said these distinctions were *not* illusionary. The command of God pointed man to his position and woman to hers, as God created them male and female in the beginning—not two A's equal and interchangeable, but an A and a B not to be equated, sanctified *in their particular place* in relation to each other.

> It is here we see the order outside which man cannot be man nor woman be woman, either in themselves or in their mutual orientation and relationship.[29]

This order of creation also prescribed an order of *succession* from Adam and Eve. A preceded B, B followed A, preceding and following, superordination and subordination. Man as superordinate does not enjoy privilege or advantage over the woman, nor should he engage in self-glorification, but is simply

> taking the lead as the inspirer, leader, and initiator in their common being and action...Only as he accepts her as fellowman, only together with her, can he be the first in his relationship to her—the first in a sequence which would have no meaning if she did not follow and occupy her own place in it.[30]

Barth acknowledged that this divine order might seem restrictive and unfair to women, but God's commands it, so "that's the way it is, folks." In response to the feminist challenges of his time, he said:

> It is understandable that woman should protest and rebel against this exploitation, although she ought to realize at once that here, as elsewhere, protesting and rebelling are one thing and the way from disorder to order quite another. It cannot be a question of women attaining their rights as opposed to man and his, but of man's understanding of the order and sequence and therefore the obligation in which he is the first, of his primary submitting and rendering obedience to the common law instead of standing upon his own rights...By simply protesting and rebelling, woman, even though she were a thousand times in the right, does not affirm and respect the order under which she also stands and by which alone she can vindicate her rights.[31]

Barth's whole argument was made on his literal reading of the Genesis statement that man shall rule over women and the few texts attributed to Paul that speak of women submitting to their husbands, both of which we shall challenge later in the book. He conveniently ignored the many Pauline texts that talk of breaking down graded differences between men and women to a discipleship of equals. Describing how women should feel about being subordinated and restricted within the marriage relationship, he said:

> This order gives her her proper place, and in pride that it is hers, she may and should assume it as freely as man assumes his...Properly speaking, the business of woman, her task and function, is to actualize the fellowship in which man can only precede her, stimulating, leading and inspiring. How could she do this alone, without the precedence of man? How could she do it for herself and against him? How could she reject or envy his precedence, his task and function, as the one who stimulates, leads and inspires? To wish to replace him in this, or to do it with him, would be to wish not to be a woman...Why should not woman be second in sequence, but only in sequence? What other choice has she, seeing she can be nothing at all apart from this sequence and her place within it? And why should she desire anything else, seeing this function and her share in the common service has its own special honor and greatness, an honor and greatness which man in his place and within the limits of his function cannot have?[32]

The style of argument is so familiar it makes me cringe each time I read it. Barth's decorative words paint a picture of the honor and glory of women such that a woman who rebels is portrayed as an ungrateful wretch. As in Rousseau's view, woman is almost divine when seated high on a pedestal, with accolades and honor far greater than man, so long as she stays on that pedestal where she has been put, not of her own asking but by men. This kind of language traps women into silence, making them feel guilty if they ask for anything more than confinement to domesticity in a private sphere.

For Barth, this divine order was inviolable even though, in a fallen world, such inequality of place might lead to a "genuinely and irreparably deplorable" situation for women. Even then, the order cannot be challenged, so women, like their medieval sisters—"hospitals for men's souls" against the temptations of fornication—must accept another male "servicing" role as their "natural" place regardless of personal consequences, to preserve the male soul by her "goodness":

> There can be no shadow of sadness and resignation and therefore no spark of rebellion even in relation to a tyrannical or weak man. In face of an erring man the mature woman will not only be sure of herself in her quiet self-restriction, but she will also know her duty and witness toward him. Successfully or otherwise...she is in her whole existence an appeal

to the kindness of man…She puts him under an obligation to be kind…He can and must take such a one seriously. If anything can disturb his male tyranny and therefore his male weakness, if anything can challenge him to goodness and therefore to the acceptance of woman, it is encounter with the self-restricting woman.[33]

No wonder in Christian churches today, domestic violence has been so devastating. Submission to male tyranny and abuse as *duty* and *witness* was the sign, according to Barth, of a "mature woman" who knows her proper place.

I once wrote a college essay critiquing Barth's imprisonment of women to what he read as a "divine order." My professor graciously agreed that Barth was a product of his time, but assured me his views on men and women had been culturally superseded. He thought I was being intolerant, critiquing his views as problematic rather than allowing "the past to be the past." But Barth's thinking has *not* been relegated to the past. His ideas on almost everything are still *very* influential in theological circles, and his ideas of women are heeded along with his other ideas, forming a new generation of theologians who gently but firmly put women in their subordinate place. We only need to listen to the Promise Keepers for a few moments to see reflections of these final words from Barth:

> She will endorse the strength of the strong man which is the strength of his sense of responsibility and service, and successfully or otherwise she will negate the tyranny of the tyrant…(She) knows and takes her proper place, not in relation to man but in relation to the order. She realizes that between man and woman there can be no question of claim and counter-claim or the brutal struggle for power, but of rivalry only in regard to the right following of the path common to both but specifically allotted to each. Therefore, while she compares herself to the man, she will not compare her place and right to his. If she is challenged by him, it is not whether his attitude and function might not equally well be hers, but whether she is truly fulfilling the position and function assigned to her…By (this) she asserts rather her independence, showing her mastery, her true equality with man. [34]

We cannot leave our discussion of women role models without mentioning one more woman. If Lilith and Eve fared badly, perhaps that other great woman of the Bible will do better.

> Hail Mary, full of grace, the Lord is with thee.
> Blessed art thou among women
> And blessed is the fruit of thy womb, Jesus…

Jaroslav Pelikan said "You could copy on an eight-and-a-half-by-eleven sheet everything there is about Mary in the New Testament…to get from skimpy evidence to what she has become is an astonishing example of how an idea can develop out of small beginning."[35] Yet Mary, like Eve and Lilith, steps on a rollercoaster, alternately elevated and demoted. Robert Sullivan asks,

> Why are two billion Hail Marys said daily? Why did five million people, many non-Christian, visit Lourdes this year to drink the healing waters? Why did more than 10 million trek to Guadeloupe to pray to Our Lady?…How can it be that Mary adorns the banners of liberals who seek a greater role for women in all churches, and also those of conservatives who would keep ministries all-male? What is it about Mary?[36]

The easy answer is that she was Jesus' mother. As twelfth-century theologian Bernard of Clairvaux advised, "If you fear the Father, go to the Son, if you fear the Son, go to the Mother."[37] If she was so honored for her mothering, surely she is the antidote for negativity about women stemming from Eve? We shall see.

What do we know of Mary from the New Testament? Paul refers to her only to acknowledge Jesus' origins—Jesus "born of a woman, born under the law" (Gal. 4:4). He does not call her a "virgin," the term for any young, unmarried woman. The earliest Gospel, Mark, does not mention Jesus' birth but moves from John the Baptist to the baptism of Jesus. Mary and Jesus' brothers in Mark 3 suspect, with the crowds and Scribes, that Jesus is deranged and try to restrain him. When Jesus is told his mother and brothers are in the crowd, he calls the *crowd* his family. When the neighbors took offense at his preaching, Jesus agrees that prophets are not honored in their own country, among their kin, *in their own house* (Mk. 6:1−6)!

Although they give differing accounts, the Gospels of Matthew and Luke, written later than Mark, talk of Mary's virginal conception, announced to Joseph in Matthew and to Mary in Luke. Matthew writes from *Joseph's* perspective—his vision, his dilemma over a pregnant fiancée, hiding her until the birth, and their escape to Egypt. Only Luke describes Mary's reaction to her pregnancy, accepting her role as servant of God. Luke keeps track of Mary. He records Jesus' consecration in the temple where Simeon tells Mary that "a sword will pierce your own soul also" (Lk. 2:35). He mentions an incident when someone praised the body that birthed Jesus, and Jesus' reply, "Blessed rather are those who hear the word of God and obey it" (Lk. 11:27−28). He records the young Jesus' rebuke to his mother in the Temple that he must be about his father's business (Lk. 2:21−40). He includes Mary with the Twelve in the upper room (Acts 1:14) and describes her as present at Pentecost (Acts 2:1−4). In John's Gospel, she is unnamed. As "his mother," she finally persuades Jesus to do something about the shortage of wine at a wedding (Jn. 2:1−11); she and his brothers accompany him to Capernaum (2:13); and she waits at the cross with other women and John, whom Jesus calls her "son" and she his "mother"(19:25−27).

These scant references are all we have in the Bible of the woman who would become first in the hearts of Christians seeking access to her son. There is an ambivalence in Mary. Mark 3 shows her questioning Jesus' mental stability.

Luke records her ambivalence about his birth: "But Mary treasured all these words and pondered them in her heart" (Lk. 2:19). At the temple, she did not understand why Jesus wanted to be with the teachers (Lk. 2:21–40), but seems to have joined his cause. She was at the cross (Jn. 19:25–27) and with the Twelve after Jesus' ascension (Acts 1:14). The only extended opportunity to hear from Mary is her dialogue with the angel at her conception, and her dialogue with Elizabeth during her pregnancy, including her song (Lk. 1:46–55) modeled on Hannah's song (1 Sam. 2:1–10).

Despite, or perhaps *because* of, this lack of information, the cult of Mary—Mariology—grew. She was continuously reinvented to fit what people needed of her. Justin Martyr, toward the end of the first century, was first to interpret her as the Second Eve:

> The firstborn of the Father is born of the Virgin, in order that the disobedience caused by the serpent might be destroyed in the same manner in which it had been originated. For Eve, an undefiled virgin, conceived the word of the serpent, and brought forth disobedience and death. But the Virgin Mary, filled with faith and joy, when the angel Gabriel announced to her the glad tidings...answered, "Be it done to me according to thy word."[38]

His contemporary, Irenaeus, reiterated the parallel—bad woman, good woman—saying that since the human race was sentenced to death by a virgin's disobedience, it was saved by a virgin's obedience. By the fourth century, when virginity was the ideal, sin, sexuality, and death depicted Eve, but obedience, virginity, and eternal life were Mary's credentials. Man fell through Eve but was redeemed through Mary.

As Mary became elevated compared with Eve, the Church had to fill in the blanks about her in the New Testament. Since Jesus was conceived from God's uncontaminated seed, Mary's resumé must be cleared of original sin and any human sexual contact. She was declared Mother of God at the Council of Ephesus in 431 C.E. Later church decrees insisted that she was not just a virgin *before* Jesus' birth but a perpetual virgin never involved in sexual intercourse. The brothers of Jesus were first declared children of Joseph's first marriage, and then identified as cousins in Jerome's fourth-century Latin translation of the Bible.[39] Mary's hymen was declared intact before, during, and after delivery, not damaged or torn. Had her hymen not been intact, or had she been shown to have engaged in intercourse, she would be no better than Eve (woman), that "cauldron containing the hell of lustfulness." Her delivery was painless, as opposed to Eve's curse, "because she conceived without carnal pleasure" and delivered Jesus like a ray of light "the way spirits pass through the body without resistance."[40]

Because Augustine had declared that original sin came with pregnancy from contaminated seed, concern in the Middle Ages about Mary's original sin caused *her* conception to be declared "free from original sin" as well from her mother's womb. Belief in her immaculate conception was reaffirmed by the papacy in 1854, and her assumption into heaven, formulated in the sixth century, was affirmed in 1950, removing her from the stain of death, the consequence of Eve's sin. Vatican II (1962–65) sought to change this otherworldly image Mary had acquired, but the pendulum swung back with Pope John Paul II. His traditional view of Mary and his devotion to her, signified by his motto *Totius tuus* (completely yours), has encouraged her ever-higher elevation and her ever-increasing apparitions and miracles. Speculation hovers as to whether the pope might make another pronouncement, giving Mary, creator of miracles and ultimate mediator between humanity and her Son, a more significant role in salvation. Many Catholic theologians are concerned about this move from scholarship and normal devotion to Mary through the church, and statements from Vittorio Messori, the pope's collaborator, do little to ease fears:

> The old lady who rattles her rosary beads in the darkened corner of a church is wiser than all the professors at the Pontifical universities, because venerating Mary is the best way to take Mary's son seriously. And the Madonna, when she appears, appears to shepherds, not professors.[41]

The Mary created by the church remains an ambivalent, puzzling model as perfect woman and mother. Sinless and pure, free from sexual contact and desire, she is what Eve, and every other woman, can never be. She is "pure woman" in contrast to all other "impure" women. While she is a mother, she is both supreme virgin and supreme mother, an impossible feat for any woman. While a perpetual virgin who birthed God's offspring without sexual contact may be good for celibate priests, what does this image say to women looking for a role model—pure, self-denying, eternally nurturing, ecstatic in the performance of her tasks, "divinely" submissive and humble? And what do we know of Mary's mothering techniques anyway? On what do we base our claims she was the perfect mother?

Mary reinforces women's ambivalence. How does Mary as *virgin* and *mother,* saved from sexual use, and the ultimate female image of a church rigidly opposed to birth control, function as comfort for a South American woman dying from her fourteenth pregnancy in as many years, or a poor black woman fearful of another child she cannot feed or clothe? As perfect, understanding mother negotiating on their behalf with the men that count—her Son and his Father—what has she achieved for them? She functions for the most part not as a *liberator* from hopeless situations, or as a *critic* of church assumptions about women that assign them to such fates, but as "ideal woman" in a *patriarchal* society, knowing her "proper" place in relation to her men and operating within it. She can understand, comfort, soothe the dying, hopefully influence her Son through motherly persuasion, do miracles through her connections, and promise a reward in another life, but she cannot overthrow the system that puts women—and her—in that submissive, passive role.

Fearing "popery," Protestant church fathers treated Mary with the same uneasiness she probably experienced back in the neighborhood as a pregnant girl. Stripped of ethereal credentials, devoid of a miraculous or mediatory roles and definitely in the background, Protestantism simply saw her as a "good" mother, submissive and humble to God's will. Not only does she unquestionably and joyfully accept the divine assignment to be pregnant and unmarried with an unlikely story in a culture that put such women to death, she also utters the self-abasing question "Why me?" Despite scant comments in scripture, the Christmas Mary has "spoken" volumes in books, plays, and films about her motherly experience. Her relative silence in the Bible allows each generation to use her afresh for their own purposes, continually writing and editing her ambivalent script. Just as you feel you can grab onto Mary as a foremother, she doesn't quite materialize.

This is a shame, because there are wonderful words attributed to Mary that are profoundly relevant today. While her cousin Elizabeth's greeting "Blessed is the fruit of thy womb" is said repeatedly around the world, Mary's reply, paralleling the prayer of Samuel's mother Hannah, is rarely heard (Lk. 1:48–54).

> [God] has looked with favor on the lowliness of his servant. Surely from now on all generations will call me blessed…[H]e has scattered the proud in the thoughts of their hearts. He has brought down the powerful from their thrones, and lifted up the lowly; he has filled the hungry with good things, and sent the rich away empty.

Mary's song tells of her hopes for Jesus—that in this Man, her Son, all unjust systems of the day will be upturned. Mary, herself poor and marginalized like three quarters of her people, *knew* about oppression. Her song has become a central theme of hope for Christians struggling against oppression in many countries today. If only those two billion "Hail Marys" had included the *rest* of the conversation between those two women, Mary's words might revolutionize the world!

Thus ends the tale of three women. Lilith, the shadowy figure behind the Christian story, gives birth to a demonic universe. Eve, mother of all living, brings down the whole of humanity she produced. Mary, the *ultimately* perfect mother, circumvents all her female bodiliness in order to produce *only* the offspring of God. The road from Eve to Lilith to Mary is a long one, involving centuries of their reconstruction into ambivalent models of womanhood for Western Christian culture. Their deconstruction will not be rapid and it becomes more complex and subtle when women *appear* on the ground floor of things to be recovering their place, while the structures and assumptions of centuries about women remain as strong as ever in the basement.

CHAPTER 4

Stepping Out of Their Place

Whether marriage establishes between the husband and wife a perfect equality of rights or conveys to the former a certain degree of superiority over the latter, is a point not left among Christians to be decided by speculative argument. The intimation of the divine will, communicated to the first woman immediately after the fall, is corroborated by various injunctions delivered in the New Testament…Let not pride or ignorance be for a moment permitted to suggest, that the Father of the universe, in allotting obedience to the wife, has displayed a partial regard to the welfare and comfort of the husband. Eternal wisdom, incapable of error and of caprice, has in this dispensation consulted her happiness no less than that of her associate…To which of the two parties would it be wisest and best that the preeminence should be assigned?…Man…has been furnished by the Creator with powers of investigation and of foresight in a somewhat larger measure than the other sex…he should be the person to whom the superiority should be committed.

"The Female Instructor"(1815)[1]

My research in the British Library for women lost from history turned up this 1815 treasure *The Female Instructor: Advice To the Fair Sex Both Before and After Marriage*, assuring readers that God's will, intimated at the fall and backed up by the New Testament, was unequivocally clear that men were superior. This message has boomed throughout history from sermons in pulpits, priests in confessionals, fathers to daughters, husbands to wives. Women have heard with their ears, obeyed with their actions, but, like Mary the village girl, pondered them deep in the privacy of their hearts.

46

In every century, such pondering produced a handful—often a host—of women strong enough to resist forgone conclusions about them deduced by men with privileged access to God's mind. Women's resistance has taken many shapes, depending on women's access to power. These women shared in common a feeling, often not even shaped into words or causes, that women were of equal value to men, at least in God's sight if not in the eyes of the world; that injustices were perpetuated against women by descriptions of their inferiority; and that something had to be done about it without delay, even if it led to danger or death. These feelings, by another name, are feminism.

In this chapter, we'll browse back again through Christian history, alighting briefly in a few tents, homes, convents, and public places where women experienced these feelings strongly enough to try to change the world, the church, or even their assigned domestic sphere. Many stories are lost; some are only found on the edges of men's stories; others have earned fame—or infamy—for women stepping out of assigned roles or causing disruption in the world of men. By hearing the variety of ways women have challenged established rules of how things are, I want to show that feminism cannot be captured in one definition, no matter how broad. It certainly is not limited to a few twentieth-century expressions, but has been with us for centuries.

Women who question the rules do not always share the same vocabulary, worldview, or causes. Some of the negativity toward feminism today is caused by the fact that "norms" are held up—positive and negative. "Feminists think this…" "feminists do that…" The difficulty with norms is that exceptions immediately pop up, making nuisances of themselves for our neat definitions. It's like trying to get all the tentacles of an octopus into a bucket at the same time! In this chapter, the tentacles will *hang out,* so the stories of women "resisting" can define their own brand of feminism. Our twentieth century judgments of how they *should* have acted don't count. We must listen to how *they* saw their place and role, *their* sense of injustice, and *their* assessment of how best to protest within *their* specific and often limited circumstances. We have seen how women's subordinate place has been defined in Christian history. Now we will listen for "feminist" foremothers who refused to be silenced by such unjust restrictions.

The book of Esther in the Hebrew Bible tells of two royal women, Vashti and Esther, who, in their own way, protested their fate as disposable property of the king. Ahasuerus, mighty king of Persia, had thrown a party for his staff, and ordered Queen Vashti to parade before him and his drunken friends wearing the royal crown—some suggest it was *all* she was to wear—to show off her beauty. Vashti refused, and the angry king forbade her to enter his presence again. He feared some fallout, however (Esth. 1:17–19):

> For this deed of the queen will be made known to all women, causing
> them to look with contempt on their husbands, since they will say, "King

Ahasuerus commanded Queen Vashti to be brought before him, and she did not come." This very day noble ladies of Persia and Media who have heard of the queen's behavior will rebel against the king's officials and there will be no end of contempt and wrath!

The need for spin doctors suggests the king's order was demeaning and Vashti's response inspirational for other women in the same situation. The king circulated the provinces, holding up Vashti as an example, to reinforce every man as "master in his own house." He then ordered virgins brought to his harem, to choose her replacement. Esther, a Jewish woman, became queen. However, when she heard of a plan to destroy the Jews, she entered the king's inner court to dissuade him, even though no one, under pain of death, could go in uninvited—not even a queen. When the king saw her beauty, his heart was softened. To make a long story short, the Jewish ethnic cleansing plan was averted and anti-Jewish activists put to death.

Both these women knew their tenuous situation in a court society where rebellious or disobedient women were dispensable. Vashti attracted the inevitable consequences for her resistance. The Bible is silent about her reasons. Did she overestimate her power over the king or her position as queen? Had she resisted before, but miscalculated his humiliation in front of his staff? Or had she simply had enough, saying no to a system that made her a plaything for her husband? Esther also risked death, but *used* the power she and Vashti had over the king as objects of his desire for a greater purpose. Despite double jeopardy as woman and Jew, and with Vashti's fate clearly in her mind, she gambled on her beauty and won a reprieve for her people. Some feminist critics might object to Esther using her looks to get what she wanted from her man, but they would miss the point. Feminism is not about certain right and wrong ways to act, but about *acting* and protesting, in whatever form might succeed in the limits of the situation.

At the other end of the power spectrum was Jephthah's daughter (Judg. 11). Jephthah, renowned for guerrilla tactics, led the Gileadites against their enemies on the condition that he be made leader if they won. Desperate for victory, he promised God a sacrifice of the first person to meet him on his return home from victory. It was his only daughter—the worst-case scenario. The Bible does not discuss the morals of the bargain or make the vow God's idea, but Jephthah, as ruler of his household, *could* make such a deal with the lives in his possession. Jephthah blamed his daughter for his predicament. "You have become the cause of great trouble to me. For I have opened my mouth to the Lord, and I cannot take back my vow." The daughter replied, "do with me according to what has gone out of your mouth."

I want to grab this girl and tell her she has value, that he has no right to take her life—it says so in the Ten Commandments, doesn't it? But this is *my* protest from a society where the courts would uphold my intervention. The daughter with no name knew she had no power to prevent her fate, but made a request. Realizing she would die childless, she begged time to bewail her virginity with her women friends. The women went to the hills for two months, and then the daughter was killed. There is no intervention from God as there was with Abraham's son Isaac. Only in the last sentence does a splinter of light pierce the dark horror of the story. Her women friends—perhaps her mother among them—refused to let this pass unprotested, even though the "deal" seemed satisfactorily settled for Jephthah. After thirty-nine verses about Jephthah's "problem," the story ends:

> So there arose an Israelite custom that for four days every year the daughters of Israel would go out to lament the daughter of Jephthah the Gileadite. (vv. 39–40)

Powerless women did the only thing they could to resist the murder of a young girl. Having supported her through sorrow and death, they established an annual period of mourning to remember her. Here is feminist protest in the shadow of evil. Jephthah's actions might have been acceptable in the culture, but it did not make his daughter's death right in the eyes of these women.

When Paul preached the new freedom in Christ from Jewish and Roman laws that graded men over women, Jews over Greeks, and slaves over free people, he might not have been prepared for the many women who heard this not just as freedom *to* follow Jesus, but freedom *from* subordination in marriages arranged for them from puberty, often with pagan husbands. Many such women were martyred for their rebellion, drawing an additional charge besides being Christian, that of resisting their proper place in the patriarchal household and modeling a female counterculture.

Thecla, described in the *Acts of Paul and Thecla*,[2] did exactly that. She refused a lucrative marriage arranged by her widowed mother and ran off to join Paul. Her mother begged Thecla's fiancé to talk sense into her about that strange man Paul

> …who teaches deceptive and subtle words…disturbing the city of the Iconians, and your Thecla too; for all the women and young people go to him. "You must," he says, "fear one single God only, and live in chastity." And my daughter, too, like a spider at the window, bound by his words, is dominated by a new desire and a fearful passion; for the girl hangs upon the things he says, and is taken captive.[3]

When Thecla rejected her fiancé's pleas, he had Paul and her arrested. Her mother, furious that Thecla would jeopardize their security and resist her proper role of marriage, joined the crowd calling for her punishment when she refused to recant:

> Burn the lawless one! Burn her that is no bride in the middle of the amphitheater, so that all the women who have been taught by this man may be struck with terror![4]

Paul was beaten and driven out of town. Thecla, her guilt greater for upsetting the social order, was condemned to burn. She was brought to the arena, stretched naked on a pile and the wood ignited, but heavy rain allowed her escape. She was arrested again, this time for resisting the advances of a noble- man who no doubt thought this single woman was "unclaimed" property, she was thrown to wild beasts. When this badly wounded woman was released, many believed in God as a result of her courage. Thecla was prepared to die— twice—rather than deny her freedom, like her Christian *brothers,* to follow Christ as a single person, even though she was a woman.

Thecla's decision to resist marriage inspired a trail of other women to do the same, despite threats of persecution. Their vows of celibacy were declara- tions of independence and spiritual freedom, and many went bravely to death for their resistance against Roman societal codes. Two hundred years later, celibate women living in solitude or in monastic communities still called them- selves "new Theclas." By then, however, celibacy had become the *superior* choice over marriage, and the title "male woman" began to appear for such women, revered not as *women,* but because they had become "manly" by rejecting their female functions.

It might seem strange to suggest that women who *denied* their female functions, becoming "male," were feminists, but theirs was a rebellious resis- tance against their only option—becoming the property of a man often not of their choosing. Feminism is about women being able to *choose* for themselves how they will live their lives, as men do, and choice depends on what options are available. When I talk of such women choosing the celibate life over mar- riage, I am not saying marriage was bad. There are many women who found their place within patriarchal marriages in these times, but since the law gave a husband complete ownership over a wife, her happiness and safety de- pended solely on his goodwill, which sometimes was *no* security! The single life in the safety of a community of women offered not an alternate choice, but a choice! "New Theclas" chose this life over marriage for a variety of reasons. Paula, a wealthy Roman widow, joined church father Jerome in exile and personally financed one monastery for men and three for women. Queen Bathildis, the English wife of a French king, became a nun once her son had become king. Queen Etheldreda of Northumbria became a nun *against* her husband's will, founding a monastery to care for the poor and sick, while Irmina, a German princess, became a nun when her betrothed fell off a cliff while struggling with a rival for her hand.

By the Middle Ages, women had gained no new autonomy in marriage. Girls were married according to their father's choice. Only half survived child- bearing, and half their children died in infancy. Medieval gynecological texts highlight the horrors of childbirth when doctors and midwives had little more than poultices and potions. The convent remained an option, but while earlier "new Theclas" had *chosen* this alternate way of life to resist an arranged marriage, the convent life was now being chosen *for* girls by their parents. Many were placed in convents as young children—the family's "tithe" to the church—or against their will as a solution for unmarried or unruly daughters. It is interesting how many religious women whose names *did* survive in church history for making a difference, did not want convent life, yet, strong as they were, negotiated options for themselves *within* these confines of high walls *and* male hierarchy.

Something else was stirring in the Middle Ages—bubbling hot spots in the cauldron of ecclesiastical order. The papacy had lost touch with the people, and its power was corrupted by the embarrasing situation of two popes in two different cities. Devout lay people reacted against the institutional church and wanted other ways to live their spiritual lives free from its control. Women especially, who had no power in the church, responded to this diverse spiritual movement across Europe. While many still entered monastic communities, many others chose to live a life of piety as individuals or in small communities without a monastic rule. Some saw their calling to prayer, others to work with the needy. Some chose a celibate life, others remained in celibate marriages, and widows chose not to remarry. The consensus among such women was that demands of home and family were an insuperable impediment to holy life. One could not obey both an earthly husband and Christ.

One such subversive group of women who would eventually bring down the wrath of the church on themselves were the Beguines, lay women in the Netherlands living in small communities in cities. They had no vows, were celibate, and engaged in prayer and ministry to the poor and sick—the active *and* contemplative life. They did not renounce property or commit for life, had no organizational structures, supported themselves by weaving and sewing, and attended local churches. The movement swept Europe in the twelfth and thirteenth centuries as a way independently minded women without the considerable dowry required to enter some convents could live spiritual lives free of an overlord, be it husband, father, or priest. Around 1300, there were three hundred Beguines in Strasbourg out of a population of 20,000! Not surprisingly, Church hostility mounted against this growing trend of "religious" women outside of male ecclesiastical control, and the cry of "heresy"—that generic charge for anything threatening church authority—led to their persecution. By the fourteenth century, their communities were forbidden, and the women were forced into convents under male supervision. Their male counterparts, the Beghards, were allowed to continue by agreeing to submit to ecclesiastical direction!

A major issue in the Middle Ages was the problem of women "teaching." Teaching was the sole domain of men in holy orders. Hadn't Paul said a woman should not teach (1 Cor. 14:34–37; 1 Tim. 2:11–15)? What then should be the fate of women who claimed to see visions or hear God speak to them? Prophecies and revelations were a hot commodity during periods when society and the church were in disarray. Churchmen were willing to listen to strange voices, even women's voices. Thus, when there were two popes and two papal seats during the fourteenth century—a major crisis of authority—uneducated women claiming mystical insights, visions, and messages from God (living saints) were encouraged. These women differed from the Beguines in that, while they pursued this "vocation" as unmarried women outside the cloister, they submitted to the control of a male confessor priest.

Catherine of Siena was one such "living saint" who attached herself in 1363 to a Dominican lay order dedicated to the poor. Her extraordinary life-style and rejection of the social order disturbed clerics, who put her under the control of a Dominican priest. Their roles reversed when *he* became convinced of her saintliness, submitted to her teachings, and began promoting her to the world! Catherine went on to inspire reform in the Dominican order and beyond; she was canonized in 1461 and declared a Doctor of the Church in 1970. While Catherine's visions gave her power in the church during a period of popularity of such eccentric female models of sanctity operating independently, there has always been a fine line between what was hallowed as ecstatic prophecy and what was condemned as consorting with the devil.

> What witches could do through demonic agency was possible for holy women through the ministry of angels, but the goals of their amazing flights were diametrically opposed; while witches gathered at their Sabbath to worship the devil and trample on the Christian faith, the holy women traveled to Jerusalem to venerate the cross and were transported invisibly to various places to convert sinners or perform acts of charity.[5]

Church theologians charged with detecting special powers in holy women were *also* responsible for detecting women possessed by the devil. With a stroke of the inquisitor's pen, the scales could fatally tip. The specter of the inherently weak and deceitful female, the daughter of Eve, hovered in the shadow of even the brightest "living saint."

This was the fate of Joan of Arc. This peasant girl began hearing voices from God at thirteen telling her to lead the French army against the English. Her village suspected "witchcraft" and tried to force Joan into a marriage. In 1429, when the English laid siege to Orléans, seventeen-year-old Joan appeared before the French dauphin with her "message." After many examinations for demon possession, she was permitted to lead the army. The French were desperate to try anything! Clad in "white armor" and men's clothes, Joan led 6,000 soldiers into besieged Orléans. She rode into battle at the head of her army and the English retreated. Hailed as a heroine and gift from God, Joan unsuccessfully urged the apathetic dauphin, now king, to completely expel the English from France. After attempting a few more battles without his support, Joan was captured by the Duke of Burgundy's troops, secretly allied with the dauphin *and* the English. The King made no attempt to rescue her, and the Archbishop of Reims blamed her capture on her refusal to take orders. While she had been allowed to "step out of her female place" when her spiritual connections were useful, the scales tipped when she assumed an ongoing place in this male world after she had helped the king and his cronies gain power. The "saint" of Orléans was on her way to becoming a witch.

Joan was tried for heresy, imprisoned, and "sold" to the English. At her trial, she defended herself against her "crimes": forsaking clothes of the feminine sex against divine law, to wear those of a man; committing cruel acts of homicide; convincing simple folk she was sent from God and had knowledge of divine secrets; and holding serious doctrines scandalous to the Catholic faith. She was passed to a church court to be tried as a heretic for claiming God spoke to her, but refused to say what her voices had said. Interrogators then focused on proving her a witch, that her voices were the devil; and on her dressing in male attire "against nature," familiar charges for women "out of place." Public opinion sided with Joan. Finally the verdict came:

> The visions and voices were either "human inventions" or the work of devils; that Joan's evidence was a tissue of lies; that she was blasphemous toward God and impious toward her parents; schismatic as regarded the church.[6]

Joan refused to recant, and her male attire became for her *and* her opponents the "symbol" of her resistance. The bishop offered her communion if she wore a dress, but Joan refused, claiming God would hear her mass without priestly assistance.

Finally taken to the scaffold, Joan, in a moment of fear, "confessed" that she lied about her revelations, had worn an immodest outfit "against nature," and grievously erred in her faith. The English were furious at her "confession," thus the bishop, while releasing her from excommunication, condemned her to life in prison for sins against God. It was not over. Joan was found in male attire again—she had been abused by her captors and left without her dress. Declared a relapsed heretic, she was burned May 30, 1431, maintaining to the last that her voices were from God. At her death, the mood changed. In 1456 when her trial was reopened, she was declared innocent and canonized in 1920. Saint or devil, the line was a fine one for women, and Joan had been pushed across it.

At the Council of Trent in the 1550s, the Catholic Church reaffirmed its doctrines after the challenges from reformers. Opportunities for women to follow a spiritual call outside of convent or marriage were forbidden. The council decreed that only the church should interpret scripture. Spanish churchman Bartolemé Carranza de Mendoza, a member of the council, argued that while scripture was like wine and not meant for the inexperienced, it could be "watered down" with commentaries and guides so some parts could be read by the laity. Mendoza's catalogue of suitable lay readings was listed in the Church's Index of Forbidden Books, and he was imprisoned for seventeen years. His opponents were particularly concerned about *women* reading scripture, since the divine word was a man's issue—"like arms and money." Even if women *could* read Latin, they would inevitably misinterpret it.

> No matter how much women demand this fruit (the Scriptures) with insatiable appetite, it is necessary to forbid it to them, and apply a knife of fire so that the common people cannot get at it.[7]

By 1559, vernacular translations of scripture and devotional guides were banned, no doubt influenced by the reformers' cry of scripture for everyone. Women were back under control. Contempt oozed from Luis de Maluenda's pen:

> The literal, let alone the spiritual meaning of the Epistles, is difficult for wise men to understand. How much more so for the silly woman who neglects her spinning and has the presumption to read Saint Paul. Holy angels, what a tempest! What business has a silly woman, however pious she may be, reading the Epistle of St. Paul![8]

Teresa of Avila, our last "living saint," was caught in this pendulum swing. Born in Avila, Spain, in 1515 when "living saints" were still celebrated, Teresa reached adulthood as they were being silenced. The child Teresa had become rebellious and "worldly" after her mother died, so she was placed in a convent at sixteen and joined the Carmelites at twenty. It took her twenty more years to accept this "spiritual" home and begin her mystic life of ecstasies, visions, and finally a "spiritual marriage" with Christ. Teresa would reform her order, found the "Barefoot Carmelites," write books about spiritual life, and be canonized. How did she survive in this period of hatred against visionary, teaching women? By using strategic political tactics that enabled her to maintain a voice even when what she did was condemned—subversive resistance while playing the game!

Since "diabolical sexual possession by the devil" had become the Inquisition's preferred verdict for female ecstatics in Teresa's time, her visions rang alarm bells for her nervous confessors, who had her document her experiences. Teresa was in a bind. Her confessors controlled her access to confession and absolution, and, as an unlearned woman, she could not claim "voices from God" without drawing their anger. She knew all about politics:

> We are living in a world in which we have to think of people's opinions of us if our words are to have any effect.[9]

Her survival strategy was to *adopt* the going stereotypes of female ignorance, timidity, and physical weakness. She argued that women like her received more spiritual favors because they were *weak*; that God intervened with visions because of their *incompetence*; that women interpreted scripture more simply because of *inferior* intellects; that she needed her confessors, yet that Paul's words should not tie her hands when other scripture encouraged women to use their gifts, however small. Thus, she avoided charges of ignorance or diabolical delusion by encouraging the hierarchy to "see" her through *their* spectacles.

In *The Way of Perfection*, her inner convictions peep through:

> Lord of my soul, you did not hate women when you walked in the world; rather you favored them always with much pity and found in them as much love and more faith than in men.[10]

This line was censored by Teresa's confessor and her own hand in the original drafts. Teresa knew the minefields and made concessions to male authorities, knowing the alternative was silence. At her canonization in 1622, she was called a *virile* woman with deeds not of woman, but of glorious man. When made patron saint of Spain, she was praised for overcoming her sex:

> This woman ceased to be a woman, restoring herself to the virile state to her greater glory than if she had been a man from the beginning, for she rectified nature's error with her virtue, transforming herself through virtue into the bone [Adam's rib] from which she sprang.[11]

Her election as the first woman Doctor of the Church in 1969 brought an ironic, but vindicating, accolade. Teresa had succeeded in being heard against all odds. The Promoter General of the Faith wrote:

> The difficulties in conceding the title of Doctor to holy women which have customarily been adduced, based on Pauline texts and historical reasons arising from former heresies, have disappeared in our times…Certainly, since the circumstances of our times have changed, not only in civic life, but in the very life of the Church, it seems opportune to concede the title of Doctor also to certain saintly women who have excelled in the eminence of their divine wisdom.[12]

For one brief, bright, shining moment of medieval history, the tables against women seemed to turn. The Renaissance allowed some high-born women in royal and ducal courts the option of marriage *and* an intellectual life outside of a convent. Such women became patrons of arts and learning, entered theological and philosophical debates, protected and financed those demanding church reform, and began asking "feminist" questions as part of the broader critique of society. One woman's questions would shake up male assumptions and begin the *Querelles des Femmes* (The Woman Question) debate, which lasted for centuries in many languages. Could a woman be virtuous? Could she do noteworthy deeds? Was she the same species as man?

Christine de Pizan, born in 1364, was educated in Charles V's court in Paris where her father was court physician. Her father thought education did not "handicap" women, although her mother wanted her to spin like other women and not get into science and learning. Christine was married at fifteen and widowed at twenty-six, with three children and a mother to support. She began writing for royal patrons, perhaps the first woman to support herself as a writer since antiquity. Some of her poems were the usual court tales of unrequited love, but in *L'Epistre au Dieu d'Amour* (Epistle to the God of Love), Christine attacked the antiwoman literature circulating in the courts declaring women "monstrosities of nature." She challenged Boccaccio's popular *Concerning Famous Women,* a catalogue of notable women from antiquity in which Boccaccio had singled out women with "virtues" of chastity, silence, and obedience against women in public life, who were suffering terrible punishments for entering that male sphere. Christine argued that female virtue, rather than being *exceptional,* was universal! Way ahead of her time, Christine also "read" scripture with a critical woman's eye and found, contrary to public opinion, few tales of evil women and many of good, faithful women. Christine's writing did what no other had done—defend women against attacks on their sex at a time when women were not even *aware* of the possibility of an identity of their own.

The debate that followed Christine's challenge weighed women's essential worthiness against their essential deficiency. Remember that the Renaissance had revived the musings of Greek philosophers, including their ideas about women. The church also argued women's natural inferiority, inclination to vice, and sole purpose as childbearers. The *new* challenge was that women shared the same mental and spiritual capacities as men, could excel in wisdom and action, and were not less perfectly human than men. Men who supported women's equality advocated for their education—a great step forward—even though education was limited to "acceptable" topics. Since a court woman's role was to inspire male gallantry and be an "occasion of beauty and delight" without which courtly gentlemen could not function, they could read the church fathers and the philosophers, but only those parts about "womanly" virtues— modesty, chastity, manners, cleverness, prudence, efficiency, beauty, charm, and agreeable conversation:

> Above all…in her ways, manners, gestures, and bearing, a woman ought to be very unlike a man; for just as he must show a certain solid and sturdy manliness, so it is seemly for a woman to have a soft and delicate tenderness, with an air of womanly sweetness in her every movement, which, in her going and staying, and in whatever she says, shall always make her appear the woman without any resemblance to a man.[13]

You can hear the sounds of troubadours, of chivalry and gallantry in these courtly descriptions of women. Poets waxed lyrical about "Fair Ladies" on high pedestals who were their patrons. Such women became almost divine, but only if they stayed on those decorative pedestals away from man's world.

However, these literary notions of noble, inaccessible women were about to be challenged for what they were—romantic talk with little concern for the subjugation of women. Into the debate sailed Henricus Cornelius Agrippa's amazing 1529 treatise, *Declamation on the Nobility and Preeminence of the Female Sex,* which was immediately translated into French, English, Italian, and German.[14] Agrippa argued that the oppression of women, supported by doctors, philosophers, the Bible, theologians, and lawyers, was based on custom. Customs were arbitrary, not universal "truth," and opposite conclusions could equally be reached! Arguing from canon law, Greek, Jewish, and Roman theory, and against Aristotle and the church fathers, he concluded women were not equal to men, but *superior!*

Since Agrippa's argument goes against everything we've heard thus far, it deserves a thorough look. He named Adam and Eve as the *basis* for myths about women. Since sexual distinction existed *only* in bodily parts, not different souls, the superiority of one sex over the other deduced from the nature of the soul was false. He then turned the creation stories upside down. According to him, woman were infinitely superior to the "ill-bred masculine race," even in name—Eve meant "life" and Adam "earth." Women's place in the order of creation was higher, since creation moved toward perfection.

> For when the Creator came to the creation of woman, he rested himself in this creation, thinking that he had nothing more honorable to create, in her were completed and consummated all the wisdom and power of the Creator; after her no creation could be found or imagined…woman is the ultimate end of creation, the most perfect accomplishment of all the works of God and the perfection of the universe itself.[15]

The creation of woman completed a circle, since feminine Wisdom was the *first* creation.

> The Lord created me (Wisdom) at the beginning of his work, the first of God's acts of long ago…before the beginning of the earth.[16]

Woman was thus created in Paradise with the angels, but man made *outside* Paradise with the animals and *transported* to Paradise for the creation of woman. Hold your breath! Agrippa proved this from experience. Because of their heavenly origins, women do not suffer vertigo as severely as men, and their eyes are not troubled by looking down from great heights! Women were also made not from clay, but from material already endowed with life and soul, and thus were more receptive to divine light than men, as evidenced by their refinement and extraordinary spiritual beauty. Their beauty, however, was not *only* spiritual. Agrippa waxed lyrical about woman's body as well! God made nothing more beautiful than woman, thus they deserve the highest esteem and honor.

Women's *virtue* was also superior. Agrippa's arguments make us smile, but are no more fantastic than those for male superiority already filling ecclesiastical halls.

> Women are more modest than men; their long hair conceals shameful body parts, women do not need to touch these body parts when they urinate, these parts do not protrude in women as they do in men, women are loathe to expose their body parts to a male physician and have been known to choose death rather than do so, women float face down in water when drowned, their heads (the supreme part of the human body)

are never bald, they secrete menses from the lower parts of their bodies while male secretions are from the face, they are always clean after one washing (while men continue to dirty the water no matter how many times they wash and change the water), and when they fall they fall on their backs and not on their faces.[17]

Agrippa rejected Aristotle's biology, saying women also contributed to the fetus, their fluid being *more* efficacious. Mothers bestowed more wisdom than fathers on children and were loved more, a denial of the Aristotle/Aquinas claim. Women were stronger because they procreated earlier and were inclined to sex even when pregnant or after delivery. They could even reproduce *without* a man, as the virgin birth proved!

Agrippa claimed humans received original sin from Adam's seed, not through Eve, citing Romans 5:12 and 1 Corinthians 15:42–49, which "blame" Adam. *Adam* was forbidden to eat the fruit before Eve was created, sinning in *full knowledge*. Eve ate in ignorance, deceived by a serpent who recognized superior divine light and was envious. Atonement came through the *offending* gender, with Christ taking male form and male priests continuing this action. Christ *chose,* however, to be born of woman *without* male help. Mary did not surpass her sex; female sex surpassed male sex. While Aristotle said men were more courageous, wise and noble, God chose the *foolish* things to confound the wise, the *weak* to confound the strong, according to Paul. Aristotle declared that the best in humanity determined the superior species, so Agrippa voted Mary the *best* and Judas the *worst*, making females superior in morality, martyrdom, faithful relationships, prophetic powers, scientific and philosophic endeavors, literary skills, leadership, inventiveness, and courage.

Agrippa concluded that women were not active in public affairs because of male tyranny under guise of "natural" and "divine" law, excluding them from public office, courts, and inheritance:

> As soon as she is born a woman is confined in idleness at home from her earliest years, and, as if incapable of functions more important, she has no other prospect than needle and thread. Further, when she has reached the age of puberty, she is delivered over to the jealous power of a husband, or she is enclosed forever in a workhouse for religious.[18]

Women were also excluded from preaching, despite God's words that "Your daughters also will prophecy," and despite the presence of women leaders in the early church. Man-made laws declared women inferior:

> And so these laws compel women to submit to men, as conquered before conquerors, and that without reason or necessity natural or divine, but under pressure of custom, education, chance, or some occasion favorable to tyranny.[19]

Such tyranny was based on scripture:

The curse of Eve is continually in their mouth. "You will be under the power of your husband and he will rule over you." If it is responded to them that Christ has put an end to this curse, they will make the same rebuttal again, from the words of Peter, adding to them also those of Paul: "Women are to be subject to men. Women are to be silent in church."[20]

Agrippa conceded that scripture might suggest an "order" in the church, just as it favored Jews. However:

God has a preference for no one, for in Christ, there is neither male nor female, but a new creation.[21]

In this astounding analysis, Agrippa took the romantic notions written about women at the time,and suggested their authors "put their money where their mouths were" by critically reflecting on the theological, physiological, and psychological assumptions held about women. It is incredible that Agrippa's description of systemic subordination of women, which feminists "discovered" in the seventies, lay forgotten for so many centuries. Even in 1937, when Emile Telle claimed Agrippa had been ignored "even by suffragettes," he was not unearthed.

Some commentators have suggested Agrippa's exaggerated arguments were tongue-in-cheek. Satire, however, is not without serious intent, a calculated way to challenge within limits of social acceptability. Comedians ridicule our folklore so it can never be taken seriously again, and extreme arguments are often the only way to expose the flaws in our assumptions. Agrippa saw through the arguments for a divinely authorized natural order based on Adam and Eve and reinforced by Paul, despite the overwhelming evidence in scripture and history for the opposite. No matter how amusing his arguments might have been, they did what he intended—showed that things can be as easily read one way as the other, and the view that predominates depends on who is in power.

So why was Agrippa not fêted throughout history for his theology? Because this window of opportunity for women would disappear again with Catholic and Protestant reform. Catholicism would reiterate traditional teaching about women—marriage or convent. Protestants would do away with convents, but make marriage the *only* role for women, removing their chances for a scholarly career. Women *could* study scripture, pray, and teach children, but only in the home, because of Eve. What this meant in the lives of women, who basked in a brief, bright moment of opportunity before the fall back again, is seen in Olympia Morata's story, born as Agrippa's treatise swept her world, and dying as the pendulum swung back.

Olympia Morata was born in Ferrara, Italy, in 1526, daughter of a classics professor who taught her Greek and Latin. At fourteen, she became tutor-companion to the daughter of Renee, Duchess of Ferrara. Renee, a French princess trapped in an unhappy marriage to an Italian duke, also carved her niche in history, despite opposition from her husband and the pope, by creating a haven for church reform in her court. The brilliant Olympia took advantage of her studies and was soon considered equal to the scholarly women of Greek antiquity. There is no doubt how she saw her future:

> In such is the excellence of study, how could the needle and spindle, the appendages of my sex, render me insensible to the sweet language of the Muses? Too long did I resist their voice, as Ulysses did the sirens' spells. My efforts were powerless. The distaff and shuttle speak no language to me, and have for me no attractions. I therefore bid them adieu forever.[22]

However, the duchess's court had been tagged by the Inquisition as "a hotbed of heresy." Twenty-two-year-old Olympia, at the height of her scholarly fame, left court to care for her father, and returned to find rumors had turned the court against her. She was dismissed. Olympia does not expand on the rumors, but says she was prevented from reading the Old and New Testament, something not off-limits for her *male* colleagues, reform-inclined or not. Since the Inquisition was involved, Olympia's life was in danger. Perhaps her "crime" was that dangerous habit of *women* reading and interpreting scripture. Olympia's scholarship trespassed the church's boundaries for women, and in the court purge of reform supporters, she was a double target.

Her career over, Olympia "in her disgrace" married Andreas Grundler, a German doctor, and fled to Schweinfurt to escape persecution. Encouraged by Curione, professor at Basel and her tutor in Ferrara, she continued her writing, corresponding with reformers across Europe. In 1553 when Schweinfurt was besieged, they barely escaped with their lives. Andreas found a professorship in Heidelberg and Olympia, now a German Protestant wife, continued writing and tutoring at home while Curione assembled a new library for her. The trauma had weakened her, and she died a year later at age twenty-nine.

Curione published her writings in 1558, titled "The Orations, Dialogues, Letters, and Poems, both Latin and Greek, of Olympia Fulvia Morata, a Learned and Almost Divine Woman." Three editions followed. She was obviously revered by her colleagues, but has now disappeared from history. Her crime of teaching and studying scripture as a woman expelled her from Catholic Italy, and German Protestantism, which she espoused in Schweinfurt, turned her into a pious Protestant wife at home. In her few later biographies, Olympia's brilliant scholarship becomes "frivolous," then simply the talents of a "clever child." She is transformed from a famous philosopher and theologian to faithful wife and martyr, finally disappearing from history because a good Christian woman is not necessary to record! Only in this decade has she been reclaimed as a brilliant woman who, for a brief moment, defied the heritage of Eve.

Protestant women, unlike their Catholic sisters, *could* read scripture, but they were, because of the fall, assigned to the home *under* the rule of their husbands—like "a nail driven into the wall" was Luther's phrase. Any woman wishing something different had to negotiate it *within* these limits. For some women, even reading the Bible at home became subject to husbandly rule. Anne Askew was such a woman, who tried to maintain her spiritual life as a well-educated English woman of the 1500s married against her will to a wealthy but uneducated neighbor. Anne "demeaned herself in all things like a Christian wife" but her Bible reading angered her husband. Encouraged by the priests, who forbade women reading scripture, Anne's husband demanded she give up the "heretical practice," but she would not. Forced from her home and family for this "disobedience" after the birth of their second child, Anne went to London hoping for religious freedom, but the Bishop of London and the Lord Mayor had been warned of this "dangerous heretic." Anne was summoned to answer for her beliefs and ordered to prison, but friends secured her release. During the reign of Henry VIII the ruling clergy wanted a public scapegoat. Anne was arrested again, repeatedly questioned, and, refusing to give up reading the scriptures, was burned at the stake after being tortured on the rack until her joints were "almost plucked asunder." Anne would not renounce her habit of reading scripture for herself, that dangerous habit feeble-minded womanhood was wont to do rather than listen to the priest. Her original "crime" however, was reading it against the will of the uneducated man her father had chosen to "rule over" her.

As we have already seen, the Enlightenment of the 1700s challenged the dogmas of the church, taking on the new science and man's rational mind as its guides. Rousseau sketched the Enlightenment vision of an intellectually and morally self-sufficient man living in an ordered society modeled on the patriarchal family. In all the talk about everyone being free and equal, no one remembered to ask about the women! Rousseau thought egalitarianism destroyed differences—sexual, class, and ethnic—threatening ordered society. Thus, he declared those who were subordinate had to surrender liberty "for their own advantage" to avoid a "clash of wills." It doesn't take much figuring to work out *who* he meant. Rousseau, like Barth, made much of the "complementarity" of men and women in a mutual domination, but somehow this meant that men monopolized the public space and "headed" up the private sphere of the home as well!

Mary Wollstonecraft in England (1759–97) was singularly unimpressed with Rousseau's happy domestic scene of subordinate women "reigning" in their limited territory. It had not been her experience! Mary's father had been drunken and abusive, leaving his children penniless. She left home at nineteen, worked as a governess, teacher, and companion, and taught herself French and German. Angry at the fate of young girls and women, she established a girls' school at Newington Green, and joined a network of liberal thinkers, including William Godwin. Despite shared objections to the institution of marriage, Godwin married the pregnant Mary. In response to Rousseau, Mary picked up her pen in protest and wrote the first sustained argument for feminism, *The Vindication of the Rights of Women,* a passionate plea for equal rights and opportunities for women. She argued that talk about individual rights applied only to males, and that women were excluded because they were said to be "naturally" weak and in need of protection. This myth of women's natural weakness was due to social conditioning and could be corrected by education extended equally to boys and girls, followed by equal rights for women. Mary's book of 1792 drew both praise and criticism. Like most attacks on women who step out of place, it was critiqued not on its argument, but on the author's lifestyle—a "philosophical wanton" and "a hyena in petticoats." By making Mary evil, immoral, and "unfeminine," her work could be dismissed by respectable men and women alike.

Mary *had* lived an unconventional life, resisting the "family" model of her childhood with involvement in the French Revolution, several love affairs, one illegitimate child, and two suicide attempts. When she died at thirty-eight while giving birth to a second daughter, her husband wrote *Memoirs of Mary Wollstonecraft* with great love and respect, but this cast even more scandal over her name. Early nineteenth-century feminists in England judged her a risky champion for women's rights, sidestepping her as a role model. Mary would not be vindicated until 1889, when Susan B. Anthony and Elizabeth Cady Stanton put her name *first* on the dedication page of their *History of Women's Suffrage*. Mary's protest, the first demanding women's equality not just in the spiritual realm, as the church sometimes conceded, or in the fantasy of literary musings on courtly love, or in Rousseau's limited "honor" of home and motherhood, but in the whole realm of being human, foreshadowed the beginning of the two great women's movements that take the official title of "feminism" and move us into the next chapter!

CHAPTER 5

A Feeling Finds a Name

When the ivy (wife) has found its tower (husband), when the delicate creeper has found its strong wall, we know how the parasite plants grow and prosper…Alone they but spread themselves on the ground, and cower unseen in the dingy shade. But when they have found their firm supporter, how wonderful is their beauty.[1]

Anthony Trollope

Women don't consider themselves as human beings at all. There is absolutely no God, no country, no duty to them at all, except family…I have known a good deal of convents. And of course everyone has talked of the petty grinding tyrannies supposed to be exercised there. But I know nothing like the petty grinding tyranny of a good English family. And the only alleviation is that the tyrannized submits with a heart full of affection.[2]

Florence Nightingale

Two views of women from two famous Victorians—take your pick! The glories of the Victorian domestic scene as the "natural" sphere for a happy woman depends on who's doing the talking.

The Victorian period of our grandparents and great-grandparents left its name on furniture, fashion, and morals, to say nothing of spreading its expansive colonizing tentacles over half the world. The diminutive queen who lent the era her name gazes down on town squares in Africa, Australia, India, Canada, and hundreds of islands in between. Even where Britain didn't reign, the Victorian influence penetrated, and the beckoning far-flung shores of the Empire where the sun never set on its brave men were inversely proportionate in size and opportunity to the narrow confines of hearth and mind for the

Victorian wife. The helpless child-bride, confined to frills and foibles, became the cherished possession of Victorian male society. The more delicate and empty-headed she was, the more ladylike she appeared. Removed from participation in the world and outfitted in restricting clothes signifying her life of leisured affluence, such women were elevated on the highest pedestals like porcelain "priestesses of virtue," the final touch in the family image. As Florence Nightingale said of this, her world:

> A woman cannot live in the light of intellect. Society forbids it. Those conventional frivolities which are called "her duties" forbid it. The Family uses people, not for what they are but for what it wants them for...this system dooms some minds to incurable infancy, others to silent misery.[3]

For the husband busy in the sordid world of business, the wife was the symbol of "home," untouched by trade and undefiled by worldly sins. This "housekeeper for his soul" soothed and protected him from the outside world. Such guardianship did not include intellectual stimulus; the best caretakers hovered silently. The wife was the "household nun," and "guardianship" her religion of self-renunciation. As Elsa sang in Wagner's *Lohengrin*, a wife should "fade into her husband and become as nothing, totally absorbed." A wife *did* literally become a nonentity, *legally* passing out of sight to become a "covert nature included henceforth in her husband":

> Her personality is so far merged in his, that she cannot bring a suit any more in her own name, for it is a name no longer known to the law.[4]

Mrs. Ellis's best-selling Victorian marriage manual, *The Women of England: Their Social Duties and Domestic Habits*, assumed such subservience as "natural":

> In her intercourse with man, it is impossible but that women should feel her own inferiority, and it is right that it should be so...she does not meet him on equal terms. Her part is to make sacrifices in order that his enjoyment may be enhanced. She does this with a willing spirit but she does it so often without grateful acknowledgment. Nor is man to be blamed for this.[5]

In fact, women should rejoice in this assigned role of keeper of a man's soul because *without* this task they would be nothing:

> Woman, with all her accumulation of minute disquietudes, her weakness, and her sensibility, is but a meager item in the catalogue of humanity; but, roused by a sufficient motive to forget all these, or rather, continually forgetting them, because she has other and nobler thoughts to occupy her mind, woman is truly and majestically great...Never yet, however, was woman great, because she had great requirements; nor can she ever be great in herself—personally, and without instrumentality—as an object, not an agent.[6]

Ellis' writings were quoted widely as the "Bible" for good women, and the woman's information highway of the time, the Victorian novel, embellished the image.

Although the domestic world was woman's natural assignment, it was not *really* hers. The husband was master of the house. Babies were handed to wet-nurses and nannies because of the delicate nature of the middle-class mother. In the early 1800s, a mother had no rights to her children, however irresponsible the father. In 1839, the Custody of Infants Bill was passed in England giving a woman rights to children up to seven years old. A wife could not seek divorce until 1857, and then only for desertion and cruelty, not adultery. Divorces were prohibitive for wives with no legal property until 1870. Such total dependence stole all responsibility from women, leaving them doll-like in purposeless lives. In Ibsen's 1879 play *A Doll's House*, Nora is a plaything in her husband's house as she was Papa's doll as a child. When she tells her husband Torvald she cannot raise children until she educates *herself*, he tells her a woman's duty is, before all else, as a wife and mother. Nora replies:

> I believe that before all else I am a reasonable human being, just as you are—or, at all events, that I must try and become one. I know quite well, Torvald, that most people would think you right, and that views of that kind are to be found in books: but I can no longer content myself with what most people say or with what is found in books. I must think over things for myself and get to understand them.[7]

From such frailty and inconsequence, the cult of the "invalid" sprung. The "angel of the home" constantly languished and faded, hovering between this life and the next. Healthiness raised suspicions about virtue and breeding, hinting at dangerous masculinizing tendencies.

> More fragile than a child, woman absolutely requires that we love her for herself alone, that we guard her carefully, that we be every moment sensible that in urging her too far we are sure of nothing. Our angel, though smiling, and blooming with life, often touches the earth with but the tip of one wing; the other would already waft her elsewhere.[8]

Of course, this "affliction" did not infect poor, working-class women who "did" for the languishing mistresses, further proof of the condition's link to breeding! Yet many women could not abide this prison they inherited. Why were they destined to be the clinging vine, especially when the *vine* often held up the tower? The challenge was to find ways to share in the greater arena of life without being ostracized, and a few middle-class women managed to pick their way between the minefields of convention on both sides of the Atlantic. Often the most repressive of times spawns the greatest rebellions, and the Victorian era produced that worldwide women's movement that gained the woman's vote. In this chapter, we'll go behind stage to see the *personal* struggles of a few of the women who stepped out of place and into history.

Florence Nightingale glides through history's half dark with her lamp, treading a path between wounded Crimean soldiers. We do Florence a disservice and lose a passionate foremother if this is the only image we carry of her. We need to hear her pain, anger, and frustration at the "destiny" assigned her by birth, and her struggle to fight against it. Florence was born in 1820, second daughter of William and Fanny. Fanny epitomized the Victorian wife, beautiful, vacuous, and extravagant. The Nightingale household "languished" suitably in accordance with the tastes of the era. A misplaced letter or tense relationship necessitated smelling salts and country escapes for women of "sensibility." Florence was an unhappy child, strange, passionate, and obstinate, hiding a "monstrous" secret that she was "different." She escaped into dreams to numb this guilt and terror.

Fanny lived to launch her daughters into society, but Florence, at seventeen, received a secret "call" from God. When the family "went abroad" soon after, Florence was in despair, trying to deduce her call and make her life "worthy" while constantly being set up for a "suitable" marriage. She rejected several suitors and, seven years after her call, a second call came to work in hospitals, but without follow-up details. Eight years would pass before she "knew." Meanwhile, overcome with guilt, she told her diaries God's silence was punishment for her "sin."

> This morning I felt as if my soul would pass away in tears, in utter loneliness in a bitter passion of tears and agony of solitude. I cannot live—forgive me, oh Lord, and let me die, this day let me die.[9]

At twenty-nine, after refusing another suitor, Florence rejected Victorian marriage altogether because it would deny her the chance to answer her call. She was severely dejected at her either/or option:

> To be nailed to a continuation, an exaggeration of my present life without hope of another would be intolerable to me…that voluntarily to put it out of my power ever to be able to seize the chance of forming for myself a true and rich life would seem to me like suicide.[10]

She decided to go to Kaiserswerth in Germany, a religious training center for hospital care. When her mother and sister heard her plan not to marry or stay with them, they became "ill," insisting her duty was at home engaged in pursuits proper to her station. Florence was thirty! Struggling to obey, she despaired of the monster she had become:

> What am I that their life is not good enough for me? Oh God what am I? The thoughts and feelings that I have now I can remember since I was six years old. It was not I that made them. Oh God how did they come? But why, oh my God, cannot I not be satisfied with the life that satisfies so many people? I am told that the conversation of all these good clever men ought to be enough for me. Why am I starving, desperate, diseased on it?…My God what am I to do?[11]

This wonderful human being in the image of God, with a call outside the "natural" role for women, despaired like thousands of women have done. If *she* could not accept what other women were happy to bear, there must be something wrong with her! Florence finally went to Kaiserswerth and found her calling. When she tried to return to a London hospital, the family trapped her again with *their* "illnesses" and *her* guilt. Channeling her rage at the Victorian family into *Cassandra,* a novel about a Victorian girl, Florence bemoaned that after vacuous days of looking at pictures, reading little books, and taking afternoon drives, women suffer at night

> the accumulation of nervous energy, which has had nothing to do during the day, making them feel every night when they go to bed, as if they were going mad. The vacuity and boredom of this existence are sugared over by false sentiment. Women go about maudling to each other and preaching to their daughters that "women have no passions"…if the young girls of the "higher classes" who never commit a false step…were to speak and say what their thoughts employed on, their *thoughts* which alone are free, what would they say?[12]

Cassandra, "who can neither find happiness in her life nor alter it, dies," slain by the Family. She welcomes death, divine freedom at last!

At thirty-three, Florence finally extracted herself from her family to reorganize a London Women's Hospital. Her vocation had begun. She introduced reform, and her advice was sought for other hospitals by friend and politician Sidney Herbert. When the Allied armies landed in the Crimea, Florence, at Herbert's request, took nurses there, transforming nursing and eliminating wound infection. With Queen Victoria's support, Herbert presented Florence's findings to the British Cabinet. When war ended in 1856, Florence returned to England. Just forty, she took to her bed as an "invalid," organizing reform and founding nursing schools from there through Herbert and other go-betweens. Her "delicate" constitution held until she was ninety!

The women's rights movement was gaining ground in England during Florence's lifetime, advocating women's vote and control of their destiny, children, and property. Florence did not join the movement, seeing her call, not to women's issues, but health. Again, this reminds us of the scope of feminism and the many places women sit along its continuum. Florence's writings are remarkable feminist statements reflecting her struggle to choose beyond her destined role of Victorian wife. Yet, unlike her predecessor Mary Wollstonecraft, who sought to secure women's control of their destiny out of *her* experience of poverty under an alcoholic father, aristocratic Florence had connections and money and could choose to refuse marriage, not needing it for survival. Property ownership, access to children, or a public voice were not her "problem." Initially, she did not think women needed a vote, since it had not affected *her* ability to achieve what she wanted from the "respectable" confines of her private drawing room through powerful, public men—a clever compromise of gender rules. Later she would admit that *ordinary* women might need a vote.

On the other side of the ocean, women had defended the homesteads while their men fought the American Revolution. Abigail Adams cautioned her husband John, a drafter of the Constitution:

> Remember the Ladies, and be more generous and favorable to them than your ancestors. Do not put such unlimited power into the hands of the Husbands. Remember all men would be tyrants if they could. If particular care and attention is not paid to the Ladies, we are determined to foment a Rebellion, and will not hold ourselves bound by any Laws in which we have no voice, or representation.[13]

Abigail's words were not heeded, and women of the new Republic found their role very similar to their British sisters. Guardians of the male soul, they were divinely ordained subordinate to husbands because of the fall. No "true" woman would challenge this, they were told, since their *real* power lay in the "feminine" influence they wielded on husbands in private. Once again, men could be generously complimentary of their women just so long as women stayed in the place men had assigned them. Theologian Horace Bushnell assured his 1869 audience in his *Women's Suffrage: The Reform against Nature:*

> Why, if our women could but see what they are doing now, what superior grades of beauty and power they fill, and how far above equality with men they rise, when they keep their own atmosphere of silence and their field of peace, how they make a realm into which the poor bruised fighters, with their passions galled and their minds scarred with wrong—their hates, disappointments, grudges, and hard-worn ambitions—may come in, to be quieted, and civilized, and get some touch of the angelic, I think they would be very little apt to disrespect their womanly subordination.[14]

Although Bushnell was enamored with the "superiority" of women and their "power," he did not convince all women, and their capped energy bubbled out in a variety of rebellious ways. When the religious revivals of the 1700s called for holy living across America, women trespassed on a new arena not quite public, not quite the home—the church. With no state churches in America, religion was part of private, not public, life and thus an acceptable place for women, especially as they were "guardians of the family soul." They usually did not gain leadership roles, since women were not supposed to teach, but they established women's groups and Sunday schools, became involved in charitable organizations, and raised money for missions. From this jumping-off point, the more adventurous became involved in *public* social problems—prostitution, slavery, and the demon drink—which touched on their role in the family. They soon discovered their voice was hampered without the ability to vote for social reform.

Church women reached out to prostitutes, first to redeem their souls, but then to advocate better justice for them in a society that excused "respectable" men who sought their services. These wise and crafty women with little public voice found an extremely effective way to control the industry—publish names or initials of men seen visiting brothels:

> We think it proper even to expose names, for the same reason that the names of thieves and robbers are published, that the public may know them and govern themselves accordingly. We mean to let the licentious know, that if they are not ashamed of their debasing vice, we will not be ashamed to expose them.[15]

In the standards of their day, these women trod the fine line of Victorian "refinement" by speaking publicly on such "indelicate" subjects, but they justified their boldness with their moral outrage at this threat to the family they were charged with protecting.

The temperance movement provided another window of opportunity for women to enter the public area "undercover," as it were. When evangelical churchmen moved against the liquor trade, women could only play supporting roles, since reform involved political and legislative action and they had no vote. This frustrated women, since drunken *men* were the problems and *women* and children the victims, yet women had no direct way to influence their domestic predicament. The idea of demanding the women's vote began to form in many reforming minds. Susan B. Anthony, Elizabeth Cady Stanton, Lucretia Mott, and Lucy Stone all began their advocacy for the vote in the Temperance Movement. When Susan, a delegate to the 1852 Temperance Convention, was not allowed to speak, she and Elizabeth left to form their own society. When other women would not take such a "radical step," and voted men should join as well, Susan and Elizabeth resigned and the group disintegrated. The 1853 World Temperance Convention in New York did not allow women to speak or help with organization, so the women labeled it the "Half World's Temperance Convention" and held their own. One woman who *did* try to address the Convention was drowned out by protest. An editorial the following day read:

> First Day—crowding a woman off the platform.

> Second Day—Gagging her.

> Third Day—Voting that she shall stay gagged. Having thus disposed of the main question, we presume the incidentals will be finished this morning.[16]

The women once again took matters into their own hands. The "Women's Crusade" of 1873 entered the saloons, bastions of male solidarity, to hold prayer meetings and plead for their closing. Women's fear was real. Liquor was more available after the Civil War and alcoholism a growing problem. Since a wife had no legal right to money or to her children, a husband could drink their money away and still be the legal guardian of the family. Women who might not feel comfortable—or safe—in the more militant suffrage movement could get involved in temperance reform because it affected their family concerns. The Women's Crusade became the Women's Christian Temperance Union (WCTU) in 1874. Men were not admitted into leadership for fear they would take over as they did with the previous movement; thus the WCTU's great successes was to allow women a glimpse of their power and leadership despite biblical injunctions to the contrary:

> The Crusade had an emotional impact equivalent to a conversion experience and moved these women to feminist principles, whether they recognized them or not...[it] was a liberating force for a group of church-oriented women who could not have associated themselves directly with the equal rights or suffrage movements.[17]

When Frances Willard became president, she saw the WCTU's potential to tackle the more fundamental issue—women's ability to influence legislation about the liquor trade with a vote. She steered the movement in that direction, not on a platform of women's rights, which would earn the label of rebellious women pitted against God's order for the family, but that the women's vote would protect *homes* from the evils of the liquor trade. Thus, the movement attracted more conservative women, by cultivating images of pious, chaste, and moral women, and made women's suffrage "respectable" to women taught to see the vote as a *threat* to God and family—"I'm not a feminist, but..." women. There is nothing new under the sun!

> The challenge that faced these Nineteenth century women was formidable: to claim self-fulfillment for women without condoning egotistical selfishness; to affirm the human being's social connectedness and care for neighbor without endorsing denial and sacrifice to the point of self-negation; to demand that women be respected as full persons, with rights and opportunities enjoyed by men, without thereby implicitly embracing the male system and male values that denigrated women's traditional activities and concerns.[18]

Abolition of slavery was another "nursery" for the emerging women's movement. Quaker women took the lead, since Quakers had no problem with women in leadership—the Spirit of God spoke regardless of sexual organs! Sisters Sarah and Angelina Grimké lectured against slavery across New England, and, in preparing their arguments, realized the rights they sought for slaves were not granted to *women* because of "what the Bible said." Sarah wrote an article in 1838 rejecting biblical interpretations that denied a woman's ability to be her own moral guide:

> The first duty, I believe, which devolves on our sex now is to think for themselves...Until we take our stand side by side with our brother; until we read all the precepts of the Bible as addressed to women as well as to man, and lose...the consciousness of sex, we shall never fulfill the end of our existence.[19]

The sisters drew hostile opposition from clergymen. It is one thing to oppose inequities but another to challenge long-standing biblical interpretations about women! Opposition also came from those who saw the "women's issue" as harming the abolition cause. The sisters were accused of forgetting the dreadful wrongs done to the slaves in their selfish crusade against "some paltry grievance" of their own, the paltry grievance being that *women* could not vote or be full citizens or have a say in legislation that gave their children, property, and income to their husbands!

In 1837, the Congregational Ministers of Massachusetts issued a "pastoral letter" of concern against the sisters:

> We invite your attention to the dangers which at present seem to threaten the female character with widespread and permanent injury. The appropriate duties and influences of women are clearly stated in the New Testament. Those duties, and that influence are unobtrusive and private, but the sources of mighty power. When the mild, dependent, softening influence upon the sternness of man's opinions is fully exercised, society feels the effect of it in a thousand forms. The power of a woman is her dependence, flowing from the consciousness of that weakness which God has given her for her protection. We appreciate the unostentatious prayers of women in advancing the cause of religion at home and abroad; in Sabbath-schools; in leading religious inquirers to the pastors for instruction; and in all such associated efforts as become the modesty of her sex…but when she assumes the place and tone of man as a public performer…she yields the power which God has given her for her protection, and her character becomes unnatural. If the vine, whose strength and beauty is to lean on the trellis-work, and half conceal its cluster, thinks to assume the independence and the overshadowing nature of the elm, it will not only cease to bear fruit, but fall in shame and dishonor into the dust.[20]

Sarah's response, *Letters on the Equality of the Sexes,* went to the heart of the problem, reading scripture from a male point of view. She *too* wanted women to move in the sphere the Creator made for them, but which sphere was God's divine intent and which a manmade construction?

> No one can desire more earnestly than I do, that women may move exactly in the sphere which her Creator has assigned her; and I believe her having been displaced from that sphere has introduced confusion into the world. It is, therefore, of vast importance to herself and to all the rational creation, that she should ascertain what are her duties and her privileges as a responsible and immortal being.[21]

Sarah argued that men who translated the New Testament from its original languages changed the intent of the words through their "official" interpretations and commentaries. She went back to the original Greek and Hebrew and recovered the Genesis 1 creation story ignored for centuries, arguing that men and women were *both* in the image of God; that dominion was given to *both* over other creatures and not each other; and that equality of the sexes was part of Jesus' teaching:

> Men and women were CREATED EQUAL; they are both moral and accountable beings, and whatever is *right* for man to do, is *right* for woman.[22]

Sarah cleverly enlisted an American clarion call to her cause—a city set on a hill—pointing out there were no gendered roles spelled out in the command for men and women to be shining lights to the world, as the ministers who opposed her argued:

> The influence of women, says the Association, is to be private and unobtrusive; her light is not to shine before men like that of her brethren: but she is passively to let the lords of the creation, as they call themselves, put the bushel over it, lest peradventure it might appear that the world has been benefited by the rays of her candle…"her influence is the source of mighty power." This has ever been the flattering language of man since he laid aside the whip as a means to keep woman in subjection. He spares her body; but the war he has waged against her mind, her heart, and her soul, has been no less destructive to her as a moral being. How monstrous, how anti-Christian, is the doctrine that woman is to be dependent on man! Where, in all the sacred Scriptures, is this taught?[23]

Little by little, the "aha's" of Church women, realizing their powerlessness without legal rights or the vote, rose to an audible rumble. Set a few good women, pushed to their limits, around a table with a pot of tea, and they can change the world with their cry "Enough is enough"! At the 1840 World Anti-Slavery Convention in London, Lucretia Mott and the other American women delegates were excluded from the main hall for the voting sessions but permitted to observe from the balcony! Elizabeth Cady Stanton was also present, honeymooning with her delegate husband. This fiasco fueled the friendship between the two women, which lit the bonfire of conviction that women were in as much need of emancipation as slaves. With Lucretia's sister and friend Mary Ann McClintock, they decided over tea in July 1848 to place an advertisement in the *Seneca County Courier* inviting interested parties to attend a convention to discuss social, civil, and religious conditions and rights of women. To their amazement, three hundred people filled the Wesleyan Chapel in Seneca Falls, New York, on the appointed day! Since men came as well, the women-only plan was abandoned and Lucretia's husband elected chairperson.

Elizabeth presented her "Declaration of Sentiments," modeled on the Declaration of Independence:

> We hold these truths to be self-evident; that all men and women are created equal; that they are endowed by their Creator with certain inalienable rights; that among these are life, liberty, and the pursuit of happiness…The history of mankind is a history of repeated injuries and

usurpations on the part of men toward woman, having its direct object the establishment of an absolute tyranny over her. To prove this, let facts be submitted to a candid world.[24]

The Declaration was accompanied by twelve resolutions about women's grievances. All but one passed unanimously. The controversial one—that it is the sacred duty of the women of this country to secure to themselves their sacred right to the elective franchise—passed by a small majority. The first American women's movement was on its way. Their task was immense—to prove women's equality with men and thus their *right* to a vote; to diffuse the idea that women *already* voted through influencing husbands at home, and to shatter the decorative Dresden figurine of ideal womanhood as fragile, child-like, and passive.

From the start, the movement battled widespread fear that "radical, un-feminine aggression" by women would damage other causes in which they were involved. The media and the church did its best to fuel a negative image of these "monstrous women" out of their place. Some in the Movement wanted to concentrate on citizenship for African American men while others wanted to work for suffrage for *all*—African American men and women and all women. The latter were asked not to spoil the "Negroes' hour," despite the fact that half the African Americans were *women!* Sojourner Truth, encouraged to consider the "good of her race" first and be patient a while longer, saw the difficulties:

> If colored men get their rights and not colored women theirs, you see the colored men will be masters over the women, and it will be just as bad as it was before.[25]

When the vote was given to African American men only, the women's movement split, and Elizabeth Cady Stanton formed the National Woman Suffrage Association, advocating votes for all. By 1890, the groups merged again, but it would take until 1920 for women's suffrage in America to be ratified. This struggle for the woman's vote was not limited to England and America. New Zealand gave women the vote in 1893, the first country to do so. Australian women received the vote in 1902, followed by Finland (1906), Norway (1913), Denmark (1915), and Russia (1917). Canada was the first North American country (1918), followed by the United States (1920). England gave the vote to women over thirty in 1918, and to those over twenty-one in 1928. That same year, Equador became the first South American country. Ceylon was the first Asian country (1931), and Senegal the first African country (1945).

Men had been involved in the struggle for women's suffrage in America since the beginning. Lucretia's husband, made Chairman at the first Seneca Falls convention, affirmed the validity of women's complaints:

> He has compelled her to submit to laws in the formation of which she has no voice...He has made her, if married, in the eyes of the law, civilly dead. He has taken from her all right to property, even to the wages she

earns…In the covenant of marriage she is compelled to promise obedience to her husband, he becoming to all intents or purposes her master—the law giving him power to deprive her of her liberty, and to administer chastisement…He closes against her all the avenues of wealth and distinction which he considers most honorable in himself…He has denied her the facilities for obtaining a thorough education, all colleges being closed against her…He has created a false public sentiment by giving to the world a different code of morals for men and women by which moral delinquencies which exclude women from society are not only tolerated, but deemed of little account to man. He has usurped the prerogative of Jehovah himself, claiming it as his right to assign for her a sphere of action, when that belongs to her conscience and to her God. He has endeavored in every way that he could to destroy her confidence in her own powers, to lessen her self-respect, and to make her willing to lead a dependent and abject life.[26]

Such men were exceptions among clergymen, most of whom were outraged at this violation of the God-given nature of women, and the gross attack on scriptural laws. Women's conventions were interrupted with the usual "proof texts" from the Bible—Paul told women to be silent in church and consult their husbands at home; Paul did not let women preach and usurp man's authority; Adam was formed first, then Eve. Rather than seriously consider the women's learned arguments from scripture, the opposition painted them as "monsters" any God-fearing woman should dread—man-hating, angry, uncivilized spinsters out to destroy men, religion, and the family. The Seneca Falls convention drew charges of "insurrection among women, blasphemy, legalized adultery, and free love." That Angelina Grimké, Elizabeth Cady Stanton, Lucretia Mott, and many others raised families and were married to men who supported their passion and their grievances was conveniently overlooked.

Who were some of these women who had the courage to defy the odds in the American struggle for women's suffrage? Lucy Stone's mother milked eight cows before delivering Lucy, and at her birth cried, "Oh, dear! I am sorry it is a girl. A woman's life is so hard." Lucy watched her mother raise nine children, slaving endlessly in house and farm while bowing to the "one will in the house," her husband's. Rebelling early over the woman's lot, Lucy worked and saved to go to Oberlin College, where she had to practice her public speaking in the woods, since woman were forbidden to speak in public. After graduation, Lucy lectured on abolition for the Anti-Slavery Society on weekends and advocated for women's rights under her own steam during the week. Before coming into a town, ugly rumors of a masculine woman wearing boots, smoking a cigar, and swearing like a trouper would precede her. Lucy would appear before her stunned audiences, dainty and dressed in a black satin gown with a white frill at the neck. *The Boston Post* ran a poem promising fame for the man who "with a wedding kiss shuts up the mouth of Lucy Stone."

Henry Blackwell earned the honor, despite Lucy's conviction that marriage for women was synonymous with the slavery she denounced. They wrote their own marriage vows, impressing the minister so much he published them for other couples:

> While we acknowledge out mutual affection by publicly assuming the relationship of husband and wife…we deem it a duty to declare that this act on our part implies no sanction of, nor promise of voluntary obedience to such of the present laws of marriage as refuse to recognize the wife as an independent, rational being, while they confer upon the husband an injurious and unnatural superiority.[27]

Lucy kept her own name because to become a wife was to *disappear* in the eyes of the law. Henry and daughter Alice devoted their lives after Lucy's death to the ongoing battle for women's vote. In a three-generational moment, Lucy, aged seventy, wrote to her daughter:

> I trust my Mother sees and knows how glad I am to have been born, and at a time when there was so much that needed help at which I could lend a hand. Dear Old Mother! She had a hard life, and was sorry she had another girl to share and bear the hard life of a woman…But I am wholly glad that I came.[28]

Sojourner Truth (1777–1883) entered the women's movement from an entirely different place than her white sisters. Born a slave, she won her freedom in 1827 and became a traveling preacher. She was active in the abolition movement, but saw the women's movement, despite its white, middle-class majority, as crucial for black women's vote. At a women's rights convention in Akron, Ohio, men were ridiculing the white women on the platform as "naturally" weak and delicate, not *able* to take the roles and responsibilities of men. Sojourner took the floor:

> The man over there says women need to be helped into carriages and lifted over ditches, and to have the best place everywhere. Nobody ever helps me into carriages or over puddles, or gives me the best place—and ain't I a woman? Look at my arm! I have ploughed and planted and gathered into barns, and no man could head me—and ain't I a woman? I could work as much and eat as much as a man—when I could get it—and bear the lash as well! And ain't I a woman? I have born thirteen children, and seen most of 'em sold into slavery, and when I cried out with my mother's grief, none but Jesus heard me—and ain't I a woman?[29]

Her challenge was a momentous one—that feminist issues are different depending on where you stand, and certainly different from the underside. This "correction" was made again with the women's movement of the '60s as black, Hispanic, and Asian women challenged their white sisters.

Elizabeth Cady Stanton (1815–1902), like the Grimké sisters, identified the root of the problem for women and crossed an unthinkable line by publishing *The Women's Bible.* The closets were opened, and her spring-cleaning brought shock waves across respectable Christian society. Elizabeth, raised in a strict Puritan home, was brilliant, religious, and devastated when, after a good education, she could not attend Union College with her male friends. In 1840, she married Henry Stanton, a man involved in moral and social reform who offered her in marriage an alliance of "affection and abolition." Their honeymoon was spent at the World Anti-Slavery Convention in London where Elizabeth met Lucretia Mott, and the rest is history! Elizabeth's fifty-year friendship with Susan B. Anthony began in 1851, with Susan the strategist and public speaker and Elizabeth the philosopher and speech writer. They shaped the women's movement from Elizabeth's kitchen, Susan feeding one or other of Elizabeth's seven children while Elizabeth worked on Susan's speech!

Elizabeth brought to the movement a brilliant mind, a classical education, and a healthy skepticism. At Seneca Falls, she described her vision for women:

> Let woman live as she should. Let her feel her accountability to her maker. Let her know that her spirit is fitted for as high a sphere as a man's, and that her soul requires food as pure and exalted as his. Let her live first for God and she will not make imperfect man an object of reverence and awe. Teach her her responsibility as a being of conscience and reason, that all earthly support is weak and unstable, that her only safe dependence is the arm of omnipotence, and that true happiness springs from duty accomplished. Thus will she learn the lesson of individual responsibility for time and eternity. That neither father, husband, brother or son, however willing they may be, can discharge her high duties of life, or stand in her stead when called into the presence of the great Searcher of Hearts...[30]

At first she offered positive readings of scripture for women, but later turned to severe critiques of the interpretations that had distorted or smothered its intent. She challenged the Ten Commandments from a slave woman's perspective in her 1860 book *The Slave's Appeal.* To honor father and mother is impossible for illegitimate children of Southern masters and slave mothers. Thou shalt not kill means nothing for robed clergy who preach on Sunday and condone lynching, beating, and degrading of slaves through the week. Thou shalt not commit adultery falls on deaf ears for men buying trembling girls from auction blocks. Thou shalt not steal accuses every slave owner who steals both men and women.[31]

Elizabeth became increasingly convinced that women's low self-esteem and oppression stemmed from biblical interpretations that needed challenging. The 1878 National Woman Suffrage Association convention had passed resolutions about such interpretations:

> *Resolved,* That as the first duty of every individual is self-development, the lessons of self-sacrifice and obedience taught women by the Christian Church have been fatal, not only to her own vital interests, but through her, to those of her race.

Resolved, That the great principle of the Protestant Reformation, the right of individual conscience and judgment heretofore exercised by man alone, should now be claimed by women; that, in the interpretation of Scripture, she should be guided by her own reason, and not by the authority of the church.

Resolved, That it is through the perversion of the religious element in women—playing upon her hopes and fears of the future, holding this life with all its high duties in abeyance to that which is to come—that she and the children she has trained have been so completely subjugated by priestcraft and superstition.[32]

When no women were appointed to the American Revising Committee for the 1885 revision of the King James Version of the Bible, even though there were women experts in the field, Elizabeth was appalled. Now over seventy, she took matters into her own hands and appointed her own revision committee! Herself a student of science, Darwinian evolution and German biblical criticism, she had studied biblical Greek since the age of eleven and was equipped to ask hard questions. As she observed:

When those who are opposed to all reforms can find no other argument, their last resort is the Bible. It has been interpreted to favor intemperance, slavery, capital punishment and the subjection of women.[33]

The resulting *Women's Bible* was not a total revision. The committee extracted all Bible passages dealing with women—one tenth of the text—and reassembled them with commentaries. The challenge was twofold: Have Bible teachings advanced or retarded emancipation of women? Have they dignified or degraded the mothers of the race?

Of Jephthah's daughter it observed that, if the women's movement had reached her, she might have said to her father, "Self-development is a higher duty than self-sacrifice and should be a woman's motto henceforth."

These loving fathers in the Old Testament, like Jephthah and Abraham, thought to make themselves specially pleasing to the Lord by sacrificing their children to him as burnt offerings. If the ethics of their moral code had permitted suicide, they might with some show of justice have offered themselves…by what right had they to offer up their sons and daughters in return for supposed favors from the Lord? The submission of Isaac and Jephthah's daughter to this violation of their most sacred rights is truly pathetic. But, like all oppressed classes, they were ignorant of the fact that they had any natural, inalienable rights. We have such a type of womanhood even in our day.[34]

The wise and foolish virgins who came to the wedding feast with and without extra oil for their lamps became a lesson in self-reliance for women.

In their ignorance, women sacrifice themselves to educate the men of their households, and to make themselves ladders by which their husbands, brothers and sons climb up into the kingdom of knowledge, while they themselves are shut out from all intellectual companionship, even with those they love best; such are indeed like the foolish virgins.[35]

The *wise* virgins equipped themselves with education and self-sufficiency, so that when the "marriage feast" comes—changes in the status of women—they will be ready to take their proper place.

The Women's Bible addressed the "problem" texts right in the introduction:

The Bible teaches that woman brought sin and death into the world, that she precipitated the fall of the race, that she was arraigned before the judgment seat of Heaven, tried, condemned and sentenced. Marriage for her was to be a condition of bondage, maternity a period of suffering and anguish, and in silence and subjection, she was to play the role of a dependent on man's bounty for all her material wants, and for all the information she might desire on the vital questions of the hour, she was commanded to ask her husband at home. Here is the Bible position of women summed up.[36]

Eizabeth declared these texts so overused by clergymen and politicians that even *women* accepted them as "the Word of God," making their emancipation impossible. When clergy tell women not to take part in antislavery campaigns or women's movements because they "undermine the very foundations of society," the majority of women stand still with bowed heads, accepting the situation.

Elizabeth had already resurrected the Genesis 1 creation story in a resolution at Seneca Falls:

Resolved That woman is man's equal—was intended to be so by the Creator, and the highest good of the race demands that she should be recognized as such.

In *The Women's Bible,* she expanded on the original equality of the sexes:

The masculine and feminine elements, exactly equal and balancing each other, are as essential to the maintenance of the equilibrium of the universe as positive and negative electricity, the centripetal and centrifugal forces, the laws of attraction which bring together all we know of this planet.[37]

Since Genesis 1:27 said the image of God was male and female, how was it possible women were an afterthought, and why was the "afterthought" story selected for use rather than the one where women and man were created together and equal? By taking seriously the *first* story, the second story can be read differently. Eve was *impressive!* Didn't the serpent communicate with her because of her intelligence? Didn't he tempt her, not with jewelry or luxuries, but with the promise of knowledge from the gods, arousing a thirst for knowledge not satisfied by chatting with Adam or picking flowers? Eve, the superior performer, ate the fruit *because* wisdom was promised. Adam, who *received* the command *not* to eat, did nothing. Expanding on the "fall," the committee marveled that the inferiority of woman could be deduced from such a story. Although I have already quoted this passage, it's worth repeating!

> All this time Adam standing beside her interposes no work of objection…had he been the representative of the divinely appointed head in married life, he assuredly would have taken upon himself the burden of the discussion with the serpent, but no, he is silent in this crisis of their fate…Having had the command of God himself he interposes no word of warning or remonstrance, but takes the fruit from the hand of his wife without a protest…The subsequent conduct of Adam was to the last degree dastardly. When the awful time of reckoning comes, and the Jehovah God appears to demand why his command has been disobeyed, Adam endeavors to shield himself behind the gentle being he has declared to be so dear. "The woman thou gavest to be with me, she gave me and I did eat," he whines—trying to shield himself at his wife's expense! Again we are amazed that upon such a story men have built up a theory of their superiority![38]

The Women's Bible went through seven printings in six months, and produced outrage in expected circles. When charged with the heinous but familiar crime of consorting with the devil, Elizabeth declared that "his Satanic Majesty" was not invited to join her Revising Committee, which consisted of women alone! As to the suggestion that it was "ridiculous" for women to attempt a revision of the scriptures, she asked, "I wonder if any man wrote the revising committee of Divines to stop *their* work on the ground it was ridiculous for *men* to revise the Bible."

> We have many women abundantly endowed with capabilities to understand and revise what men have thus far written. But they are all suffering from inherited ideas of their inferiority; they do not perceive it, yet such is the true explanation of their solicitude, lest they should seem too self-asserting.[39]

The Women's Bible also asked the feminist question, often in tongue-in-cheek form, about whether *all* the Bible was transparently edifying and useful, or was it trapped in the context of its ancient society:

> Indeed the Pentateuch is a long painful record of war, corruption, rapine, and lust. Why Christians who wish to convert the heathen to our religion should send them these books passes all understanding. It is most demoralizing reading for children and the unthinking masses…[40]

Elizabeth's book also disturbed some in the suffrage movement, which relied on the support of conservative men and women. Elizabeth was condemned by many as destructive to the cause. At the 1896 Convention of the National American Woman Suffrage Association, a motion was made to dissociate the movement from *The Women's Bible.* President Susan B. Anthony, knowing this also meant dissociation from Elizabeth, left the chair to speak against the resolution:

> The question is whether you sit in judgment on one who had questioned the divine inspiration of certain passages in the Bible derogatory to women. If she had written approvingly of these passages, you would not have brought in this resolution because you thought the cause might be injured among the liberals in religion. In other words, if she had written your views, you would not have considered a resolution necessary. To pass this one is to set back the hands on the dial of reform. It is the reviving of old time censorship, which I hoped we had outgrown...This resolution, adopted, will be a vote of censure upon a woman who is without peer in intellectual and statesmanlike ability; one who has stood for half a century the acknowledged leader of progressive thought and demand in regard to all matters pertaining to the absolute freedom of women.[41]

Despite her pleas, the resolution to dissociate was adopted. Elizabeth last appeared at a national convention in 1892, delivering at seventy-seven her greatest speech, *The Solitude of Self,* summing up her convictions:

> A woman was first and foremost an individual and not to be denied any of the rights of choice and development which men expected to have as individuals, and not to be judged solely in regard to her duties as a mother or wife any more than man was as a father or husband.[42]

That, to me, is what *all* rebellious women thus far have fought for and what it means to be "feminist," in whatever form the commitment to advance that principle takes. Elizabeth's Bible however, would lie forgotten until the 1970s when feminists rediscovered her timely arguments.

CHAPTER 6

In Our Own Voices

Woman was created to be a wife and mother; that is her destiny...For this she is endowed with patience, endurance, passive courage, quick sensibilities, a sympathetic nature, and great executive and administrative ability...[The] woman's rights party, by seeking to draw her away from the domestic sphere, where she is really great, noble, almost divine, and to throw her into the turmoil of political life, would rob her of her true dignity and worth...[1]

"The Woman Question," 1869

As I became conscious of my oppression as a woman, I found myself entering a state of rage...Like many women, I have been used to lying to myself. To tell myself that I wanted what I did not want, or felt what I did not feel, was a habit so deeply ingrained in me, I was never aware of having lied. I had shaped my life to fit the traditional idea of a woman, and thus, through countless decisions large and small, had sacrificed myself. Each sacrifice has made me angry. But I could not allow myself this anger. For my anger would have told me that I was lying. Now, when I ceased to lie, the anger I have accumulated for years was revealed to me.[2]

Susan Griffin

When Betty Friedan, *summa cum laude* graduate of Smith College and mother of three, wrote *The Feminine Mystique* in 1963 about "a problem that has no name," *Life* magazine called it "an angry, thoroughly documented book that in one way or another is going to provoke the daylights out of almost everyone who reads it."[3] Everyone in the early '60s *knew* that only neurotic women wanted careers, independence, and higher education along with marriage, children, and a home in the suburbs. Wasn't the American housewife the envy of the world with her labor-saving devices? Yet, when *McCalls* magazine ran their 1956 article "The Mother Who Ran Away," it brought the highest readership of any article. Suddenly people realized *hosts* of American women at home with three and a half children were miserably unhappy. What had Betty stumbled upon? An intelligent woman, she had struggled like many women through history with the discrepancy between what people said should make her "truly happy" and her own experience. Guilty about her "feelings without a name," she surveyed the two hundred women who graduated with her from Smith College and found a common bewilderment.

Despite '50s families like "Ozzie and Harriet," women were asking, "Is this all?" Magazines assured them there was no greater destiny than catching a man, cooking his meals, dressing in feminine clothes to keep their marriage exciting, toilet training, and keeping sons from delinquency. Yet their foremothers had *fought* to go to college and vote. In the 1920s, 49 percent of women went to college, but only 38 percent by the late '50s. Sixty percent dropped out to marry, and others feared a degree would hinder their prospects. Girls went steady at twelve, bought padded bras at ten, and advertisements for little girls' dresses declared "She too can join the mantrap set."[4] If a woman questioned all this, something must be wrong with *her*—sexually based, some would say, or stirred up by a college education. Betty "named" the problem, and, like a new disease, when it has a name, it could be spoken about. A collective sigh went around the suburbs as a weight lifted off women's hearts. I am not alone, not stupid, not dysfunctional.

What had happened in the forty years since women gained the vote? Angry "feminists" wanted to be like men—"penis envy" in Freudian terms. What Freudians failed to distinguish between was women's envy of male *organs* and male *options*. Men could have careers, public life, *and* marriage. It was *this* that women craved, not body parts that gave privileges to one group, not another. Margaret Mead's research on the South Seas Islands had shown that island *men* envied their women:

> In our Occidental view of life, woman, fashioned from man's rib, can at the most strive unsuccessfully to imitate man's superior powers and higher vocations. The basic theme of the initiatory cult, however [in the South Seas] is that women by virtue of their ability to make children, hold the secret of life. Man's role is uncertain, undefined, and perhaps unnecessary.[5]

She was demonstrating how the superiority of one sex over the other was *culturally* determined, not eternally decreed by some "order of creation," but some used her research to promote instead a

> return to the Garden of Eden; a garden where women need only forget the "divine discontent" born of education to return to a world in which male achievement becomes merely a poor substitute for child-rearing.[6]

This "feminine mystique," as Betty called it, preached that woman's highest goal was to fulfill her femininity. Women's *problems* were rooted in envying men instead of accepting their natural *difference* fulfilled in sexual submission, male domination, and maternal love, which *somehow* included cooking, cleaning, washing diapers, and foregoing education and adult stimulus. Farnham and Lundberg's *Modern Woman: The Lost Sex* warned that education "masculinized" women with dangerous consequences to home, children, and good sex! Career women sank as villains, while mothers soared as heroines. Colleges began directing women's education toward training as wives and mothers, and those institutions that did not bow to this trend were placed on the defensive. Adlai Stevenson's 1955 commencement address at Smith College assured graduating women they need not worry about politics and public issues because their role was unique—influencing their men and boys:

> Far from the vocation of marriage and motherhood leading you away from the issues of our day, it brings you back to their very center and places upon you an infinitely deeper and more intimate responsibility than that borne by the majority of those who hit the headlines and make the news.

He outlined women's task:

> This assignment for you, as wives and mothers, you can do in the living room with a baby in your lap or in the kitchen with a can opener in your hand. If you're clever, maybe you can even practice your saving arts on that unsuspecting man while he's watching television. I think there is much you can do about our crisis in the humble role of housewife. I could wish you no better vocation than that.[7]

Fifties domesticity had reverted to the Victorian home where wives waited in beauty and peacefulness to soothe troubled male souls. *Seventeen* magazine enthused:

> What profession offers the daily joy of turning out a delicious dinner, of converting a few yards of fabric, a pot of paint, and imagination into a new room? Of seeing a tired and unsure man at the end of a working day become a rested lord of his manor?[8]

Milton had described this bliss as "He for God only, she for God in him." The *Ladies Home Journal* jazzed it up '50s-style:

> If he doesn't want me to wear a certain kind of dress, then I truly don't want to either. The thing is, whatever he has wanted is what I also want…I don't believe in 50–50 marriages.[9]

The difference from the Victorian sanctuary, however, was that women now did *all* the work—from polishing floors to providing "male comfort." Women's natural "destiny" had acquired a host of extra tasks along the way!

Why *did* women go home again after efforts made on their behalf earlier in the century with the vote and their entry into male arenas during the war?

Because the '50s demanded the Victorian either/or choice—marriage without career, or career without marriage. Men could have both but women one, preferably the former. The jaunty career women of the '30s and '40s was gone. We all knew even the brightest man wanted a pretty girl at home. As one woman reflected:

> I now realize that in the back of my mind there was always the assump-
> tion, even when I was getting my graduate degree in education, that any
> work I did was temporary, something to do until I assumed my principal
> role in life which was to be the perfect wife and mother, supported by my
> husband.[10]

I entered university in Australia at the end of the Fifties, and remember struggling with the *either/or* choice. In my family, education was important and I was encouraged to achieve, yet deep down I knew that "good" Christian women abandoned such achievements after marriage to be full-time house-wives. There were two exceptions I had figured out. If a woman did medicine, she could acceptably combine career *and* family "after all that study." The other was missionary wife. A woman's education *should* be put to use in the mission field where the locals could mind the children. It always struck me as puzzling how the "faithful" back home revered missionary wives who sent their children to boarding school in another country for years, yet would gos-sip a local woman out of town if she put her child in day care for a few hours to take on a career!

Why did women's choice revert to *either/or?* Any single argument falls short. The war had catapulted women into *both/and* roles—factories, industry, support services for the armed forces, running family farms and businesses, and rearing children as single parents. After the war, these independent women were sent back home to produce babies postponed during the war; care for physically and psychologically wounded men; and restore the security of fam-ily life for a healing of the nations. The GI bill flooded colleges with veterans, and schools reduced female admissions. Like their Victorian foremothers, women became moral guardians again, but *sexy* guardians this time. Marriage was the way to reverse the sexual laxity of wartime, and, since the Pill was not yet easily available, marriage was also the safe way to have sex. Since it was billed as women's life goal, couples married early and began their families. Consuming became patriotic, and the "American Dream" of an affordable home where good housewives did everything themselves produced the "suburbs."

Motherhood was promoted as women's natural fulfillment—and also ful-filled postwar national needs. *Modern Woman: The Lost Sex* defined femininity as a

> receptiveness and passiveness, a willingness to accept dependence with-
> out fear or resentment, with a deep inwardness and readiness for the
> final goal of sexual life—impregnation.[11]

Childless couples were pitied if infertile, suspect if by choice. Numerous studies popped up blaming mothers if they didn't get it right! "Maternal deprivation" became the buzzword for anything short of fulltime mothering. Didn't Dr. Spock, Pied Piper of children, say only mothers at home could give the permissive attention required for healthy childhood? Yet mothers were *also* blamed for being both overprotective and harboring "unconscious hostilities" toward sons, damaging their masculinity! Some tried the two-career family, but the priority of the man's career for "male identity" was so universally assumed that academic institutions and businesses would not employ husband and wife. Women who "wanted more" were guilted out of careers by pressure from family and friends to do the "right" thing by their children, rather than negotiate, dodge, and weave to accomplish both dreams. Wanting a career was antimotherhood.

Women who accepted these rules reflect with amazement now. Memoir after memoir analyzes why they did not protest.

> I am a mid-life woman. Like most women of my generation, I gave over much of my adult life to marriage and motherhood. Like so many others, I awoke one day from the childhood dream…that being some man's wife and some child's mother would occupy my mind and my hands for the rest of my life. And I lay on my couch, listened to music, and wept with despair.[12]

When writer Mary Lythgoe Bradford, a full time instructor in English with plans for a Ph.D., told her department head she was getting married, he was angry because she had signed a contract and university policy required *married* women to be part-time or resign. When her husband moved cities to do *his* Ph.D., she automatically followed:

> I have often wondered why I was so quick to give up my own plans. I can't really blame my gentle and open-minded husband. I am sure he would have supported me if I had applied at one of the many universities in the area instead of getting on as clerk-typist at the Library of Congress. It was part of the culture of the time. A Master's degree for a woman was rare in my circles, and though I was praised for it, most people expected me to settle down with children and live happily ever after.[13]

For ten years she stayed home with her children. When the last was in school, she became ill, and her doctor's diagnosis was "Mrs. Bradford, when will you get back to your teaching? There is no illness like that of unused talent."

Even today, my husband and I still wonder why we never even *discussed* what my role would be—whether I would combine career and children. It was just *assumed* that they didn't mix. My husband would have been supportive if *either* of us had thought to question the "way things were," yet I remember struggling with an unvoiced sadness when a man who graduated with me was appointed junior lecturer at the university. I had outperformed him throughout graduate school and was envious that he could use his skills and *also* be married. But at the same madly ambivalent time, I eagerly anticipated the publicized bliss of full-time domesticity. So, like many women before me, I learned the adapting game, negotiating "dreams" between chores and children. I read autobiographies looking for glimpses of women verbalizing my unspoken thoughts. I lived vicariously through others changing the world and found ways to change mine within the limits. Albert Schweitzer was an inspiration when my children were young. Once asked how he accomplished so much, he said he waited at first for a free hour, then realized hours never happened and began using the minutes! I finished a theology diploma by distance education, studying late or when the babies napped. One day, desperate to finish a book, I sat in the middle of the floor surrounded by babies and toys—I had my sister's children as well that day—and held the book high with one hand as they crawled happily over me. If my abandoned microbiology degrees taught me anything, it was how to open a screw-top jar with one hand, keeping the other free for a book or a baby!

Despite the conscious and unconscious compromises I had made to fit into a system that demanded an *either/or* choice of women—marriage or career—I still remember the moment when the magnitude of the compromise struck me. We were driving in the country when our children were teenagers. I had made a comment about something I don't even remember now, and the association of ideas suddenly shook everything into place like glass pieces in a kaleidoscope. I saw clearly for the first time. Why didn't we even *consider* if I could do both? I had turned down an offer to do a Ph.D. in microbiology, settling for the shorter Master's because my fiancé's career might take us away from the university before I finished; and what did I need a Ph.D. for anyway, if I was going to be a wife and mother? When my professor made it impossible for me to complete my Master's before my marriage, I convinced myself and those around me that *I* had been the victor by refusing to be manipulated by him, rather than questioning a *system* that demanded I abandon one dream for another. When the whole picture fell in place that day years later, I began to cry. The weeping continued inside me for days, a dull ache as I finally grieved what I had unnecessarily lost. I can look back at many other paths I took, negotiating around a supportive family—some call this "God's plan" for me as a convenient way to justify the system in which women were caught— but a hollowness still comes with the reality that my options were removed as a woman in love who wanted to marry but, unlike her man, could not have both. This is what feminism is about—ensuring that women are not denied the option to use their God-given gifts because of someone else's rules.

Some women who have been fortunate not to encounter resistance don't understand these feelings until they are faced with another person's story. Feminist theologian Sheila Greeve Davaney recalled her "moment of truth" at a weekend for women students at Union Theological Seminary.

I began the weekend surprised by and suspicious of the feminist statements I was hearing. I was convinced that these were the carpings of women who simply had not made it. But as I listened to the stories of woman after woman, to the tales of pain and humiliation and of courage and determination, a new awareness began for me. I was deeply troubled by my own ignorance and what had been my facile dismissal of the pain of others. And I felt as well the beginnings of that anger that invades every woman when she recognizes her own oppression. It would take years for this awareness and anger to be given full expression; but though I did not recognize it then, my weekend in New York was a turning point of my consciousness of myself as a woman…I began to understand more fully the dynamics of sexism. Such understanding felt almost like a physical assault. So many things that had once appeared trivial now took on ominous proportions.[14]

When awareness comes, there is no going back. Ripples make wider circles as the evil of legitimized subordination of women sink in, changing one's whole perspective of the world. For some women, anger at having lived their lives by someone else's rules and at missing opportunities to realize their dreams leaves them bitter and cheated. They cannot face the fact that their self-sacrifice was unnecessary and so refuse to support feminist ideas that challenge the only identity they had as women. At the other end of the continuum, women who realize the injustice of a system are energized to transform the world so that never again will women—or anyone else—be excluded by so-called laws of "nature" described by those with power to enforce such laws.

Betty Friedan challenged women to listen to their inner voices and find their identity, fitting love, children, and home with other choices as well. Her voice seeded the Women's Liberation Movement of the '70s, and other voices joined hers through books, magazines, conferences, and political action. "Women's Lib" was soon applied to anything smelling of women stepping out of place, and its evil ramifications were preached especially in religious circles. "Bra-burners" became the caricature, reminding us of the Suffragists in the last century who were scathingly labeled "Bloomers" for adopting that modest-by-our-standards skirt with long pantaloons rather than restricting Victorian corsets. Their eighteenth-century sisters who joined male literary groups in London were, in their turn, denounced as "blue stockings," the hose *men* wore to such events rather than formal black stockings. And Joan of Arc was burned at the stake for wearing men's clothes as much as anything else—and so on and so on.

Like any movement, one size did not fit all. Throughout this book, I have argued that feminism is a continuum of feminisms with many places for women to stand. Sixties feminists saw a world geared for male players and wanted to play like men, with the same rights and opportunities. The next generation of feminists argued that there was a distinct "women's experience" common to all women but different from men's. Books describing this female "way of knowing" rushed off presses, and women's conferences mushroomed as women shared together how they saw the world. But the "common experience" didn't seem to include everyone. Just as powerful men in the past described what was "female"—weak, insatiable, etc., *feminist* leaders were creating their package of what automatically went with being a woman, and it didn't fit everyone.

I remember spending three uncomfortable days at a church women's conference where it was assumed *all* women had a repressed desire to dance unrestrained with other women and return to a womblike place of origin reconstituted with candles and chanting. Red wool bands around our wrists symbolized our common symbol of menstrual blood. I hated it! It felt spooky, a bit frightening, but mostly downright silly. I met many interesting women but felt increasingly less at home, not brave enough to admit my feelings since everyone else seemed to find some lost sanctuary under considerable pressure to conform. Power structures were alive and well, no matter how often it was said that when women lead, everything is egalitarian. Admitting I was uncomfortable and longing to be home with my husband would have "proved" I was sucked into male values, unconscious of my starvation. I shared my feelings much later with other women, who sighed with relief because they felt the same way! It is one thing to agree women should be paid like men and that airline stewardesses should not be fired for gaining weight, but another to substitute one set of dominant gender "rules" for another.

The idea of a common "woman's experience" that sublimates all differences between women was also challenged by women of color in the '70s. Just as Sojourner Truth broadened the nineteenth-century white middle-class women's movement with her "ain't I a woman" challenge, they claimed *their* experience of oppression was not limited to gender, but blended with race and class oppression as well; thus white feminists could not describe their feelings *for* them.

> Simplistic definition of women's liberation is a dismissal of race and class as factors that, in conjunction with sexism, determine the extent to which an individual will be discriminated against, exploited or oppressed. Bourgeois white women interested in women's rights issues have been satisfied with simple definitions for obvious reasons...placing themselves in the same social category as oppressed women, they were not anxious to call attention to race and class privilege.[15]

Thus, African American women coined the term *womanist* for *their* feminism, encompassing *anything* that worked for women's welfare—race and class issues as well. This criticism was necessary for feminism, allowing feminism to include other discrimination—sex, race, class, age—and opening itself to Asian, Hispanic, Native American, and poor women, who added color and texture to the ever-growing feminist quilt.

It is important for Christian women to recognize the diversity of the feminist movement begun in the '70s, so that they do not "throw the baby out with the bathwater" if a negative image of "feminists" has been embedded in their minds. It is like the many expressions of Christianity. If people feel so passionately about something that it energizes them to commit strength and time to it, the *way* they pursue it will reflect their personal needs and concerns. It is one thing to agree that a male-biased society has diminished women around the globe, but another to decide how this should be reversed. Many women have worked *within* the regular structures of marriage, family, and society, often not calling themselves feminists but agreeing with its arguments. They have gathered with other women for short periods in retreats, or sought other women's support in an emotional rather than practical way. They have enjoyed both men and women, expressing their sexuality in a mixed environment while making sure those relationships respect an equal basis of power. Others have concentrated on spending their time with other women as much as possible, refusing to waste energy fighting a male-oriented society that has not changed. Others—"radical feminists"—believe the structures of society *depend* on oppressing women to survive, and thus a totally *new* order is needed. These are all different models of feminism, and we need to find our place somewhere within them.

I want to spend time talking about "radical feminists," since this is the feminism that bothers many church women. By the '80s, Women's Studies programs were established in many universities, and, like any other academic discipline, the broadest limits of the topic were explored. "Radical" feminism (radical meaning "of the roots") found its home there, often seen as the "pure" feminism. Radical feminists see patriarchy as a *value* system created by men to sustain male power and female subordination and *needing* violence against women for its survival. The "family," held together by highly publicized ideas of romantic love, is a tool of this patriarchy as an *economic* structure with women as unpaid labor serving men. Women's "labor" includes sexual favors, owned by the husband until the recent legislation against rape in marriage, and still owned by men in countries where women cannot file rape charges against husbands. Many radical feminists see the religious and political resistance to women becoming mothers outside a "traditional family" as protecting patriarchy's "family." The challenge for radical feminists, therefore, is not just to address the *evils* of patriarchy, but to oppose male power that keeps it in place through majority representation in politics, religion, medicine, and law.

Some radical feminists even argue that sex has been *defined* by patriarchy, and women who live with men collaborate to keep the heterosexual experience dominant in society, silencing lesbian women as deviant. "Lesbian" does not exclusively refer to women who choose women as sexual partners, but to women who seek all aspects of their identity *primarily* in relation to other women, rather than being defined as women *primarily* in relation to men. Radical feminists like Adrienne Rich argue that society's emphasis on intimacy as a male–female *sexual* experience ignores the history of women who have shared rich inner lives bonded together in friendships far broader than for sexual reasons. They are not denying that many men need women, and vice versa, but argue that this need must be affirmed in ways other than "power over" and the right to take whatever they want. Radical feminists therefore call for an *alternate* culture created for women, which puts their interests rather than men's at the center of their society with separate communities, networks of women-run businesses, and women-operated health care, even women-only religion. When radical feminist Sonia Johnson ran for President in 1984, she claimed:

> One of the basic tenets of radical feminism is that any woman in the world has more in common with any other women regardless of class, race, age, ethnic group, nationality—than any woman has with any man.[16]

Radical feminism draws different responses from women in general. Those who have lived in situations of violence at the hands of men—fathers, husbands, factory foremen, political leaders—as many women across the world have done, find the arguments liberating. They also sound a voice of liberation for women who have been excluded, overtly or subtly, from "normal" society because of sexual orientation. Yet many women who have lived happy lives with men they love and care for find their radical conclusions—even while agreeing that patriarchal society has oppressed women—vindictive and untrue. Such women believe it a fallacy to say *all* men are violent and *all* women peacemakers, or that certain characteristics—cooperation, collegiality, intuition, niceness—are synonymous with being female, and other negative values—competition, hierarchy, rationality, or violence—synonymous with being male. They are also not convinced "woman-oriented" social structures will "naturally" avoid discrimination and oppression, as if dominance is only a male thing.

Again, I come back to my repetitious theme. Feminists come in many shapes and sizes according to their particular views and experiences, yet none represent *all* of feminism, just as Christians are not all Lutheran! Radical feminists have often been painted as the "norm" for feminism, by radical feminists themselves who believe that they are the "pure" feminists and that all others are shams, and by those who oppose feminism, equating all of it with these radical positions. It reminds me of Christianity's considerable history of heresy trials. So many Christians have felt they can define "true Christians" in their own narrow, judgmental terms, condemning the rest. I do not agree with all feminists, and they do not all agree with me. But I also do not agree with all *Christians*—some ideas are downright harmful in my opinion—yet I do not reject Christianity or the label "Christian," nor can I deny others their right to express their faith in ways that are helpful for them. And we must never forget that those called radical often become, in retrospect, heroines!

By the late 1980s, polls showed the *majority* of American women sup-ported feminist ideals but did not call themselves feminists. They saw the need for a strong women's movement, but only 39 percent believed the current movement represented their views. The numbers were even lower among younger women. Feminist theorists disagreed on the reasons for this.[17] Susan Faludi's 1991 bestseller *Backlash: The Undeclared War Against American Women*[18] blamed a subtle, antifeminist message through the '80s from the media, politicians, and church leaders, ranging from claims that women had gained equality so there was no need to seek equal rights any more, to conclu-sions that American career women were miserable, barren, and lonely—even angry and dysfunctional—as a result. Susan blamed the religious right's political influence with its "biblical" model of family values, and tirades such as Rush Limbaugh's "femi-Nazi" journalism, all of which left ordinary women uneasy, confused, and anxious. This clever backlash, argued on American traditional values, which also were *God's* values, was internalized by women without access to other views, shaming them into rejecting the feminist movement. Naomi Wolf in *The Beauty Myth: How Images of Beauty Are Used against Women,*[19] more specifically blamed subtle societal pressures to diet, dress a certain way, and work out, coalescing into a national mood defining how women should look and behave. Both urged women to band together to resist such coercion.

But a new breed of young '90s feminists have argued a different reason for "feminist fall-off." Born after the '60s, they have grown up in a world that gave them college and workplace, even if not yet equal representation on boards, corporations, and in Congress.[20] These women took Women's Studies courses taught by the "radical feminists" of the '70s and found the arguments not reflective of their '90s experience. They have reacted against the "patriar-chy" of their *women* professors, who penalized classroom dissent or criticism of their radical feminist stances. The young feminists did *not* view men as the enemy, women as perpetual victims, sex as a form of violence, and hetero-sexual sex as a sell-out. They did *not* think women were "naturally" women-oriented or the world totally structured on female oppression and male domination. While they acknowledged some of these problems still existed, they saw *other* causes worthy of their attention as feminists—revised childcare laws, birth control and abortion rights, and parity in politics and business. Some even espoused right-wing politics!

These women asked, "Is it obligatory to subscribe to certain policies to be a feminist, or does feminism transcend the political and ideological lines of the 'old guard' feminists?" Susan Faludi and others have called these women "faux feminists"—false feminists:

> They denounce the second wave of feminists and their concern with violence against women, delight the media, pander to the right wing, and set young women against older women.[21]

Yet the questions of the '90s feminists are valid. Is there only one way to be feminist, or do we each express feminism in our own way and context? When the word *feminist* was first used in the April 1895 *Athenaeum,* it described a woman who "has in her the capacity of fighting her way back to independence." Susan Faludi's 1991 definition is not much different:

> [Feminism] asks that women not be forced to "choose" between public justice and private happiness. It asks that women be free to define themselves—instead of having their identity defined for them, time and time again, by their culture and their men.[22]

The young '90s feminists would agree. They *too* want the freedom to define themselves, not be defined by others, even other feminists. While they believe strongly in the principles of feminism—the freedom women have sought to define themselves from earliest times—they hesitate to use a title that they see currently aligned with only *one* expression of a worthy history of strong women.

Once again, feminism's power is its diversity—its ability to advocate for the freedom of all women to live a full life of equality with men in whatever form or circumstance they choose. As we have seen through history, rebellious women who protested have been silenced because they did not have other voices to protest with them. For the first time for centuries, women are gaining representation across many disciplines and places of power, supported by both men and other women. It seems impossible that this momentum could be lost again, but the impossible is no stranger to history! Women cannot afford to pit themselves against each other, arguing about whose feminism is the "pure" or correct one. That happened in Christianity, and its cause has been weakened by division within itself more than by those who opposed it! Women—and men—need to respect other women's journeys even when different from their own, in the larger vision that all women—and men—can have life, and have it abundantly! That was the message of Jesus.

Speaking of the message of Jesus, just as the women's movement of the last century caused Sarah Grimké and Elizabeth Cady Stanton to question male interpretations of the Bible used to keep women in subordinate positions in the family, the feminist movement of the '60s would do the same. As Betty Friedan pondered her "feeling without a name," Valerie Saiving was doing the same. One of a rare breed of female theological students at the University of Chicago, she sat through endless discussions as men defined what was wrong with the human condition, and why humans needed God. After her doctoral studies were finished, she published her nagging suspicions in a 1960 article in the *Journal of Religion:*

> I am a student of theology; I am also a woman. Perhaps it strikes you as curious that I put these two assertions beside each other, as if to imply that one's sexual identity has some bearing on his theological views. I

myself would have rejected such an idea when I first began my theological studies. But now, thirteen years later, I am no longer certain as I once was that, when theologians speak of "man," they are using the word in its generic sense. It is, after all, a well-known fact that theology has been written almost exclusively by men. This alone should put us on guard, especially since contemporary theologians constantly remind us that one of man's strongest temptations is to identify his own limited perspective with universal truth.[23]

Valerie's concern was the way her peers were describing what was wrong with humanity. From the beginning of Christianity, theologians have discussed this question, coming up with different solutions according to their experience. Fifties theologians were identifying the problem as anxiety and loneliness. Man, unlike other creatures, was free to make choices and not be bound to conditioned responses like animals. He could stand apart from his world and survey it, manipulating and organizing it for his purposes. *Sin* therefore was man's temptation to overcome his anxiety about making the right choices and staying in control, by magnifying his own power, righteousness or knowledge.

> Man knows that he is merely part of the whole, but he tries to convince himself and others that he *is* the whole. He tries in fact to become the whole. Sin is the unjustified concern of the self for its own power and prestige; it is the imperialistic drive to close the gap between the individual, separate self and others by reducing those others to the status of mere objects which can then be treated as appendages of the self and manipulated accordingly.[24]

If anxiety was man's problem, which led to sinful pride and domination, where man tries to lord it over others, what was the remedy? According to Valerie's colleagues, it was to espouse the opposite—"completely self-giving love," taking no thought for one's own interests but seeking only the good of the other.

Valerie felt uncomfortable with this assessment. It didn't make sense to her as a woman. While anxiety about maintaining power and control over others might be a problem for the '50s male, it was not something '50s women experienced. Valerie's nagging doubt that something was wrong with this picture took thirteen years to mature into a challenge to male theology. Using Margaret Mead's work showing a different male–female relationship in the South Seas, Valerie argued that societies conditioned girls and boys in different ways. Little girls grew up knowing they would be like *their* mothers simply by waiting for their bodies to mature. Boys knew from early days they were not like mothers and needed to develop their individuality. Femininity was about "being"; masculinity was an endless "becoming"—career, sexual maturity, performance—molding an individual to stand competitively and successfully compared with others. Men were rewarded for what they *became;* women grew into their destiny as wife and mother.

This process of defining what they would be was anxiety-producing for males, Valerie argued, and thus male theologians identified this anxiety as the "problem" of being human in a society where public achievement, competition, and control over nature was highly valued. Sin was the striving for power, exploitation, self-assertiveness, and the use of others as objects, all of which tried to overcome anxiety and fear. The *remedy* was to do the opposite—love sacrificially and surrender to the other's needs—what '50s women had done for years! Thus the "generic" human problem described by Valerie's colleagues was in fact the *male* problem! Valerie argued that the *opposite* was true as the *female* problem, not a temptation to power over others, but constant *surrendering* of their power and self-identity to other's needs as wives and mothers. Their *sin*—the "fall" from their original creation in God's image—was better described as *giving up* that image, lack of self-definition as God's creation, dependence on another for definition, lack of pride in its best sense, diffuseness, triviality, and lack of focus, and underdevelopment and negation of themselves as people. A woman's *remedy* was not *more* surrender, *more* submissiveness, *more* sacrificial loving, but becoming a person in her own right, not defined by another, responsible for herself as the image of God. If man's redemption was to seek relational self-sacrificing love after the anxiety-ridden experience of independence and individuality, woman's redemption was to seek independence and individuality after a life of sacrificial giving and self-denial in relationships.

Valerie's brave argument was addressed to the theological "giants" of the time. Like Elizabeth Cady Stanton before her, she protested that if only men write theology and interpret the Bible, only male experiences of being human before God will be described. Universal claims made about humans through Christian history have not been "generic" descriptions, but ideas about male experience applied to everyone. Such doctrines were also culturally limited because they reflected the way different societies and periods of history have defined the virtues of men. The sex and the context of the theologian *mattered!* Valerie had stumbled on what would become feminist theology—the challenge to "read" the Bible through the eyes and experiences of women as well as men. Ahead of her time, her paper was reprinted once but then ignored until the '70s when women were becoming teachers in theological departments, and the blossoming feminist movement would provide a nurturing soil for such feminist questions to be asked of theology. At last, through feminist theology, the sisters of Eve would find a way to retell their story!

CHAPTER 7

Introducing Feminist Theology

A man and a lion were discussing the relative strengths of men and lions in general. The man contended that he and his fellows were stronger than lions by reason of their greater intelligence. "Come now with me," he cried, "and I will soon prove that I am right." So he took him into the public gardens and showed him a statue of Hercules overcoming the lion and tearing his mouth in two. "That's all very well," said the lion, "but proves nothing, for it was a man who made the statue."

Aesop's Fables (The Lion and the Statue)[1]

Valerie Saiving, like the lion in this story, discovered that the way a story is told depends on who is telling it. Some of us will cheer along with Joshua as the walls of Jericho fall down, but a few might harbor twinges of illicit sympathy for the Canaanites who had to share their land simply because someone else's God promised it to the Israelites. Native Americans and Australian Aborigines might side with the Canaanites too, since they have had personal experience of their homeland being taken by others, and their perspectives on the story might make the rest of us aware for the first time that, while stories are usually told by the winners, they are not the whole story. The meaning of any story is decided in the interaction between the story and its reader.

Biblical scholar Marcus Borg calls feminist theology the single most important development in theology in his lifetime, because it gives another vantage point, another lens from which to look at the Christian tradition.[2] Feminist theology challenges the way those in power have told the story for centuries and suggests we look at the statue of the strong man Hercules from the perspective of the one overpowered and silenced—in this case, women. While feminist theology is new, it is also very old—ever since Eve—as the last six chapters have shown. Every time a woman protested the way the Bible or the church described her and her place was an event of feminist theology. Theology is "talking about God." Feminist theology is talking about God from the perspective of women who believe they *also* are made in the image of God—equally human.

While Valerie Saiving raised the question of the male domination of theology, Vatican II (1962–65) provided women an opportunity to keep the question alive. This momentous Catholic council called by Pope John XXIII was a breath of fresh air. It heard petitions from women's groups; priests argued that women should not be reproductive machines trapped without safeguards against pregnancy; nuns shed habits, took part in civil rights marches, pursued graduate studies, and even sought representation on the all-male church committees that determined their role! However, despite the advances, women theologians were still not admitted to the Catholic Theological Society of America even though lay *men* were, and women were not permitted to become priests. Denied a voice at the center, theologically trained women protested from the margins. A women's ordination organization was formed, providing a forum for women to formulate feminist theological arguments together. In a way, the Vatican was a *benefactor* of feminist theology as this incredible group of lay women theologians in seminaries and universities became angry enough to change the world!

Mary Daly, a lecturer at the Jesuit Boston College, published her groundbreaking book *The Church and the Second Sex* [3] in 1968, tracing the history of misogyny in Catholicism. Misogyny means "hatred of women," a disdain that views women as not just morally and intellectually inferior to men, but as the source of evil in the world. Mary's concern was that women did not even recognize this hatred, so conditioned were they to accept their sex roles and stereotypes as theological "truth." This truth was disguised with flattering platitudes idolizing them and making their domestic role appear noble, while their pedestals *prevented* them from participating in society. Without access to other ways to think, women felt like traitors to husband and children if they rebelled. As one lay woman told the council:

> You may omit all the pedestals and incense honoring women. All women really want is to be treated in the church as the full human persons they are. [4]

Mary echoed French writer Simone de Beauvoir's thoughts in her book *The Second Sex* [5] published earlier in the century—that Christianity oppressed women by promising rewards in the afterlife for obedience in this life. The illusion of equality and female sovereignty *in the home* kept women as men's possessions, glorified *only* in this narrow role. Both Simone and Mary blamed the interpretations of Eve that cast women as inferior afterthoughts, transmitters of sin and temptation incarnate, rather than part of a team in God's image multiplying and replenishing the earth, a task wider than reproduction.

Reminding readers of papal decrees affirming male rule because women's "nature" best fitted house work, subjection, and motherhood, she voiced the unspeakable—some women have *difficulty* being defined by motherhood alone. If work rewarded men in society, women might *also* enjoy respect for their professional excellence. They might *delight* in a self-image rather than being absorbed into their husband's image. Besides, if subordination was "natural" for women, why did the church need to insist so strongly on it? "Learning to behave naturally" is an oxymoron!

Mary's book was a reaction to a Vatican II backlash, which wanted to preserve the "eternal feminine" myth. Two priests had argued in *Woman is the Glory of Man*[6] that spiritual and mental distinctions between sexes *dictated* that women's psychology was founded totally on a primordial tendency to love and be submissive—and also harbor illusions about themselves! Women's lighter, simpler brains had less capacity for deduction, and attempts to discipline their "intuition" with male logic made them "masculine." Women were "most womanly" when utterly humble and completely surrendered, not self-creative, active, and searching. They could accurately be described exclusively as virgins, brides, or mothers, even though men were not exclusively defined as virgins, husbands, and fathers. God placed women in the family, and they were neurotic and unhappy outside it. Lest we forget, it started with Eve:

> She [woman] has not lost the dispositions of impressionability and mobility which Eve had manifested in the initial drama of humanity. She remains fragile, more subject to an unreflected impulse, and more accessible to seduction. [7]

Mary saw women's lack of resistance as caused by a number of things: their powerless position; a lack of opportunity to protest; an ignorance of the roots of their frustrations; and a self-interest when the system worked for them, blinding them to the plight of other women. Most of all, there is a psychological mechanism in oppressed people that eliminates that to which they cannot aspire. Women accepted their limited existence as normal and acted in the way they were described—a self-fulfilling prophecy that in turn "proved" their role was grounded in "nature." This myth overrode their creative potential and uniqueness, so that they could not see themselves in any role beyond the Catholic marriage manual's portrait:

> Nothing gives a man greater satisfaction and sense of fulfillment than a realized sense of importance. Men want recognition. They thrive on it…Nothing like this is natural to the woman. If she is aggressive or domineering it is because she has been made so, and that is not good. Two egotists do not easily make a harmonious pair.[8]

Mary identified three theological roots for women's problems:

(1) The maleness of God, that bearded man of Christian art. While the beard was optional, maleness never was, as if there was some divine purpose

for a male appendage. Yet maleness, as we shall see, is only one biblical metaphor among many for God, who has been described as rock, shield, lover, fortress, shepherd, potter, and nurturing mother, to name a few.

(2) The church's obsession with the fall and original sin, both blamed on Eve. This sin-haunted view of life encouraged negative attitudes to creation, world, sexuality, and women as symbols of sinful sexual desire. Marriage was reduced theologically to producing and educating offspring, with women inferior or complementary to the male norm. The emphasis on sin to be punished or forgiven overshadowed other ways to think about God and humanity, such as alienation seeking reunion and disharmony needing restoration, both biblical images which celebrate creation, women, and sex as *good.*

(3) A disproportionate emphasis on the status of the male priest and sacramental orders. Women were excluded from ordination because of their inferior feminine nature and subordinate position in the order of creation assigned since Eve. Women could not preside over men or represent the male Christ in the mass. Arguments created to justify such exclusion perpetuated negativity toward women. Mary advocated a change in the priestly role from the male who substituted for Christ in the mass to people in mission in the world. The end point of this line of thought is "Why have *any* division between priest and laity, *any* separate caste?" Many Catholic women who began in the women's ordination movement finally reached this conclusion, seeing the *caste system* itself as a problem.

The difference between Mary and Simone was hope versus despair. Simone saw the church unworthy of mature humanity and rejected it. Mary, optimistic after Vatican II, longed for radical transformation but was fired from Boston College! Three months of petitions and student marches accomplished her reappointment, promotion, and tenure, but her 1973 book *Beyond God the Father*[9] displayed less hope and signaled her move out of the church. She described the basic problem:

> There is a worldwide sexual caste, involving birth-ascribed hierarchically ordered groups whose members have unequal access to goods, services and prestige and to physical and mental well-being. Caste systems are hard to change, and are interdependent units, so that to change one unit is to alter all. This caste system is perpetuated with consent of the victims as well as of the dominant sex, consent obtained through sex role socialization—a conditioning process begun at birth and enforced by most institutions.[10]

The church called this gender caste system "natural," the "divine plan." Pope Paul VI had described *true* women's liberation in the wake of the '60s women's movement, not as equality with the other sex, but recognition of true feminine personality—the vocation of a woman to become a mother! This was not only a Catholic attitude. Influential Protestant theologian Karl Barth in this century would also declare woman "ontologically" subordinate to man, meaning "that's the way it naturally is, folks."

Mary's second book urged women in the church to abandon the male-created images, language, theological methods, and value systems. Like the question of ordination, it was not a matter of being *included* in the structure, but changing the structures altogether. Even though theologians agreed that God was not *actually* male, the symbols and language still conveyed this meaning. Because the "ideal male" image was the predominant metaphor used to describe God, the "maleness" of God and Christ sanctioned the "rightness" of male rule in society. Once this theological sexism is recognized, nothing is the same again. Mary urged church women to rid themselves of this internalized patriarchy, which produced guilt, inferiority, and self-hatred, and form "sisterhoods" to support each other against the opposition that would follow—social disapproval, guilt at opposing men, resistance from women who saw feminists as threats, opposition from token women in church positions whose power might be weakened, false feminine humility in aiming low, female ambivalence toward success, self-depreciation in fighting all causes but their own, and an emotional dependence that prevented women from protesting alone. To strengthen her point, Mary turned Eve and the fall upside down. The new fall was up—women tasting the fruit of the "knowledge of God" forbidden by patriarchy, and bringing men with them from innocence to adulthood.[11]

While Mary exposed the history of the subordination of women within the church, Catholic theologian Rosemary Radford Ruether, also encouraged by Vatican II, traced sexism beyond Jewish and Christian history to religious changes in the first millennium B.C.E.[12] Prior to then, tribal culture held a holistic view of everything bound together and interconnected—man, woman, nature, culture, gods, and goddesses. As cities developed and public affairs dominated over tribal households, a dualism of opposites with male public roles taking precedence emerged. Women's domestic sphere became separated from men's public life. Half the race—men—were freed for what society called "productive work," while the other half—women—serviced this "freedom." The duality remained in existence, but women's service role had now been argued as something "natural" and unchangeable. Rosemary called for the liberation of women, linking her challenge with the emerging liberation theology movement. In 1968, South American Catholic bishops had challenged the church to resist any status quo that preserved the poor as an eternally oppressed caste. Rosemary made her parallel challenge on behalf of women that all oppressive systems be banished. She argued it was not enough for women to take on masculine traits "valued" by society at the expense of "devalued" feminine ones, but rather that they should describe a new humanity valuing both, eliminating all distinctions that divided and discriminated. For the church, this meant dissolving male-female, clergy-lay and sacred-secular distinctions. The word was out! Western religion, including Christianity, was profoundly sexist with its promotion of male images of God and its teaching on the "natural" subordination of women.

Feminist theologians have gone in many directions since then, challenging different expressions of women's subordination in different countries and contexts and in different ways. More recently, non-Western feminist theologians have challenged *Western* feminist theologians for not hearing the voices of women from the Two-Thirds World. Diversity has become the heart of feminist theology—many colors, many sounds, many struggles, many grounds. The search for justice and dignity for all women is initiated and resolved in as many ways as there are women, since feminist theology begins not in a textbook with a set of eternal doctrines, but in everyday experiences of women struggling for liberation, calling on God to help them and not side with the oppressors.

African feminist theologians are concerned about how the church will address widowhood rituals and inheritance customs that disadvantage women, and the lack of education for women in the church. Many see feminists as a small class of elite women struggling against male domination, saying abstract things of little concern to ordinary daily life. Massacres of helpless women and children in Rwanda and Burundi need a theology that emphasizes the sanctity and preciousness of *ordinary* lives. In a culture where widows are married to the deceased's relatives to keep property in the family, biblical stories like Orpah, and Judah's daughter-in-law can be used *against* women. Thus, these need interpreting in ways that do not reinforce oppressive customs. When other *women* impose female circumcision on girls and encourage divorce or polygamy when wives are barren, feminist theology needs to confront not only male perpetrators but women as well. And when Western feminist theologians impose their interpretations on African ritual practices without "hearing" their African feminist sisters' views, it is Western feminist theologians who must be challenged.

In Asia, the struggle of women involves not just discrimination and subordination, but domestic violence and trafficking in various forms—as prostitutes, mail-order brides, overseas contract workers, domestic helpers, and entertainers. Feminist theology in Asia is concerned with the systemic "sin" that allows such abuse of women; whether and how churches contribute to this subjugation of women; and what biblical interpretations reduce the image of women so as to allow such treatment to persist. While older Asian women find the story of Ruth and Naomi useful for perpetuating daughter-in-law subservience, the voices of modern young Asian women who find this story oppresses and restricts them must also be heard. Rejection of traditional religions has left Asian women in limbo between Western Christianity and their roots, such that a liberation theology for women might mean reuniting them with their *cultural* roots and indigenous spirituality. When a Korean feminist theologian summoned the spirits of her ancestors as her "great cloud of witnesses" at the 1991 World Council of Churches Assembly in Australia, the outrage from some churches dealing heavily in saints and icons made it clear *whose* ancestors were acceptable and whose "not." The experience of Korean "comfort women" under Japanese soldiers still haunts many Korean families, drawing Korean feminist theologians into an alliance, not with white Western feminists, but with black womanist theologians whose grandmothers understood what it meant to be "surrogate" wives, mistresses, and mothers for the conquering race.

Even in the shared American setting, African American and white feminist theologians think differently. Womanist theology has emerged as the theology of African American women and their different struggle from white women. Upper-class white feminist women cannot begin to understand the reality of a poor, uneducated, single mother; nor do they have access to cultural images, language, and story for a theology of liberation for women—and men and children—reflecting their unique experience. With the high death rate among young men, womanist theologians reflect on the survival of the *whole* community, and their women's issues have more to do with holding families together as linch-pins rather than individuality and self-expression.

Despite the diversity, there is one issue all feminist theologians face wherever they are. What do you do with Bible texts about women that seem to affirm subordination and inequality? As we have seen, arguments against women, while borrowing from their cultural settings, have been grounded in and authenticated by "what God says" in the Bible. How do we interpret scripture written in patriarchal societies in a way that is liberating for women and affirms their equality with men in God's image?

You don't have to be a feminist to agree that men are the heroes of most Bible stories. If we want to hear the story of the women of Bible times, we have to go backstage, or focus on the *extras* on the set, watching the plot from their off-stage perspective. This idea of getting *behind* the text, seeing the life situation out of which the Bible story arose, is not something feminist theologians have invented, but is basic to contemporary biblical scholarship—"biblical criticism." This does not mean *criticizing* the Bible, but investigating seriously the circumstances of the stories to decipher the way the text might be read more faithfully. Let's look first at how this is done in general, then see what feminist theologians do differently.

When a preacher says "The Bible says...," it tells me more about what the *preacher* thinks than anything else. While the English translation of an ancient Hebrew or Greek text may appear straightforward, the *meaning* has been debated for centuries and interpreted in many different ways. Even before the Bible was collected together as one document, interpretation was in full swing. The technical word for interpreting the Bible is "hermeneutics"—the act of teasing out the full significance of biblical texts and unfolding hidden and obscure meanings. Over the centuries, different hermeneutical methods were popular. Jewish rabbis devised different sets of rules for interpretation, and Christians by the third century used one of two approaches, reading the Bible as allegory or in a literal or straightforward sense. The medieval period interpreted biblical texts in at least four senses: a literal meaning, an allegorical meaning, a moral meaning, and a heavenly meaning. Scholars were encouraged to look beyond the obvious meaning of a biblical story for a moral teaching or symbolic clues to a deeper spiritual meaning. During the Reformation, the reformers claimed to interpret the Bible in the common sense way, but they still brought their external cultural values and medieval views of the world to the interpretations.

By the beginning of this century, biblical criticism was well established as the preferred "hermeneutical" method, using literary techniques for interpreting old manuscripts of Bible texts. Biblical scholars tried to reconstruct events, people, communities, and religious and social practices in the time period and location of the biblical passage in order to detect what the author's intent was most likely to be. For example, when talking about Jesus as a miracle-worker, it is important to know there were many miracle-workers in Jesus' day. Thus, to argue something special about Jesus from his power to do miracles, we need to know first what was *meant* by a miracle in that culture, and then how Jesus' miracles were similar to or different from other miracle-workers. To get such information, scholars don't limit themselves to the Bible, but explore many other texts from the time period for "clues" about interpreting Bible stories. They also make comparisons *between* books of the Bible, especially when different messages are given. In the earliest letters of Paul, there is little organized church leadership, yet in 1 Timothy there is a well-developed scheme of leadership and bishops. This difference, along with other clues, led scholars many years ago to conclude that the letters *attributed* to Paul were written at different stages of the church's development and therefore not all by Paul.

Without printing facilities before the Renaissance, texts were copied by hand and comments often added for clarification or editing. Comparing different copies of the same text therefore raises questions otherwise not considered. For example, Matthew 5:22 says "Every one who is angry with his brother *without cause* shall be liable to judgment." In an earlier copy, "without cause" is absent, perhaps added later to soften the radical challenge to behavior by the Sermon on the Mount. It leads us to ask why, thus giving us clues to how the faith community might have developed in its thinking. Grammar, word structure, and the way words are used in a text also give clues as to whether the same author was responsible for more than one book, or whether a single book was always that way or a collection of writing fragments put together as a whole.

Many Bible passages were hymns and credal statements for communities before they were included in the Bible. Scholars can detect how a book was

assembled by editors merging together different songs and creeds from different ancient communities. Four sources have been detected in the Pentateuch
(the first five books of the Bible), merged in the fifth century B.C.E. Scholars
have also determined that Matthew and Luke, two Gospels written later than
Mark, used Mark as a source for information, but also another writing no
longer in existence, since Matthew and Luke have identical passages in Greek
that are not found in Mark, as if copied from an common writing now lost.
This might come as a surprise to those who assume the Bible was simply
"dictated" by God in a session of divine inspiration or written in one sitting by
a few authors, yet biblical criticism has been used for over a century now to
arrive at more accurate translations of scripture. New texts and methods also
come to light. In the 1940s, two discoveries were made in Egypt of ancient
copies of biblical and other writings that predated those currently available,
giving new insights into the texts and their times.

While these methods are in wide general use, *feminist* biblical scholars
concentrate on the social and political situation of *women* in biblical times and
how this shaped what was written about them. When the Bible tells women
how they can and cannot behave, we have to decide whether these instructions related to their *cultural* subordination in Greek, Roman and Jewish patriarchy, or whether the instructions were "divine" rules applicable to all cultural
settings, patriarchal or not. Were women not to braid their hair or wear gold
or pearls (1 Tim. 2:9) because of a divine decree for all time, or did these
suggest a particular type of "immodest" woman in that culture which would
send a negative message to onlookers? If so, what would be an equivalent
piece of advice in our day in terms of "messages" women send by their behavior?

This is not something new or suspicious that only feminist scholars do. We
make cultural critiques of the Bible all the time, often unconsciously. Few
Christians would argue that the principles of tribal warfare in the Hebrew
Bible are the *Christian* way to do battle today with our quite different military
capabilities. We simply assume they were the method of the time, now superseded, and even question the morality of war at all! Not many TV evangelists
arrested for lusting after women have cut off their hands or plucked out their
eyes, even though Jesus recommended this as a solution for out-of-control
sexual urges. We read Jesus' comments as getting our attention about the need
for drastic action to avoid temptation. Those who argue for the "naturally
subordinate" status of women as God's eternal decree, with no consideration
of the cultural societal rules about women in place at that time, obviously
forget that Bible heroes also kept slaves. Is slavery *also* God's eternal will or
"natural" order, since it was in place in Bible times? If we argue slavery was
denounced by Christians in the New Testament, so were the graded distinctions between men and women *in the same verse* (Gal. 3:28)! No wonder women
get suspicious that there is something at stake when men selectively insist on
women's subordination, yet dismiss slavery and tribal war as part of an ancient culture no longer applicable!

Just as men bring "their" reason and experience to biblical criticism, women bring *their* reason and experience as *women* to scripture to determine how to both respect *and* challenge the texts to find "good news" for women as well as men. Just like men, they do not all come to the same conclusions. Let's look at the range of ways women theologians "read" the Bible, in preparation for the next chapters, when we look at particular texts that have troubled women from the beginning.

While they would hardly call themselves *feminist* theologians, there are some women scholars who approach the Bible as an "inerrant" or "infallible" book. For them, God, through the Spirit, dictated every word, or at least ensured there were no errors or contradictions. The Bible "means exactly what it says" and can be read "literally" that is, as if written yesterday for our context. Since all verses are taken at face value, when Paul says women must keep silent, it is a straightforward, authoritative instruction regardless of the original circumstances for Paul's comment. Jephthah sacrificing his daughter in gratitude for a military victory is just as the letter to the Hebrews says—he was a great man of faith. The plight of the daughter was somehow part of "God's plan," a divine mystery not to be questioned. Since First Timothy says women must be submissive to husbands, women scholars must accept that ruling and find glory in their subordinate role. The *culture* of biblical times is "divinely" sanctioned along with God's purposes.

But such an approach is not as straightforward as claimed. It is selective and political. As I write this, today's newspaper reports the Southern Baptist Convention's addition to its statement of faith that "a wife is to submit graciously to her husband, even as the church willingly submits to the headship of Christ." However, this Ephesians passage *also* told slaves to obey their masters, yet rights of citizenship won for slaves have made such instructions superfluous. Why have citizen rights won for *women*—the vote, and their separate legal status argued on the same platforms as abolition of slavery—*not* negated these biblical instructions about women's submission? Those who insist on women's submission because 1 Timothy 2:11 says so seem to have no problem reading other passages metaphorically, and overlooking others as culturally specific. First Timothy *also* forbids braided hair and jewelry in worship (1 Tim. 2:9) and advocates drinking wine for relief for stomachaches and other illnesses (1 Tim. 5:23). Under the newspaper headlines about the Southern Baptist decision, two bejeweled women, one elaborately dressed with a flowered bonnet, addressed the Convention to support this "biblically based" command, obviously dismissing other passages on women's behavior:

> I desire then…that women should dress themselves modestly and decently in suitable clothing, not with their hair braided, or with gold, pearls or expensive clothes…Let a woman learn in silence with full submission. I permit no woman to teach or have authority over a man; she is to keep silent. (1 Tim. 2:8–13)

While most biblical scholars read the Bible selectively, weighing up what value to give texts for our very different culture, they are *open* about their selectivity. Those who insist on women's subordination "because the Bible says so," yet break this rule with other texts, ignoring them or relegating them to allegory or antiquity, are engaged not in a literal reading of scripture, but *political* decision-making, selectively naming societal relationships in a way that benefits those with power to name. Women must ask why.

The first group of women who *would* call themselves feminist theologians recognize the patriarchal underpinnings of biblical stories, yet look for ways to read them that acknowledge women's equality in the image of God. Some pick and choose, dismissing those stories operating under outmoded, even harmful, patriarchal ideas. They select stories "true" for their experience and understanding of Jesus' central message, as Luther did when he used only New Testament writings that affirmed his "gospel" of justification by faith. This approach dismisses Jephthah's murder of his daughter as a tragic story bound to a tribal era with different rituals of war and value placed on human life. Many pastors and church school curriculum writers work this way, never featuring the more difficult or disturbing stories, and folks get quite surprised when they come across them somewhere else as stories from the Bible. The *problem* with this method is that it fails to challenge the potential harm for women in stories like Jephthah's, and leaves them available for use against women. I have heard such stories used to justify Christian women submitting to sexual abuse and violence in families—"be submissive like Jephthah's daughter despite the abuse, knowing you are doing God's will, and you might win your husband by your faithfulness."

Other feminist theologians, realizing the male orientation of the texts, do not ignore the hard passages, but look for "redeemable features" in them, something liberating and hopeful to use today. While Jephthah's daughter's death shows the dark side of patriarchal power, the story ends with her women friends establishing a yearly ritual to mourn her death. *This* liberating part of the story—dependent women operating in subversive solidarity against tragedy—can inspire women today to resist, even in situations of powerlessness and injustice. While this is obviously the best way to preserve this biblical story for women, there are difficulties. First, the *story* obviously does not see the women's actions as central, but celebrates military victories where the lives of others are dispensed for Jephthah's purposes. Jephthah is mentioned hundreds of years later as one who through faith "conquered kingdoms, *administered justice* [my italics], obtained promises, shut the mouths of lions," and so on (Heb. 11:32–33). The women who mourned her death get no further mention. Again we are reminded of Hercules and the lion—it depends on who is telling the story. Second, it is difficult to separate culture and message, as if one does not impact the other. Is Jephthah's vow a bribe or a faith statement? Is the daughter sacrificed for *his* benefit or God's? By what criteria should we decide if Jephthah is a great man of faith in his time? Third, we must ask what is the *motive* of feminist theologians for redeeming such stories for women today. Is it *really* to find "liberating" biblical themes, even in the face of abuse against women, or does it simply reflect the bind women scholars find themselves in, having to "redeem" a horrific tragedy simply because it is in the Bible?

Other women scholars, like Mary Daly, who began with confidence to transform Christianity and the church, have left altogether, seeking other ways to celebrate their conviction that God is for us. In the course of their reform efforts, they decided there was *no* possibility of separating male-centered language and patriarchal thinking from the biblical message. The medium *was* the message. Patriarchal Christianity is the way *men* have described God, and, as such, it is an *inadequate* story of God's activity among humanity because it features only half the story. They believe women need to describe life with God in their own writings, using metaphors reflecting women's experience, and thus search for ancient stories and religious expressions that affirm female aspects of "divinity," or look within themselves for spirituality. Apart from the obvious problem of leaving the Christian tradition, these women, by abandoning the Bible because of its patriarchal form, have also been forced to abandon what little history they have in the Bible of God's dealings with women and any opportunity to reconstruct these foremothers as role models. They have opted for no history rather than a corrupted history.

A final group of feminist theologians see the difficulties with both these approaches. Elisabeth Schüssler Fiorenza, one of feminist theology's most famous biblical scholars, is often asked why she has not left the church. She answers that she refuses to leave the naming of God's "truth" to those who wish to do it *against* women:

> Whether we [Christian feminists] decide to move into another religious denomination or choose not to belong to any religious institution at all, we can never surrender our claim to spiritual authority. Thus Christian feminists may not give up their religious authority to define biblical religion and the Christian Church. We must never abandon our religious power to articulate a feminist religious vision of justice and liberation...I seek to assert the power of feminist theological naming to transform patriarchal religions, a power that for centuries has been stolen from us and today is threatened again in various ways.[13]

How does Elisabeth think women's religious power of naming has been stolen? By the loss of historical memory as women's stories have been excluded from history. As we have seen in the first chapters of this book, women protested all along the way, but their protests were diffused, discredited, or not recorded for later generations of women. Consequently women have to "reinvent the wheel" each century, analyzing afresh the "feelings without a name" that beset them in male-led societies, unaware that women struggled with the same questions before them. Women's religious power of naming themselves *continues* to be stolen today by those who discredit feminist theologians' right to challenge scripture and church, or who insist on "controlling" the limits of women's authority or authenticity by not allowing them to contribute to ecclesiastical debate.

Feminist theologians like Elisabeth stay firmly *within* the church, seeking to "intervene in the contest" over who has the right and authority to define biblical religion. They believe that by leaving, women relinquish that right, and also their inheritance in that vision of God's alternative world of justice, human dignity, equality, and salvation for all. *This* was the "good news" Jesus proclaimed in the midst of patriarchal oppression and dehumanization, inviting *everyone* to the table without exception. *This* is what needs to be reclaimed as the biblical message of equality between men and women. By staying, however, Elisabeth (I will use her as my example of such women) does not accept the Bible simply as a hallowed "religious" book, but as a profoundly *political* book that has been used as a weapon against women. Texts are not simply ignored or misquoted, but are *themselves* patriarchal in their original function and intent, serving to legitimate women's subordinate role and secondary status in society. Yet despite this, the Bible has *also* inspired countless women to speak out against injustice, exploitation and stereotyping, and given women a vision of freedom and wholeness to energize them to struggle against poverty, denigration, and oppression. How then we can "read" it as liberating for women?

Elisabeth's reading tool—hermeneutic—is "suspicion," and the litmus test for whether scripture can be good news for women is whether or not a text, and the traditions around it, seek to end all relations of domination and exploitation. "Suspicion" has an uncomfortable sound for many of us. We have been trained to think the Bible cannot be questioned, and that the "truths" we hold are obvious in scripture, without need of interpretation, yet we forget we are always "interpreting" when we read the Bible, using as our guide what *we* have been taught as "true." Thus we are always being suspicious of what might disagree with our beliefs. When I teach university introductory courses in Christianity, students who have grown up in church Bible studies get a little nervous. They take the course thinking it will be an easy grade, or because they want to learn more about what they believe. Since they have usually not thought much beyond their own pastor's or Bible study group's ideas, they are stunned and disturbed to discover other ways of thinking. Truth is what *they* have been taught, and all else is heresy! One student, after sitting through three-quarters of my course describing the development of Christianity from Jewish roots, through the early church, into medieval Christianity, and on to this century, wrote in her notes after the class on eighteenth-century evangelicalism, "Frankly, this is the *first* thing that has sounded Christian to me!"

Elisabeth's "hermeneutic of suspicion" *assumes* the political nature of biblical stories up front, and the probability that women's activities and opinions have been excluded or obliterated from the story. Her "critical eye" assumes we do not have the *whole* story, and perhaps only a *political* interpretation of the story—"political" in its pure sense of that which pertains to society's rules, which, in Bible times, were patriarchal. Elisabeth differs from those who see patriarchy as "benign"—the way things were—simply needing a "reread" to get around male bias. Her "suspicion," like a detective on a "missing person" case, is that something is amiss with the absence of women, and that there may have been an effort to *edit* women *out*, not just ignore them. Her advocacy on behalf of women believes that, no matter how much they were erased from biblical history, they were there—"The lords of creation do not exist independent of those they oppress"—and that God the Spirit is at work wherever people, including women, struggle for justice even though their particular struggle was not recorded.[14]

With these assumptions, Elisabeth looks for the male-centered elements in the text—language, assumptions about male and female roles, dominant and hidden players, and so on—and asks whether the text is oppressive or liberating for women today, and thus how it should be preached or interpreted. Rather than "sanitize," "ignore," or "redeem" a troublesome text, she exposes it publicly for what it is—oppressive, harmful, or inappropriate for contemporary application. Her examination of texts is also driven by remembrance, the hope of reclaiming memories of women from the male stories, and identifying and reconstructing women's struggles within those stories so they can be retold as models for women. Many women were followers of Jesus—prophets, apostles, church leaders, full participants in early missionary work—yet their stories have become one-liners, sidelines in the tales of the heroes. Such reclamation does not mean coming up with happy stories of "little women and good wives" as has been done in the past with biblical women, but stories of women struggling to hear Jesus' call to freedom and equality in an environment that precluded such freedom.

In reconstructing women's stories, feminist scholars, like other biblical scholars, search beyond the biblical writings. In the first centuries of Christianity, there were many writings—letters, gospels, books of sayings—circulating among communities across Asia Minor. There was no committee for "forbidden books," so all made the rounds, some held in honor in some communities but not in others. Gradually some writings became more "authoritative," reflecting the theology of the fledgling movement, especially when Christianity became the religion of the empire, incorporating the church within imperial government. Roman public life was male-led; thus church leadership became male, and the writings gaining the seal of approval as the New Testament collection reflected male leadership and authority. Others revolving around woman leaders were excluded. Contemporary women scholars have explored these writings, especially those describing God as both male and female, Mother and Father, Source and Silence, and featuring women in leadership roles of teaching, baptizing, healing, preaching, and administration. Other scholars have reached further back into prehistory for their background information, examining the demise of female "God" imagery over time and trying to reclaim what remains or reconstruct what was once there. This is not heresy. It is about women trying to discover the other *half* of their story by reviving the *many* images for God, including female ones, in scripture and outside of it. It's like hushing the volume of one set of voices in the orchestra for a while to hear the softer voices come through.

Despite its diversity, the gathering point of feminist theology is the recognition that men who shaped Christian concepts and language about God and humanity named women subordinate as part of God's natural order. Feminist theologians challenge this as *not* God's liberating message and look for other ways to think about God and humanity, both in the tradition and outside it. From my earlier chapters, we see how these myths about women became authoritative as "true" beyond critique, used by theologians, priests, and those with power to interpret "truth." A new generation of women theologians are now *in* these ecclesiastical and academic halls, interrupting the conversation. "Hold it. This is not the *only* way to think, and it is one-sided and downright harmful. We women see other, equally valid ways to think. Like you, we believe Christianity is good news, but good news has to be for *everyone*—women as well as men—here and now, as well as in the future."

There is a solidarity as women around the world share the struggle, rejoicing in theologies that celebrate women as good creations of God, and rejecting long-dominant interpretations of scripture that degrade and devalue them. But feminist theology is not just a "woman thing." Its perspective has benefited *all* of theology. When women started to challenge traditional ways of thinking, it encouraged others "labeled" by traditional doctrines to ask questions as well. Examining myths about women has exposed parallel myths demanding *men* be a certain way too. When women challenge traditional readings of scripture that have kept them subordinate, powerless, and poor, people can question other "isms" that keep *them* "out of the loop." Gay and lesbian people have also found the opportunity to ask questions about Bible passages that declare them sinful and perverted. Feminist theology is not an "alternative lifestyle" pitch by a few problem women, but a new, liberating way of looking at God and the world for *everyone.*

CHAPTER 8

"I Am Who I Am"

The nature of God is a circle of which the center is everywhere and the circumference is nowhere.

Anonymous

When I ask students from more conservative Christian traditions what they think feminist theology is, many tell me it's about changing "he" to "she" and calling God a woman. Braver ones, who feel they must defend God from women such as myself, will add, "Jesus called God 'Father,' so God must be male!" I understand this response, because for those who sit in church pews, this is often all that comes across about feminist theology. While the occasional pastor might refer to Mother God, and a congregation might, with resistance and mumbling, sing "human" instead of "man" in the old hymns of the faith, that's about as far as it goes. This probably does more harm than good because, without any theological discussion of the *reasons* for such corrections, it sounds like some academic special interest group messing with tradition and God—and *women* doing it doesn't help!

God is currently on the best-seller list. We have God's biography, God's history, and God's conversations with all and sundry. People want to know more about God, after a spell of wanting to know less and less, and some writers claim a fairly direct "hotline" for information! When my book group was reading Jack Miles's *God: A Biography*, one of the members kept enthusiastically telling her friends about the *autobiography* of God we were studying. How I wish, because how we think about God *matters*! Our images of God affect whether we believe in God or not, and whether we relate to God as terrified serf before the master's wrath or enlightened soul aware God is for us and with us. It affects whether we see the world as the obstacle course toward

110

heaven where God sits afar off, or whether we enjoy the world as God's good creation now.

What do you have in mind when you think of God? People say "I don't believe in God," but what do they mean? I may not believe in that God either! Most of us are fairly vague about God, holding a composite of often conflicting images from church school days. We sing that God is "up there," a friend for little children above the bright blue sky; but also ask God to live *in* our hearts permanently—"Come into my heart, Lord Jesus, come in today, come in to stay." We are urged to go to God—"Just as I am, oh Lamb of God I come," even though God is supposedly close by and concerned, watching sparrows fall and counting hairs on our heads, obviously unfazed by Christians who say the evil world needs vacating as quickly as possible.

It may come as a shock to some that whatever we say about God is metaphorical. Metaphors take the characteristics of one thing to describe *something else* when that something else is hard to describe adequately any other way. "My granddaughter is a little doll," "My brain is in shreds," "The sun is on fire today," all say something *is* something else, but don't mean for us to assume it *literally* is. I can hear you thinking, "God's not a metaphor. My God's real. He is my Father!" That is exactly what I mean. A father in our society is literally and legally defined as the male biological parent. When we call a priest or God "father," we move into metaphorical language because neither, according to our definition, is our *biological* parent. We are using human, fatherly *characteristics* to describe how we feel and think about something else—God.

Metaphors conjure up more than a "thing." They invoke feelings and experiences not adequately covered by a label—taste, sound, color, texture, and form. Metaphors are also used "in context." The writer hopes the visual image conjured up by metaphor for *her* will also be evoked in the reader. A metaphor "works"—is useful and helpful—when this happens, and does not "work" if the speaker and the hearer do not share common points of reference. If I tell my Minnesotan friends I am suffering from cabin fever, they will know what I mean and will hopefully buy me a plane ticket to Fiji. If I tell my *Fijian* friends I have cabin fever, they might assume I picked up some nasty "American" viral infection and hope I *don't* show up in Fiji! Metaphors are useful or puzzling, depending on the amount of shared meaning.

By the same token, they can be *harmful.* "God is a police officer of the soul" depends on one's experience of police officers. It is comforting if you grew up with kind London "bobbies" who find lost children and return them to their mothers, but it is frightening if your childhood was spent where police were feared by the innocent as well as the guilty! A friend who lived in Hungary during the era when people were arrested on trumped-up charges once told me that, even though she has lived in America for more than twenty years, a feeling of cold panic still rises in her stomach when she sees a police officer come around the corner. We can only talk about God in metaphors, since none of us have seen the Divine-in-Itself, and the metaphors we choose *matter* because they shape how we think about and relate to God. It also *matters* if metaphors lose their *metaphorical* status in a society over time and begin to *replace* the object described. "My granddaughter is a little doll," "my brain is in shreds," "the sun is on fire today" work wonderfully to evoke powerful comment about my relatives, mental capabilities, and body temperature, but should they become *reality*, I am in big trouble on all counts!

God is described in a many, many metaphors in scripture, both human and inanimate, lofty and humble, terrifying and loving. That fact that biblical authors used so many metaphors suggests that God is not any *one* of these in reality, not literally one and metaphorically the others. Yet many Christians who insist God is in *no* way like us humans also claim God *is,* however, male! Human maleness, by definition, indicates a biologically specific organ, so what do we *mean* when we apply maleness to God? If we do not mean male anatomy, but characteristics our society associates with males, we have *already* moved into metaphorical language and destroyed our argument that God *is* literally male.

If we insist God is *metaphorically* male, we have to ask why we chose *this* metaphor over the plethora of other biblical metaphors for God. The writers of the Hebrew scriptures experienced God in many ways, drawing from life experiences to finish the sentence "God is…"[1] They found "God-like" images in nature, animate and inanimate—eagle, lion, bear, hen, fire, light, cloud, wind, breath, rock, fortress, high tower, and shield. They found "God" models in everyday life—God as gardener, builder, shepherd, potter, healer, father, mother, lover, wise woman, old man, woman giving birth, and friend. Many of these were not explicitly male or female—potters, shepherds, friends, lovers, and gardeners. They also found models for God in their political leaders—king, ruler, lord, warrior, judge, and law-giver—and because biblical writers lived in a society where leadership was predominantly male, *these* latter metaphors usually described males, but their *application* to God was not about *maleness,* but about qualities of those roles.[2]

The Hebrew people saw God exceeding *all* creaturely distinctions. When God called Moses to lead them out of captivity in Egypt, Moses, anticipating their questions, asked God whom he should say sent him—what was the divine password (Ex. 3:13–14)? God did not confess to maleness or even resort to male metaphors, but settled for "I am who I am" or "I will be what I will be"—the unlimited possibilities of God-ness without need for limiting metaphors or human look-alikes. Expanding on this, God said (Ex. 3:15):

> Thus you shall say to the Israelites, "The Lord, the God of your ancestors, the God of Abraham, the God of Isaac, and the God of Jacob, has sent me to you: This is my name forever, and this is my title for all generations.

"Lord" is an inadequate translation of the Hebrew *YHWH* from the verb *hayah,* "to be," signifying divine mystery and freedom. Pronounced Yahweh probably, it appears some 6,800 times in the Hebrew Bible.[3] The message Moses was to convey to the Hebrew people was God's universal promise. "All you need to know is that I will *be there* for you!"

Why then did our forefathers build a *male* box for God rather than permit God to be and become whatever God chose to be and become? Why did they make a male image of God as an *idol*, when the children of Israel were reprimanded for making idols for God, which limited the possibilities of God-ness? The answer is complex, but of vital importance to feminist theology and women.

YHWH was not reduced by any qualifiers except "being," but for Hebrew writers this posed a *practical* problem. What *else* can be said about God? They resorted to metaphors—God is like this, this and this, making sure their descriptions said something, but never everything, about *YHWH*. That *YHWH* meant "becoming" as well as "being" made the task of reducing God to *any* description even more elusive. Just as they got God figured out, God could become like something not yet *known!* To express God's *majesty*, they borrowed a cultural term of respect for a social superior, *Adonai*—"lord."[4] Since their society was patriarchal, *Adonai* was, for the most part, applied to *males*—king, husband, or slave owner—but it does not take a rocket scientist to figure out that the *appropriateness* of the metaphor was not its *maleness*, but the acknowledgment of authority and respect. If *maleness* was a "given" about God, they would have vetoed female metaphors for God—a mother conceiving and giving birth to Israel, and a midwife pulling the children of Israel from the womb, keeping them safe at their mother's breast.[5]

Since Palestinians depended on sheep for the necessities of life—milk, meat, hides, and wool—the shepherd, male or female, whose voice was recognized by the sheep, and who located pastures and shelter for them, was an obvious image for God's protective care. And while shepherds protected sheep for the nomadic tribes, forts protected the Israelites once they settled in cities and towns. For people constantly under threat from neighbors, God as a strategically placed high tower was the epitome of security and safety. Neither male nor human, it evoked a powerful image of the abiding protection of God, "for you are my refuge, a strong tower against the enemy."[6]

Other Israelite metaphors for God came from deities of their past. The description *El,* chief of the Canaanite gods, was also used for the Hebrew God, especially in Job, and many elements of *El's* cult made their way into *YHWH* worship. *Elohim,* plural for *El,* became associated with Israel's God for some Israelite tribes, and both *Elohim* and *YHWH* are used in the Pentateuch. Although Israel's faith would evolve into strict monotheism (the belief in only one God), it originated with Abraham in polytheism (worship of many gods), moving to henotheism (worship of one God among many) when Abraham left Ur for the promised land. Christians have simply dismissed "other gods"—and certainly "goddesses"—as pagan or fictitious, yet Abraham grew up with these deities, each city-state in his region having one deity from a pantheon of cosmic gods and goddesses. The First Commandment suggests not the *non-existence* of other gods and goddesses, but faithfulness to a *particular* God, the "jealous" one that brought them out of Egypt (Ex. 20:1–6):

> Then God spoke these words: I am the LORD your God, who brought you out of the land of Egypt, out of the house of slavery; *you shall have no other gods before me.* You shall not make for yourself an idol, whether it is in the form of anything that is in heaven above, or that is on the earth beneath, or that is in the water under the earth.

Thus, when Moses appeared before the Israelites, they wanted to know *which* God had sent him. Why is God's early history important to feminist theology? Because when we realize God's *maleness* has not always been so but has *evolved,* and that other descriptions of God—female, inanimate, and more importantly, beyond all such limits—have also been powerful metaphors, we can challenge those who say God has to be male today.

Scholars place Abraham in Ur sometime around 2000–1500 B.C.E.[7] This ancient city in Southern Mesopotamia (now Iraq) was part of a network of Sumerian city-states. During Abraham's era, these city-states were absorbed by the one city-state Babylon into "Babylonia." Because each had its own deity, this absorption was also a takeover of many gods and goddesses by the Babylonian god Marduk. This "cosmic takeover" is described "theologically" in the Babylonian creation story *Enuma Elish.*[8] Tiamat, the female primeval watery void existing before heaven, earth, or other gods, mates with Apsu, the freshwaters, creating a new generation of gods. Their noise annoys Apsu, who wants to destroy them. Instead, son Ea kills his father Aspu and assumes power over the gods, producing a son, Marduk. The older gods persuade Tiamat to fight back, but her grandson, Marduk (Babylon's city-state god) steps forward and kills Tiamat, creating the world from her body by dividing it (the waters) into heaven and sea. He makes human servants for the gods out of the blood of Tiamat's new spouse mixed with clay. Marduk is exalted over the other gods for the slaughter of the original mother goddess, and this feat was reenacted each year with the cry "may Marduk continue to conquer Tiamat and shorten her days!"

This story tells us two things about changes of beliefs about gods and goddesses around Abraham's time. Mother Goddess Tiamat, representing prehistory fertility worship of gods and goddesses, was put to death by the male god Marduk, who then became the one god over many. Polytheism, the worship of many deities responsible for different things, was moving to henotheism, the worship of one god selected from many, this one god responsible for everything in the life of the tribe. Against this background, Abraham leaves Ur with *his* one God to create a new nation with his descendants, the Hebrew people. When the oral history of this people since Abraham was gathered together into the Pentateuch around the sixth century B.C.E., at least four sources of stories were merged.[9] Not surprisingly, scholars find snippets of the old Mesopotamian stories from Abraham's past "peeping through" Hebrew stories. The Genesis creation story has similarities with Marduk's creation story; the Genesis flood parallels a flood in the *Epic of Gilgamesh;* an Egyptian tale of two brothers is similar to Genesis 39; and the legend of Sargon is similar to Moses' birth story in Exodus 2.

The importance of this trek back into Jewish prehistory is to remind us that early descriptions of Abraham's God did not simply pop up out of nothing. Abraham's descendants had models of "God-ness" *and* "Goddess-ness" from their past history from which to describe the characteristics of their God, and, when we take a fresh look at the creation stories in Genesis—our first glimpse of Abraham's God—despite all our assumptions that the God of the Hebrew Bible was male, we find that the *Creator* God of Genesis did *not* exhibit a gender or use *sexual* functions to create, nor was this God portrayed in *any* human form! As Spirit (Wind) and Voice (Gen. 1:1–3), God spoke creation into being: "And God said, let there be...and there was. " When it came time to create humans, God created them "male and female" *in God's image* (Genesis 1:27). What image? All we know of God at this point is a voice and breath (Spirit), the breath that became the same life breath for human form. Even when God confronts Adam and Eve in the garden, it is the "*sound* of the Lord God walking" and the *voice* of God that addresses them (Gen. 1:8). Voice and breath are not restricted to any gender!

This nongendered voice continues as the metaphor for God, appropriating accessible "shape" when needed. Moses heard the "voice" of God in a burning bush (Ex. 3:4). God spoke to Job "out of the whirlwind" (Job 38:1). When Samuel heard God call in the night, "the Lord came and stood there" but there was no description of the form, simply the voice (1 Sam. 3:10). Elijah encountered God at Mount Horeb as a voice speaking after silence (1 Kings 19:11–13). In fact, when we take a serious look at the stories of God's encounter with the Hebrew people, God usually just talked! God did not appear in male or female form or demonstrate specifically male or female activity, which is not surprising given the Israelite abhorrence of "images" for *YHWH* and their belief that anyone "looking on" God would die. Yet we totally ignore this when we insist on arguing that God *is* male.

Part of our problem is the English translation "God." While the term God is supposedly generic as well as male, so long as we also use the word Goddess, God suggests the *male* variety of deity. Although the Creator God exhibited no sexuality, our English *language* gives God a gender with this term. Those who think this male label conveys a *generic* meaning only have to test "Goddess" as an alternative term and the assumed *maleness* of God becomes strikingly evident! Some feminist theologians have adopted "gender-free" words for God to shake us out of a male-oriented reading—God/Goddess, God/ess, G*d, Be-ing—but this often backfires on feminism since folks think it is "messing with God" and get nervous.

When Israel later moved from tribal communities into one kingdom, ruling metaphors depicting God became common. God by default became imaged in male terms, the divine king over earthly kings. Kings were called God's "anointed ones" (the meaning of "Messiah" in Hebrew, and its equivalent "Christ" in Greek), and in time, Israel longed for an "anointed one" (messiah king) who would *permanently* establish God's kingdom on earth. Jesus became this messiah king; thus the king metaphors for the divine followed Jesus into the New Testament. The God who had communicated as voice and spirit journeying with tribal Israelites had become the God who ruled from his exalted throne like an earthly king. Marcus Borg describes two groups of metaphors for God in the Bible that produced these two different images for God—God as monarch and God as spirit.[10] The monarchical image had the characteristics of lawgiver, judge, master, head, all-powerful, all-knowing, majestic, and dominant. Borg adds the metaphor "Father" to this monarchical group because in Hebrew society the father "ruled" the people descended from him. "Father" also referred to previous Israelite leaders, advisors to kings, high government officials, and was an honorary title for prophets and priests. Although "fathers" did father children, the *title*—used rarely in the Hebrew Bible in actuality—had more to do with rule than a hotdog-eating, ballgame-loving Dad with a covey of neighbor's kids in the Range Rover.

By the fourth century, when Christianity became the official Roman religion, these male monarchical metaphors for God dominated and had also become reality. God is *like* a king became God the King. If God *was* King, Lord, and Father, then God *was* male, and representatives of God must also be male. If Christ, as part of the Godhead, was male, and the priest "stands in" for Christ at the mass, then priests *must* be male, as if maleness made the sacrifice effective. Besides, the disciples were male, weren't they? Each of these arguments taken alone can be teased out and diffused, but the *cumulative* effect of male metaphors for God dominating all others lulls the mind into resignation after a while. Since the canon of the New Testament excluded many writings that spoke of women as church leaders, and translations of the Bible from Greek and Hebrew into Latin further removed references to *women* holding equal status in God's new community of freedom, God-ness and maleness converged early in Christian history. Images of God as voice and spirit free of gender were relegated to the margins of orthodoxy and beyond!

No doubt you noticed I sidestepped one crucial argument made for God's maleness. Didn't Jesus call God Father? I sidestepped it deliberately so I could explore it separately from Hebrew Bible references to God as Father, which have to do with tribal authority rather than parenting. The New Testament in general makes more use of the metaphor "Father" for God—two hundred and forty-five times as opposed to fifteen in the Hebrew Bible. However, of these New Testament references, over one hundred are found in the Gospel of John![11] What was John saying through this metaphor, which did not concern other Gospel writers? Scholars date John's Gospel between 80–100 C.E., written to a community recently excluded from the Jewish synagogue. This break was a rupture in the family of Abraham, to whom God had made a specific promise:

"I will be your God and you will be my people." Their crucial question was: Are we still the "family" of God to whom the promise was made?

The writer of John[12] makes it clear from the beginning what he will argue. The Word (*Logos*) that was manifested in *Jesus* existed with *God* from the beginning (Jn. 1:11–12). That Word

> came to what was his own, and his own people did not accept him. But to all who received him, who believed in his name, he gave power to become children of God.

Those who *did* believe were those now excluded from Judaism, to whom John was writing, the *true* children of God the *Father*. John continues building this grand family *metaphor* of the *true* family of God with more biological images. God *begot* the *Logos*, incarnate in Jesus. The *children* of God accept this *Son* the *Father* sent, an anointed one like God's *son* David and the *sons* of God, the Israelites. In the family metaphor, God is *Father* to both the *Son* Jesus as anointed one, and the faithful *children* of God. Jesus calls God *Father* (*abba*), a term of intimacy between father and child and tells his followers to do the same as God's *true children*. Jesus' long monologues about his relationship to God and his followers further borrow the family *metaphor*.

Some point to Jesus' use of *abba*, the intimate form of the Aramaic word "father," to argue an actual *biological* Father-Son relationship, thus Jesus' divinity. Yet John is not making a point about actual biology here. He does not distinguish between Jesus' use of *abba* and that of his followers. When Jesus meets Mary in the garden, he says (Jn. 20:17):

> Go to my brothers and say to them, "I am ascending to my Father and your Father, to my God and your God.

Abba is used by Jesus when he prays in the garden,[13] but he also invites his followers to address God as *abba*—our Father—in the "Lord's Prayer." John does not call Jesus' followers "adopted" children as opposed to Jesus as "biological" son. When Jesus asks the Father to send the Spirit, the reason given is so his followers are not left *orphaned*.[14] The fact that there is no reference to the Holy Spirit impregnating Mary, and no birth story of Jesus at all in John, is clue enough that the writer of John's Gospel was not intent here on arguing the *biological* fatherhood of God!

The term *Son of God* also does not suggest *biological* reality. "Son of God" meaning "anointed one" or Messiah was used in the Hebrew Bible for all those obedient to a divine call—Israel (Hos. 11:1); the monarch (Ps. 2:7); the angels (Job 38:7); the righteous individual (Wis. 2:18)—and Jesus. Paul says Jesus was *declared* a "Son of God" at the *end* of his mission, after being a "son according to the flesh" like David (Rom. 1:4):

> the Son, who was descended from David according to the flesh and was declared to be Son of God with power according to the spirit of holiness by resurrection from the dead, Jesus Christ our Lord.

This is not to deny a unique relationship between God and Jesus (a topic beyond this book), but to show that John was using father and son metaphors to develop a *relational metaphor,* not a biological *reality.* God the Father describes a *metaphorical* relationship with the "children" of God, just as God the Father in the Hebrew Bible is a *metaphor* of respect and authority, not "proof" of the maleness of God.

By not questioning this excessive use of "Father" in John as opposed to the rest of the Bible, Christians have over time transformed John's grand *metaphor* of family into a biological *truth—*God *is* the Father of the *begotten* Son Jesus— despite the fact that earliest theological explanations in the church for the relationship between God and Jesus focused not on biology, but on whether God and Jesus were of the same substance, that is, both God, and whether the Trinity was "three masks" (*personae*) of God. The metaphor *persona* as "mask" would in time also become "persons"—"God in three Persons, blessed Trinity"—further fueling the cumulative idea of a *biological* Father and Son, even though these *two separate* entities threatened the argument for the Trinity as One! It's not as simple as it seems to declare that God is male!

To recap, I have argued that the Hebrew vision of *YHWH,* the great "I am," disallowed images limiting or idolizing any aspect of God's mystery and freedom. I have argued that the Creator Spirit of Genesis exhibited no gender tendencies and "created" alone without sexual activity, and that male, female and nonhuman metaphors borrowed from deities of Abraham's prehistory were all used as descriptions for God. I have suggested that in time, especially as the monarchy developed, God metaphors of leadership and majesty became dominant—King, Lord, and Father—and, since in patriarchal society these were *male* roles, the assumption that God was male hovered behind them. Although "father" was a metaphor of authority in the Hebrew Bible and a relational metaphor in the New Testament, the father metaphor eventually blended with the "Son of God" metaphor to suggest a *male, biological* Godhead. By the time Christianity became the official Roman religion, *theological* arguments were in place for male priests to represent a male Godhead.

What would compound the cumulative effect of these many transformations of God into a male was the English language. When the *King James Version of the Bible* appeared in 1611, *he* was used for God, and *man* was used for humanity. Although grammatical convention at the time said the masculine *he* and *his* could refer to man *and* woman, there was no way anyone in 1611, given the cumulative trend toward "God as male" I have described, would assume the generic *he* included an option God could be *she*! In God's case, *he* meant *he*! Since English does not have a singular pronoun like the plural *them* that includes all possibilities, male and female, human and non-human, the only other choice would have been *it.* Although God obviously transcends human limits, there was no way God, now dominantly described in human metaphors, could be called an *it*! So, despite the great "I am," which defied all boxes of gender *and* humanity, and the Creator Spirit, who appeared to the Hebrew people as nonanthropomorphic speech and wind, the English God became *he*, separated by grammar and tradition from any wider possibilities of being. And so my university student last week wrote in his paper, "Feminist theologians who try and change God from *he* to *she* are misinterpreting and misreading the Bible for their own agenda. If God is *he*, how can he be a woman?"

Surely we can show conclusively if God is male by going back to the original Hebrew. *YHWH* is masculine, thus "correctly" translated *he* in English. But there is a problem that those who did French or Spanish in high school understand. *All* nouns in French, Spanish, and many other languages, animate *or* inanimate, are *grammatically* assigned a gender. A "table" is *she* in French, but since *she* means something *biological* in English, we translate table as *it*. This is why people who learn English as a second language have problems. They translate the *grammatically* masculine and feminine pronouns of their language into *his* and *her* in English, assigning sex to rocks, caves, and islands! To us, *he* and *she* are biological clues; to them, they are grammatical conventions to be memorized.

Nouns in Hebrew are like French and Spanish ones, *grammatically* assigned male or female regardless of sexuality. When translating the Bible into English, translators have to ignore grammatical genders of Hebrew words and decide on *biological* grounds whether to use *he*, *she*, or *it*. Obviously "table" is easy, but when it comes to God or Spirit, the choice is *theological*—is God male, female, or it—beyond gender? In the past, English translations made the pronoun for *YHWH* masculine singular. This was argued *grammatically* since the English *he* then included male and female, and the Hebrew grammatical pronoun for *YHWH* was masculine. Grammatically *female* Hebrew terms for God such as *ruach*—creating Spirit of Genesis 1:2, and *chokmah*—God's wisdom, were also translated into the *generic he* in English. However, over time, and with the buildup of assumptions that God was male, the generic *he* in English became the masculine *he*, and attempts now to challenge that are seen by many as changing the Bible and God—"If the King James Version was good enough for Jesus, it's good enough for me!"

When feminist theologians argue that some terms for God are feminine in Hebrew, their point is not to make God *female* instead of male, but show that Hebrew masculine and feminine pronouns say *nothing* about biological gender, and so God can't be assumed to be *male* because *YHWH* is masculine, just as God can't be assumed female because the Spirit *ruach* is feminine. Otherwise we would have to argue that French and Spanish tables are female, but English tables have no sex! Many people in the church feel it doesn't *matter* if God is called *he*, and that feminist theologians are changing God to a woman because they don't like men or male leaders. These ideas obstruct both men and women theologians who believe that not only has God been *misrepresented* for centuries by being limited to male descriptions and characteristics, but Christians have been shortchanged. Many years ago, a little book by J. B. Phillips, *Your God is Too Small,* hit the best-seller list, encouraging

Christian folk to think in broader categories about God. Feminist theology invites us to do the same today. God as a male king, lord, and father is not even a fraction of the story, or of God's characteristics. The great "I am" continues to evolve as the great "I will become" and invites Christians to break their boxes created for God, boxes long since vacated by God, if they ever contained the Divine at all!

While the dominant "monarchical" model for God has controlled theology for centuries, Marcus Borg reminds us of the other model based on metaphors equally present in the Bible but not equally promoted. He calls this model the Spirit model, with metaphors like wind, breath, word, lover, wisdom, companion, nurturer, rock, shield, and high tower that are not tied to any gender. This "spirit" image is not a remote, removed, male ruler we must fear and obey, but a nonpersonified Spirit present with us in a loving, caring relationship. This Spirit "present" brooded as creating, life-affirming Spirit over the waters at creation; led the people of Israel to safety in the exodus as the great "I am," going before them as a cloud; communicated with frightened, reluctant prophets through burning bushes and silence, encouraging them not to give up because the Divine "I am" was with them; spoke a liberating message of compassion instead of debilitating and marginalizing rules through the life of a Nazarene peasant; invited Paul on the road to Damascus to change allegiances; appeared to many folk at Pentecost, giving them spiritual power to continue after Jesus' death; and continues to speak in various ways *in* our history. God as Spirit is not "out there" but God "present" within, around, and beyond us—immanent *and* transcendent. Such a Spirit has no use for male or female labels, or even human characteristics. It is an active description, like being and loving. Spirit language needs no "other" to dominate or subdue, as does the monarchical image, which requires obedient subjects, servants, and children. It is a *relational* term. The Divine Spirit present in, with, and around us defies the "great gulf fixed" between authoritarian God and disobedient humanity, between divine and human, and meets our spirit in a mutual relationship where each affects the other.

Both images of God are in the Bible. Feminist theology is not about changing one cluster of metaphors for the other, but rediscovering the *myriad* of metaphors for the great "I am" and finding new ones that best describe our experience of God today. Feminist theology also offers a *critique* that ensures the metaphors for God *stay* as metaphors, thus optional and changeable. The father in the story of the prodigal son exhibits the unconditional love of a parent despite the rebellious actions of a child. This "fatherly" mercy reminds us of what God is like but does not say that God *is* a father, a male operating with all the characteristics of a patriarchal father. It is the merciful *action*, not fatherhood, that is Godlike and could equally be displayed by a mother or a kind ruler. The problem for feminist theologians is that, throughout church history, the metaphor has become the thing. By calling God Father, God has been transformed into the shape and maleness of a patriarchal father, and consequently the human father has been designated Godlike and thus given authority over others.

Once this "essential" connection is made between maleness and divinity, there are *practical* fallouts. It legitimates male rule in religious, political, public, and private realms, automatically subordinating women to men because they have different biological organs from men—and, it seems, from God. It also forces women to relate to a *male* God, adopting postures they would adopt in relating to *human* males, often as inferior "other." Their religious journey and spirituality becomes shaped as a woman to a man, rather than having the freedom to image God as a mother like them, a woman friend, a sister-confidant, a powerful force—all relationships that operate differently from relationships with brothers, husbands, and fathers. When no part of the sacred is imaged as "feminine," women find it difficult to express their *own* spiritual identity "made in God's image" in suitable "sacred" metaphors. While many women, myself included, have rich human models for God's love in relationships with fathers and husbands, there are also many women whose most valid experiences of love, which they extrapolate to image the love of God, have come from friendships with other women—sisters, friends, and mothers; and whose most devastating models of abuse have come from relationships with men—husbands, lovers, and fathers.

"Reimagining God" to free the Divine from male, patriarchal forms is not without its problems, as a highly publicized incident in 1993 proved. A group of women theologians organized a Woman's Reimagining Conference in Minneapolis to celebrate the midpoint of the World Council of Churches Ecumenical Decade of Churches in solidarity with women. The organizers were amazed at the huge number of women from all walks of life who showed up. Of many events offered over several days, one particular liturgy, calling God "Sophia" and drawing on sensual and biological female images, attracted the media. Church leaders, suspicious of women gathering on their own *anyway* despite centuries of exclusively male church councils, charged the conference leaders with pagan goddess worship and ritual sex, even though the feminine images for God were all in the biblical wisdom literature and the Song of Songs! The rest of the conference's content was ignored, and some of the women leaders were blacklisted or fired from positions in their denominations. The fallout has not ceased and draws more press each year as the conference reconvenes. Conservative churches have even coached women in theological arguments for a male God and sent them to the conference to combat the "evil."

Again, it's a matter of metaphors.[15] *Sophia* is Greek for wisdom (*chokmah* in Hebrew), a feminine metaphor for God used throughout the "wisdom" literature of the Hebrew Bible and the Apocrypha—Proverbs, Ecclesiastes, Job, Sirach (Ecclesiasticus), and Wisdom of Solomon. In Proverbs, Woman Wisdom

(*Sophia*) is the exalted voice speaking with divinely sanctioned authority, counseling and enticing hearers to seek her and find life. As divine Wisdom, she is depicted as wife, mother, sister, lover, prophet, preacher in Israel, and architect of the world, building her cosmic house. Wisdom (*Sophia*) is imaged as the ideal Israelite woman in Proverbs 31, just as male images of God reflected ideal manhood in Israel. *Sophia* Wisdom was with *YHWH* before and during creation (Prov. 8:29–36):

> When he marked out the foundations of the earth, then I was beside him, like a master worker; and I was daily his delight, rejoicing before him always, rejoicing in his inhabited world and delighting in the human race...whoever finds me finds life and obtains favor from the LORD; but those who miss me injure themselves; all who hate me love death.

In Sirach 24:3, *Sophia* Wisdom "came forth from the mouth of the Most High and covered the earth like a mist" at creation. In the Wisdom of Solomon, her actions are those usually ascribed to God.

> Divine Sophia has her residence in heaven. She is the glory of G*d (Wisd. 7:25–6), mediator of creation (Wisd. 8:5–6), and shares the throne with G*d (Wisd. 9:3). She rules over kings and is herself powerful. She makes everything, renews everything, and permeates the cosmos (Wisd. 7:23, 27; 8:1, 5)...She is "intelligent and holy, free-moving, clear, loving what is good, eager, beneficent, unique in her Way (Wisd. 7:22)...She is an initiate into the knowledge of G*d, collaborator in G*d's work, the brightness that streams from everlasting light, a pure effervescence of divine glory, and the image of G*d's goodness. In short, Divine Wisdom lives symbiotically with G*d (Wisd. 8:3; 7:26).[16]

This metaphor of Wisdom for God operates in the same way in scripture as metaphors of Spirit, Voice, and Word (*Logos*) for God. Word (*Logos*) described that which was eternal with God in creation, and which communicated with humanity:

> In the beginning was the Word, and the Word was with God, and the Word was God. He was in the beginning with God. All things came into being through him, and without him not one thing came into being. What has come into being in him was life, and the life was the light of all people. The Light shines in the darkness, and the darkness did not overcome it. (Jn. 1:1–5)

In the same way, Wisdom (*Sophia*) described that which was eternal with God in creation, and which communicated with humanity. However when *Sophia*, a *female* metaphor for God is offered instead of the male *Logos*, the witchhunt is on.

Paul calls Jesus the Wisdom (*Sophia*) of God who, by God's actions, become our Wisdom (*Sophia*).[17] Jesus calls himself Wisdom (*Sophia*) and is described in a variety of Wisdom roles.[18] In Ephesians 3:9–11, the Wisdom of God (*Sophia*) has an identical role to Spirit or Christ in the Church (my italics):

This grace was given to me…to make everyone see what is the plan of the mystery hidden for ages in God who created all things; so that through the church the *wisdom of God* in its rich variety might now be made known to the rulers and authorities in the heavenly places.

The Word of God (*Logos*) in John is "that from God which was in Jesus"—Christ or Spirit, present at creation, incarnate in Jesus, and *part* of the Godhead. The Wisdom of God (*Sophia*) therefore is also "that from God which was in Jesus"—Christ or Spirit, present at creation, incarnate in Jesus, and *part* of the Godhead. To dismiss Wisdom (*Sophia*) as a metaphor for the Divine, we must also dismiss Word (*Logos*). Using *Sophia* reminds us that the Godhead is not limited to masculine or feminine, or even humanness, but that every new metaphor of God expands our view of what God is like.

How then can we as Christian women talk about God? Moses asked the same question:

If I come to the Israelites and say to them, "The God of your ancestors has sent me to you," and they ask me, "What is his name?" What shall I say to them? (Ex. 3:13)

God answered:

"I AM WHO I AM" [*or,* I am what I am; *or,* I will be what I will be]. He said further, "Thus you shall say to the Israelites, 'I AM has sent me to you.'" (Ex. 3:14)

The possibilities of God-ness are limitless and certainly never to be locked in male and female shapes. The Divine "I am" invites all of us to "unlimited metaphorical imagination" by refusing to complete the sentence "I am…" in any one way for all time. Our image of God is constantly expanding as women and men from every part of the world create new metaphors for the God they meet in their contexts.

I am reminded of walking around *Uluru*—Ayre's Rock—the huge red boulder that rises dramatically from the central Australian desert. At each point around the base, you experience a different view of the rock. Aboriginal people have stories about each feature, each crevice, stories that *together* tell the story of the rock as their sacred space. If you described the whole rock only by the view of the face that looks like a kangaroo's tail lying against its surface, it would be an inadequate description. An aerial shot of the rock is also not definitive, since it is still only one view, this time from the top. This does not mean we cannot describe the rock from every place where we stand around its huge circumference. That description will be "true" for our experience, but it is not the whole "truth," and if we insist it is, the problems begin. Each new view of the rock expands our story, but none of us can encompass all the story.

CHAPTER 9

Reclaiming Eve—and the Rest of Us

The job of suppressing women in Christianity turned out to be very difficult. No matter how much it was theologically justified, shown to be a part of the nature of things, and ordained by God, women kept on displaying powers they were not supposed to have, engaging in prophecy and ministry of which they were not supposed to be capable. They were threatened, hassled, vilified, made to do penance, beaten, tortured and even burned as witches. Yet it kept on happening...They were convinced, against all kinds of emotional pressures and spiritual blackmail, that they were indeed called and spirit-guided. They were, in some sense, claiming their heritage as God's creatures, as the daughters of an Eve who was not the source of sin but of life. But they knew this not in the rejection of Christianity but by their awareness of the very heart of the Christian tradition, in which was proclaimed liberty to the captives, freedom for the oppressed, love and acceptance and blessing for the weakest and most downtrodden.[1]

Rosemary Haughton

We might be forgiven for thinking, having read the last eight chapters, that all of history has been pitted against women and that the feminist task to divert this raging river in another direction is an impossible one. But this is not so. Enormous strides have been made in the last thirty years, supported by both men and women. Women are in Congress, medicine, ministry, and corporate leadership in greater numbers, and legislation has reduced opportunities for violence and discrimination against them. Parenting has become a joint venture and house-husbands no longer a rarity. Single women are respected, not pitied.

But even as these new river banks seem to be holding, America's largest Protestant denomination on June 9, 1998 amended its statement of beliefs for the first time in thirty-five years to include:

A wife is to submit graciously to the servant leadership of her husband, even as the church willingly submits to the headship of Christ.

While husband and wife are of equal worth before God, the husband should provide for, protect, and lead the family, and the wife has

...the God-given responsibility to respect her husband and to serve as his "helper" in managing their household and nurturing the next generation.

The Southern Baptist Convention overwhelmingly rejected two amendments that husbands and wives submit to each other; and that widows, widowers, and single people were expressions of "family." The incoming president, who opposes the Convention's moderate and liberal wings, said "We needed to say something about what a *biblical* family is."[2]

This biblical family is not *Abraham's,* where his wife Sarah arranged for him to father a child with her servant. It is not the polygamous family of *Jacob,* where Jacob worked fourteen years to earn both his brides. It also does not include *Jesus* or *Paul,* because they were most likely single. It is a *specific* family model that appears only in some of the New Testament letters with the central tenet that wives submit to their husbands and, by extension, also submit to male authority in church by not teaching men and keeping silent in *worship.* [3] Lo and behold, Eve is again at the bottom of it all!

Let a woman learn in silence with full submission. I permit no woman to teach or to have authority over a man; she is to keep silent. For Adam was formed first, then Eve; and Adam was not deceived, but the woman was deceived and became the transgressor. Yet she will be saved through childbearing, provided they continue in faith and love and holiness, with modesty. (1 Tim. 2:11–15)

Variations of this model of family life are also promoted today by the religious right and Promise Keepers. Although many mainline denominations have moved from overt rulings about women's subordination to men, such images of the "good" Christian woman still hover from theologies built on patriarchal models of the family, manifesting themselves in tendencies to blame all society's ills on mothers who work outside the home, and "feminists" who are angry, aggressive, self-seeking, man-hating women.

Let's face it! Feminist theologians have a hard task dealing with these images of women's subordination to men because they *are* in the Bible, and more particularly they bear *Paul's* name, the founder of Christian theology! We all know that Paul is quoted on Christian "truth" as much as Jesus, as if they were synonymous. But right here we need to pause and put our "suspicious" feminist minds to work. Jesus never said anything about women being subordinate to men or keeping silent. He had quite a few women among his followers, and also seemed to ignore most of the Jewish rules that set them apart from men. He also made no mention of Eve and the downfall of women, or even Adam and Eve and the downfall of everyone! Even though Paul would call Jesus the New Adam, Jesus made no reference to himself as the restorer of things after the fall. In fact, his single reference to the first couple is positive—as an example of the goodness of marriage as opposed to men discarding women on various pretexts through divorce. Why then did some of the letters attributed to Paul in the New Testament, written long after Jesus' death, begin to harp on this theme of women's subordination?

In looking at Paul, we immediately find a problem! In the many letters attributed to him, he disagrees with himself on the issue of women! This, and other inconsistencies in Paul's teaching, led the majority of biblical scholars to conclude years ago that only seven letters could be *positively* attributed to Paul—1 Thessalonians, Philippians, Philemon, Galatians, 1 Corinthians, 2 Corinthians, and Romans—the rest written by later followers. The practice of pseudonymity—writing in another's name—was widespread in the Greek world, and even used as an exercise to master the style, vocabulary, and philosophical perspectives of a venerated teacher. Of Paul's *undisputed* letters, we may not have them all in their original forms. Scholars have shown that 2 Corinthians is a composite of Paul's letters written over time to the Corinthian church, and that other letters contain editorial comments from later copiers and readers, added for clarification or updating as they were circulated.[4] There was also tension within Paul himself as he carved out his theological ideas by responding to problems in the churches he founded. Since his pragmatic guideline was always to do what was best for the developing community, his advice on an issue could vary from place to place according to the circumstances.

The place to start examining these troublesome verses about women's subordination is with Paul's convictions about Jesus in the letters genuinely ascribed to him. Paul's central theme was the new freedom realized in Christ, a release from "disciplinarian" laws, both Jewish and Roman. Perhaps his most comprehensive faith statement was the following:

> Now before faith came, we were imprisoned and guarded under the law until faith would be revealed. Therefore the law was our disciplinarian until Christ came, so that we might be justified by faith. But now that faith has come, we are no longer subject to a disciplinarian, for in Christ Jesus you are all children of God through faith. As many of you as were baptized into Christ have clothed yourself with Christ. There is no longer Jew or Greek, there is no longer slave or free, there is no longer male and female; of all of you are one in Christ Jesus. And if you belong to Christ, then you are Abraham's offspring, heirs according to the promise. (Gal. 3:23–29)

This freedom from restricting civic and religious conventions for men and women, Jew and Greek, slave and free, became the baptismal formula, the confession of the uniqueness of the new community within Judaism. It is not surprising then that Jesus' followers were seen as disruptive, disdaining Jewish dietary and social rules, affirming the unmarried state "for the Gospel" for women and men, regarding women and slaves as equals of men, and refusing to participate in public festivals for Roman gods.

Paul's theology of freedom in Christ was developed around the metaphor of Jesus as the "New Adam."[5] Why did Paul go back to Adam when the rest of scripture virtually ignored the first couple? First, Adam as "original human" was an *inclusive* figure for Jews *and* Gentiles rather than a Jewish Moses or Abraham. Second, the longed-for messianic age was seen as a time when Paradise would reopen and *Adam* (humankind) would enter again. *Jesus* was this "New Adam." Third, Adam and Eve did not then have the bad press they acquired later in Christianity. Rabbis saw the *original* Adam as an angelic figure, the model of righteousness for the new age, and Paul did not blame Adam or Eve for universal sin.[6] He said:

> Just as sin came into the world through one man, and death came through sin, and so death spread to all because all have sinned. (Rom. 5:12)

Because was translated into Latin in the fourth century as "in whom" implying Adam. This fueled Augustine's doctrine that sin originated with the first couple and was passed on to everyone at conception as inevitable "original sin," an idea not held prior to Augustine nor by many of his colleagues.[7] For Paul, disobedience was a choice Adam and *every* human made, making external laws necessary, but in the new age, people restored to Adam's prior glory will have the law written "on their hearts."[8] This new age began with Christ; thus there is no longer need for circumcision or *any* distinctions and exclusions—Jew or Greek, slave or free, male or female. All are renewed in the *image of God* the Creator.[9] This idea of breaking down the barriers—religious, social, and sexual—to form an egalitarian community in Christ was not simply a nice *side* issue for Paul, but *central* to the new community and expressed in its baptismal formula. The old distinctions had ceased to count![10]

In celebrating this new freedom, however, Paul was aware of its radicality for both Jewish and Roman society, so he also pleaded with his churches around Asia Minor to find a *balance* between their rightful freedom on the one hand, and a social decency and order that did not offend "for the sake of the Gospel on the other":

> So, whatever you eat or drink, or whatever you do, do everything for the glory of God. Give no offense to Jews or to Greeks or to the church of God, just as I try to please everyone in everything I do, not seeking my own advantage, but that of many, so that they may be saved. (1 Cor. 10:31–33)

Maintaining this balance between *women's* freedom in Christ and their subordination in patriarchal society would push Paul to his theological limits and even challenge his own patriarchal presuppositions! Although we have already discussed patriarchal Greco-Roman society from which Gentile converts were coming—and gaining freedom—a reminder is in order before we look more closely at Paul's concerns about women.

In his *Politics,* the Greek philosopher Aristotle outlined the "natural rule" for the household, with three primary components of command—master over slave, husband over wife, father over children:

> The male is by nature better fitted to command than the female…It is true that in most cases of republican government the ruler and ruled interchange in turn…but the male stands in this relationship to the female continuously.

The superiority of the male was based on the superiority of the soul—possessed in highest measure in males—over the body:

> Hence there are by nature various classes of rulers and rule. For the free rules the slave, the male the female, the man the child in a different way. And all possess the various parts of the soul but possess them in different ways; for the slave has not got the deliberative part at all, and the female has it but without full authority, while the child has it but in an undeveloped form.

Since households made up the state, civic society was jeopardized if the household rule was not upheld. Aristotle made no bones about "freedom" for women:

> The freedom in regard to women is detrimental both in regard to the purpose of the *politeia* and in regard to the happiness of the state.[11]

Jewish writers Philo and Josephus, both around Jesus' era, also made it clear that *Jews,* as good Roman citizens, adhered to this household hierarchy. Philo said:

> The husband seems competent to transmit knowledge of the laws to his wife, the father to his children, the master to his slaves.[12]

And Josephus agreed:

> The woman, says the Law, is in all things inferior to the man. Let her accordingly be submissive, not for her humiliation, but that she may be directed, for the authority has been given by God to the man.[13]

Quite obviously, the freedom Paul was advocating for women flew in the face of conventional society, both Roman and Jewish. Paul had reason to be concerned at rumors reaching him about women in the Corinthian church claiming "freedom" to remain unmarried and act publicly in ways not appropriate for women! We are not talking eccentric lifestyle here, but public *offense* against the codes of the Roman household and state! So, while Paul *never* reneges on the baptismal formula that declares no *theological* distinctions between men and women, slave and free, Jew and Greek in Christ's community, he suggests there may be some *cultural* reasons for not giving offense. This distinction is vital. It reminds me of instructions to women tourists in Muslim countries not to wear shorts or show too much "flesh" because, although women in our society are free to dress that way, it is offensive to Muslim culture and sends out very different messages. This does not mean, however, that when we return home we continue to obey this rule. In the same way, those who advocate that Paul's concessions to Greco-Roman culture reflect his *theological* views and must be preserved as "divine law" miss the point. We need to watch carefully for this distinction.

First Corinthians is a good place to see Paul's argument for balance played out. Paul had received letters from Corinth outlining some issues of contention and was replying to them. It seems from chapter 7 that, besides advocating singleness as part of "freedom" in Christ, some were also arguing for celibate marriages as well. From the way Paul responds, he may have once advocated the unmarried state "for the Gospel," but these extreme manifestations now come back to haunt him. While reaffirming singleness, but not as the only or best option, he describes "freedom" in marriage as *mutuality* like everything else in the new community. The husband should give conjugal rights, but so should the wife; the husband has authority over his wife's body, as the wife over her husband's; a wife shouldn't leave her husband, but a husband shouldn't divorce his wife. This mutuality between husband and wife in sexual relations and marriage continues what Paul calls his "rule" in all the churches—mutuality between male and female, Jew and Greek, bond and free. *All* are equal in the new community, which is in radical opposition to Aristotle's hierarchical codes of one over the other.

Only after reiterating this equality Paul says "but..." While freedom is a *right* in Christ, exercising that *right* might not always be best for the community. "All things are lawful" was the Corinthian's slogan, but Paul qualifies it, "but not all things build up. Do not seek your own advantage, but that of the other," which meant don't "give offense to Jews or to Greeks or to the church of God."[14] Paul first applies this to eating food previously offered to idols, then moves on to head covering in worship (1 Cor. 11:3–16):

> But I want you to understand that Christ is the head of every man, and the husband is the head of his wife, and God is the head of Christ. Any man who prays or prophesies with something on his head disgraces his head, but any woman who prays and prophesies with her head unveiled disgraces her head—it is one and the same thing as having her head unshaved. For if a woman will not veil herself, then she should cut off her hair; but if it is disgraceful for a woman to have her hair cut off or to be shaved, she should wear a veil. For a man ought not to have his head veiled, since he is the image and reflection of God; but woman is the reflection of man. Indeed, man was not made from woman, but woman

from man. Neither was man created for the sake of woman, but woman for the sake of man. For this reason a woman ought to have a symbol of authority on her head, because of the angels. Nevertheless, in the Lord woman is not independent of man or man independent of woman. For just as woman came from man, so man comes through woman; but all things come from God. Judge for yourselves: is it proper for a woman to pray to God with her head unveiled? Does not nature itself teach that if a man wears long hair, it is degrading to him, but if a woman has long hair, it is her glory? For her hair is given to her for a covering. But if anyone is disposed to be contentious—we have no such custom, nor do the churches of God.

Biblical scholars find this passage obtuse. Since Paul contradicts himself, it is not clear whether he is speaking throughout. Some scholars think he repeats the arguments of the false teachers in verses 3–10, then refutes them with the "nevertheless" of verse 11. One thing is sure. Women were praying and prophesying in public worship, and Paul was *happy* about it. Chapter 12 and the beginning of chapter 14 reaffirm this by urging *everyone* to seek spiritual gifts, especially prophecy. His *concern*, and that of the Corinthians, was *cultural*— whether women should cover their hair while they prophesied in public. Christian "freedom" from societal rules of decorum would say they could wear it loose, short, or uncovered, but did it offend and detract outsiders from being saved?[15] The hair conventions are lost on us today. Apparently *men* could pray and prophesy in public bareheaded, but not women. Scholars are not even sure what "veiling" *meant*, but certainly loose, uncovered, or shaved hair was out! Elisabeth Schüssler Fiorenza suggests why. Flowing hair mimicked the disheveled hair of ecstatic women in mystery religions and Greek goddess worship and hinted at "unclean" women in Judaism (Num. 5:18).[16]

Paul says "Christ is the head of every man, and the husband is the head of his wife, and God is the head of Christ" in the *context* of this discussion about headgear, making a play on the word "head"! Scholars feel "head" is better translated "source" here—"one preceding and establishing the other's being in succession rather than rule over"—which makes more sense of "God as the *head* of Christ." Somehow what Corinthians wore on their heads honored or dishonored their "source," Christ in the case of man, and a husband in the case of a wife. This theme of succession is picked up in verses 8–9:

He [man] is the image and reflection of God; but woman is the reflection of man. Indeed, man was not made from woman, but woman from man. Neither was man created for the sake of woman, but woman for the sake of man.

There is *nothing* in this reference that says women were *not* created in the image of God, as later church fathers would argue to downgrade women's equality with men. It is an argument about succession—one coming from the other—and makes no case for superiority and inferiority, nor lays any blame on Eve.[17] The whole obscure passage is not about women's subordination or silencing—they are preaching and prophesying in public—but about whether they should cover their heads for *convention's* sake![18]

While it is difficult to follow the drift of verses 3–10, the old Paul emerges in verses 11–16 with "Nevertheless…" Whatever has been said, the earlier theme of mutuality and equality in 1 Corinthians overrides everything. The bottom line is: Woman is not independent of man, nor man independent of woman. Just as woman came from man, so man comes through woman, but *all* things come from God. As for "hair," Paul asks readers to judge for themselves whether women's uncovered hair is degrading. Woman's hair is her glory, given as a *covering*, and thus *all* she needs when prophesying! The obtuse parts of the passage must be judged by what *else* we know of Paul—his overall theme of balance between freedom *and* responsibility which he continues in following chapters—encouraging all to seek spiritual gifts on one hand (chapters 12–14) but in love and for the good of the community and its observers on the other (chapter 13). In all the genuine letters of Paul, he never advocates the subordination of women to men.

Just as we are lulled into this happy conclusion, we lurch awake at 1 Corinthians 14:34:

> As in all the churches of the saints, women should be silent in the churches. For they are not permitted to speak, but should be subordinate, as the law also says. If there is anything they desire to know, let them ask their husbands at home. For it is shameful for a woman to speak in church. (vv. 34–35)

But then, just as suddenly, the old theme returns:

> So my friends, be eager to prophesy, and do not forbid speaking in tongues; but all things should be done decently and in order. (vv. 39–40)

What is going on? Why does Paul suddenly contradict what he has said throughout the letter? Scholars are so sure verses 34–35 are a later addition to this chapter by an unknown writer that they are bracketed in the *New Revised Standard Version*. Perhaps they were added as a comment in a margin and later placed into the text. We don't know, but we *do* know they stand in stark opposition to everything else Paul has said! He released folk from obedience to the law; this returns them to its authority. Women were allowed to prophesy and pray freely in public; now they must keep silent and ask their husbands. It has become *shameful* for a woman to speak in church!

Most biblical scholars agree that the church that Paul advocated as a radically free discipleship of equals did not last! The balance between freedom and social convention eventually tipped, especially for women. By the second century, the church had become part of Roman society, and Paul's fluid communities were replaced by male organizations of bishops and deacons. Greco-Roman "virtues" for men and women became Christian virtues. Men's virtues operated in public—courage, strength, justice, and endurance. Women's virtues shone in private, preserving women's "shame."

> The cultural value of shame prescribed the feminine personality as discreet, shy, restrained, and timid, those qualities deemed necessary to "protect" female sexuality. In the sexual division of moral labor, honor was considered an aspect of male nature expressed in a natural desire for precedence and an aggressive sexuality. Shame, the defining quality of womanhood, was indicated by passivity, subordination, and seclusion in the household.[19]

Christian women had been returned to their "proper" space in Roman society as chaste, obediently subordinate—and silent. "Silence is a woman's glory," Aristotle said, "but this is not equally the glory of men."[20]

This gradual transition can be traced in the non-Pauline letters, all sharing a common feature not found in Paul, the adoption of the Greco-Roman "household code" of Aristotle's *Politics,* with the rule of husbands over wives, masters over slaves, fathers over children.[21] Instructions for wives to be submissive are softer in Colossians and Ephesians (dated 70–95 C.E.) than in 1 and 2 Timothy and Titus (dated by some as late as 120–140 C.E.).[22] Ephesians 5 even *begins* with Paul's mutuality theme—"Be subject to one another out of reverence for Christ"—but then develops Aristotle's rule of father over wife, slaves and children, albeit a "kinder, gentler" version, but still requiring subjection of wives but not of husbands.[23] First Peter 2–3 (dated 70–90 C.E.) best spells out what is now "God's will" for women. Since Gentiles were being converted to Christianity, Roman society was suspicious of this religion threatening to overturn the established relationships of household and state. The author therefore instructs Christian families to obey the Roman household codes and honor the Emperor:

> Conduct yourselves honorably among the Gentiles, so that, though they malign you as evildoers, they may see your honorable deeds and glorify God...For the Lord's sake accept the authority of every human institution...for it is God's will that by doing right you should silence the ignorance of the foolish. As servants of God, live as free people, yet do not use your freedom as a pretext for evil. Honor everyone. Love the family of believers. Fear God. Honor the Emperor. (1 Pet. 2:12–17)

In this new scenario, wives were to be subordinate even to non-Christian husbands. Aristotle's ideas of women as the "weaker" sex has also become part of the package:

> Husbands...show consideration for your wives in your life together, paying honor to the woman as the weaker sex, since they too are also heirs of the gracious gift of life...(3:7)

By 1 and 2 Timothy and Titus (the 1 Cor. 14:34–35 insert is dated with these writings in the very early second century), the scene is very different.

While echoes of Paul come through, the vocabulary, style, theological concepts, and themes of godliness, church order, and good works are not Paul's. The "genre"—an elder bishop passing on "sound doctrine" to the new church leader—allows the author/s to establish rules for second century church organization.[24] Household churches where both men and women used gifts of leadership have become "households" of God, managed by male bishops along the lines of a Roman household and state:

> He [the bishop] must manage his household well, keeping his children submissive and respectful in every way—for if someone does not know how to manage his own household, how can he take care of God's church? (1 Tim. 3:5)

The major concern is women's behavior—telling us that women were *still* claiming their right to lead in worship and be "free" from subordination in marriage. The author makes it clear that Greco-Roman household codes are now *Christian* household codes for both private homes and God's "household" the church. Instructions for women are clear and totally different from Paul's vision of their freedom in Christ. Eve is back, beginning to take the blame and pass it on to her "daughters" (my italics):

> I desire then, that in every place the *men* should pray, lifting up holy hands without anger or argument; also that the *women* should dress themselves *modestly* and *decently* in suitable clothing, not with their hair braided, or with gold and pearls, or expensive clothes, but with good works, as is *proper* for women who profess reverence for God. Let a woman learn in *silence* with *full submission*. I permit *no* woman to *teach* or to have *authority* over a man; she is to keep *silent*. For Adam was formed first, then *Eve*; and Adam was *not* deceived, but the woman *was deceived* and became a *transgressor*. Yet she will be saved through *childbearing*, provided they continue in faith and love and holiness, with *modesty*. (1 Tim. 2:8–15)

All is in place again! Men pray in public, and women behave like Greco-Roman virtuous women—chaste, obedient, and silent.[25] After the fresh breeze of women prophesying in 1 Corinthians, women are not permitted to teach, and must keep silent. Widows have a code of behavior so they won't "disgrace" the church, and slaves are back in their obedient place in the household.[26] Those who teach otherwise are censored:

> Teach and urge these duties. Whoever teaches otherwise and does not agree with the sound words of our Lord Jesus Christ and the teaching that is in accordance with godliness, is conceited, understanding nothing, and has a morbid craving for controversy and disputes about words (1 Tim. 6:2–4).

It is interesting how those who use 1 and 2 Timothy to subordinate women and diffuse dissent claim they are *returning* to the true teachings of Paul and the early church! Not so! It was the teachings of Paul *against* Roman household rules and Jewish Law that broke down hierarchies and barriers, making "all one in Christ Jesus" (Gal. 3:28). To "return" to these Roman codes as authoritative for women's subordination *rejects* the freedom Paul learnt from the teachings of Jesus Christ.

Dennis MacDonald, quoted earlier, argues that the author/s of Timothy and Titus *deliberately* used Paul's name to "endorse" the return of women to subordinate places of silence and obedience. They were familiar with stories of Thecla, the young woman who followed Paul and encouraged other women to resist conventional marriage, since they quoted names of people only otherwise associated with her and Paul. Constant references to false teaching—"old wives tales" and gossipy women—contrasted with the "true" teaching of Timothy's mother and grandmother—good married women—were aimed at single women (like Thecla) and widows, who taught women in their homes (2 Tim. 3:6–7):

> Avoid them! For among them are those who make their way into households and captivate silly women, overwhelmed by their sins and swayed by all kinds of desires, who are always instructed and can never arrive at a knowledge of truth.

Titus 2:3b–5 says that if women are to teach at *all*, they must

> ...teach what is good so that they may encourage the young women to love their husbands, to love their children, to be self-controlled, chaste, good managers of the household, kind, being submissive to their husbands, so that the word of God may not be discredited. (Titus 2:3–5)[27]

This problem of single women outside male control comes up again in *Didascalia*, a third-century church manual. Women in "public" ministry do not exhibit appropriate characteristics of femaleness, passivity, shyness, and restraint, and are caricatured as talkative, gossipy, and stirrers of controversy for not staying home![28] "Public" activity has become "shameful" for virtuous Christian women, now firmly regulated by Roman household hierarchies.

While neither Jesus nor Paul condemned Eve or suggested women were subordinate or inferior to men, Eve now becomes a target in this negative climate for women. From this text alone, Eve will become the *scriptural* foundation for the demise of women. It contains *all* the ingredients the later church fathers will run with:

> Let a woman learn in silence with full submission. I permit no woman to teach or to have authority over a man; she is to keep silent. For Adam was formed first, then Eve; and Adam was not deceived, but the woman was deceived and became a transgressor. Yet she will be saved through childbearing, provided they (the children) continue in faith and love and holiness, with modesty. (1 Tim. 2:11–15)

The *problem* is Christian women out of place, refusing to marry by claiming freedom in Christ like men, and teaching this heresy to other women.[29]

The author appeals to the *creation* story to argue women's proper place within the Roman household. Like Paul, the idea of succession is used—Adam was formed first—but *now* it has to do with men *over* women. A *theology* of an "order of creation," borrowed from Roman culture where man is first and dominant and woman second and subordinate, is born. Eve for the first time is not only deceived, but the *transgressor.* The Greco-Roman argument for women's subordination based on Greek "natural" law is at play—as the *weaker* sex, women are easily deceived. But Eve is also the *guilty* one while Adam is *not* guilty, a far cry from Paul's Old Adam theme.[30] The final thrust, that women will be saved in childbearing, suggests women's salvation is conditional on their role as mothers, "good" women who marry and bear children with *modesty* within a patriarchal household as opposed to "bad" women who reject marriage and family responsibilities.

It comes as a surprise to realize that the swamp of negativity toward Eve, which would engulf the church and all women so completely, was built on this one small passage written well into the second century, which sits in direct contradiction to teachings about women from Jesus and Paul. Sanctioned by these verses alone, male theologians went *back* and dusted off the Genesis story, reinterpreting it in light of Eve's *guilt,* and built a case for "man's rule" against Paul's equality of men and women. If this "curse" of Eve—man's rule over her—was so crucial, why didn't Jesus or Paul make the case against her, and why did Jesus and Paul both go in the opposite direction advocating *equality* of men and women? As Agrippa argued way back in the sixteenth century about this development of male tyranny against women:

> The curse of Eve is constantly in their mouth. "You will be under the power of your husband and he will rule over you." If it is responded to them that Christ has put an end to this curse, they will make the same rebuttal again, from the words of Peter, adding them to those also of Paul: "Women are to be subject to men. Women are to be silent in Church."[31]

While Eve's guilt began in the final days of the New Testament with one verse in Timothy, Augustine would seal her fate forever in the fourth century by blaming her for transferring sin to the whole human race through her womb, tempting poor Adam, eating first, succumbing to the snake (Satan), causing the fall, and bringing death on all, including Christ!

What then do we do with the passages in the New Testament letters that subordinate women? We read them for what they were—a return to the patriarchal subjugations of the Greco-Roman household, which both Jesus and Paul opposed. No doubt these writings were included in the New Testament because they represented the views of the church under Roman rule at the time when the canon was settled.[32] Writings that exhibited women's leadership did not make the selection. But it is not as if we do not have *another* model in scripture. The *undisputed* writings of Paul are filled with equality and inclusiveness in the new reign of God, and Jesus was forever overturning the status quo and including the marginalized in contradiction to Jewish laws. We need to shout these passages and stories telling of a radical discipleship of equals from the rooftops, and critique strongly the subordination and denigration of women in later writings. To revert to rules of subordination is to *negate* the message of Jesus! Most of the women who protested their exclusion were silenced, but we *know* they were there, because stories like Thecla's persisted in a subversive women's culture with sufficient power to necessitate strict guidelines for women's behavior in Timothy, and household "rules" in other letters. These women are our foremothers, even though their voices are dimmed.

What then do we do with Eve? Once we realize that "evil Eve" was a post-New Testament creation of celibate church fathers who needed to exclude women from church leadership and find a theological scapegoat for temptation and sin, we can exonerate Eve. But is this enough? Simply relieving Eve of blame doesn't remove the centuries of negative images about women embedded in our history and psyche whether we know it or not. We still sit in pews and hear Eve blamed, and the "punishment" of male rule over her justified. We need to confront that apple story which has absorbed artists, poets, and theologians for centuries, and take a new bite at it! To do this, we need to go back to the garden and look again, rubbing our eyes as if seeing Genesis 1–3 for the first time.

First we need to ask what kind of a story it is, and thus its "authority" today. While the creation story was once taken literally, over the last centuries discoveries of other creation stories in the ancient world, other technological ways to talk about human origins, biblical criticism, and the conviction that Genesis is not a *historical* narrative have allowed us to look at the story in a different way. Most scholars read the early chapters of Genesis as a "creation myth," a story told on many levels of meaning to convey messages about human existence.[33] In tribal days, wisdom was learned from such stories explaining one's place in the universe. Without these stories, one could not survive the terrifying, mysterious world. Myth does not ask whether events are historical facts or what is truth or fiction, but what *insights* can be gleaned. Thus we can read the creation story as a pictorial way tribal people described how they came to be, without having to establish universal orders from it, especially an "order of creation" that places men over women! If Paul had not used the metaphor of the New Adam for Christ, one wonders if the story would now receive any more attention than the story of Cain as the first murderer!

The next surprise we get is that there is no "fall" or "original sin" in the Genesis 3 story.[34] Although *Paul* talks of the first human's disobedience, he did not see it initiating *all* sin and the fall of humanity. Later Christian theology would develop the "fall" as the beginning of "original sin," but the question has always hovered in me—if Adam and Eve's fall was so significant in the scheme of salvation, and Jesus was sent to reverse it, why did Jesus never mention their sin *or* the fall? We are so used to assuming Christianity revolves around a fall and its redemption that we are stunned to find it is not in Genesis! The doctrine of the fall and original sin lost ground in the nineteenth century as the Genesis story became read as a creation myth, but Barth reasserted traditional views of both doctrines early this century that held sway until his successors returned them to story status again.[35] If there is no literal moment when all of humanity was doomed through the first man's sin, there is no need to find blame, since each human is quite capable of sinning for himself or herself! If original sin is not passed to everyone through women at conception, there is no need to vilify Eve or women anymore!

When we rub our eyes again, we find there are *two* creation stories. Genesis 1 says man and woman were created together and equal, allowed to eat *all* the food in the garden, and told to multiply and cherish the earth. Genesis 2 tells of woman created later from Adam's rib. In the history of Eve's downfall, the first story was ignored, and the second story of Eve as afterthought and "helper" became dominant, her creation out of Adam an inferior call. Feminist theologians reconstructing Eve can simply accept the first story as *their* "myth of beginnings" and be done with it. But they can accept the second story as well, once we see how "evil" and "sin" was *read* into it to make it a fall story. Being the last thing created does *not* have to mean inferior. Some theologians argue that Eve was the *crown* of creation, the finale.[36] Realizing they were naked and "covering their shame" does *not* have to signify sin and guilt since "shame" referred to one's sexual organs at the time. Eve created as Adam's "helper" does *not* have to suggest inferiority, especially when the Hebrew word for "helper" was also used of God in relationship to Israel.[37] And what was the nature of the "help" Eve was to provide? Surely that is important if we want to make Eve's task inferior. Genesis 1 gives man and woman the shared task of replenishing and nurturing the earth, and the second story says God created a "helper" for companionship and reproduction—a mutuality of roles, not necessarily one subordinate to the other.

Once we realize there is no fall, what might the expulsion from the garden mean? Many scholars see the story of Adam and Eve not as a negative story, but as a story of the way things came to be. Humans created by God rebel against "parental" control, acquire knowledge of good and evil, and leave the garden to enter the world—"growing up and leaving home." Tilling the soil and bearing children, rather than being the *punishment*, is a description of adulthood, the reality of life experienced by humans in the world. God never *abandoned* them for their disobedience, but sent them on their way, even making clothes of skins for them like a concerned parent. This is similar to other creation stories where humans are created and sent on their way to reproduce. Sin and blame are not at issue. In fact, there is no evil in the story unless we add it. Genesis does not call the serpent Satan, but a wise and cunning animal.[38] A *sinister* slant on the natural "enmity" between serpent and human was read later into the story. The tree was said to give knowledge and wisdom, a decided advantage for life! We are so busy creating a *fall* story we forget that by eating they gained knowledge![39] Knowledge of good and evil was not simply moral, but the whole gamut of living—happiness and catastrophe, success and failure, life and death. The story catalogues these *realities* of life in the world (out of Paradise)—pain in childbirth, laboring for food, and a husband's rule in a patriarchal society. Expulsion from Paradise also explained human death rather than their immortality like gods, yet having known a world without death, this dream remains as a time when they will get back into Paradise—the messianic age.[40]

What of the problematic verse for women—Eve's "punishment" of subordination:

> The Lord God said…"I will greatly increase your pangs in childbearing;
> in pain shall you bring forth children, yet your desire shall be for your
> husband, and he shall rule over you." (Gen. 3:16)

When the Genesis story is read as a fall story with Eve responsible for original sin, this text gives permission to forever legitimately "punish" Eve and all the "daughters of Eve." Read in an "order of creation" since she was created after Adam, add a pinch of misinterpretation of 1 Corinthians 11, and you have the perfect recipe for women's subordination, as in the fourth century John Chrysostom demonstrated:

> The image [of God] has rather to do with authority, and this only the man
> has; the woman has it no longer. For he is subjected to no one, while she
> is subjected to him; as God said, "Your inclination shall be for your hus-
> band and he shall rule over you." (Gen 3:16). Therefore the man is in the
> "image of God" since he has no one above him, but as God had no supe-
> rior but rules everything. The woman, however, is "the glory of man"
> since she is subjected to man.[41]

Yet *God* did not pronounce a judgment of *sin* in the story, and Hebrew scripture did not relate later sinful actions of the Israelites back to Adam and Eve. Without a fall and the need to "punish," the "curses" become descriptions of how human life is, and the story leading up to them the myth of how this reality came to be.

Carol Myers, examining the language and social context of pre-monarchical Israel when this story would have been circulating, sees the story as a wisdom tale.[42] Those who heard it recounted would recognize it as a description of how this tribal people came to be. Man tills the stubborn ground. Woman's lot involves childbirth and childrearing. By looking at the structure and words of the verse outlining woman's "role," Carol found that earlier translations had missed nuances in the words. Without going into details of her analysis, she came up with the following translation:

> I will greatly increase your toil and your pregnancies.
> (Along) with travail shall you beget children.
> For to your man is your desire,
> And he shall predominate over you.[43]

We are reminded then, not just that women work and have children, but that anguish accompanies these life tasks. In Israelite peasant culture, extra children were advantageous as workers; thus female hesitation about pregnancy had to do with the mother's life-expectancy. The text says that although a woman is reluctant to take this risk, her emotional desire for her mate naturally exposes her. The problematic "He shall rule over you" must be read in this context. Because of woman's reluctance, the will of the husband to reproduce for social and economic necessity takes over, and he will insist on sex with conception in mind. This is not an eternal rule of man over woman in everything, but a shared economic necessity to reproduce. Read this way, Israelite peasant women played an equal part, working the fields with their men and reproducing in an extended household where everyone was involved in subsistence. Gender relationships were totally different from today. Women had responsible work roles beyond childrearing as the private and public spheres merged with men and women working together, even though there might have been patriarchal rules in place. The important feature was not that roles were assigned according to gender, but that all were recognized as *equally* contributing and essential for the good of the whole.

Such reinterpretation of biblical texts is not something scandalous done by women scholars. This goes on all the time amongst biblical scholars as new information comes to light, ensuring that conclusions of previous centuries are sound and expressed in language that makes sense for modern times. The fact that *women* scholars reinterpret verses about women is not subversive, evil, or a private "agenda," but natural. Women take a closer look at what goes against their experience of womanhood to check that all is well. As Elizabeth Cady Stanton replied a hundred years ago when men said it was *preposterous* that women could interpret scripture, "Did they also write to the men doing the Revised Standard Version that it was preposterous for *men* to interpret Scripture?"[44]

What then can we say to all this as Christian feminists? Paul's theme throughout was the equality of all in the new community of God, a discipleship of equals that broke down the barriers between who was included and who was excluded. Paul absorbed this message from Jesus, who loved the outcast and marginalized and did all he could to preach compassion as the rule of behavior, rather than emphasize fine points of the law. Women were included in Jesus' company, and were counted among his closest friends. Although scripture concentrates on the actions of men, there were obviously so many women followers that they cannot help appearing throughout the story of Jesus. Not until the second-century church began to exclude women from leadership did the Pastoral Epistles—Timothy and Titus—command women's silence and exclusion from the public arena, argued on secular virtues of a "good Roman woman." The freedom for everyone in Christ, which Paul had so strongly advocated against the restrictions of the Roman hierarchical household, was lost to the same old system. From there on, the church would adopt these *secular* structures as part of the "divine plan." Eve becomes, in 1 Timothy 2:11–15, the one who "transgressed"—sinned. The fall has begun, both the doctrine developed by the church fathers, and the ongoing fall of women. Going back to the garden, the church fathers found ways to build a story of guilt, sin, and woman's complicity to such proportions that even now it is hard to believe this is not all in the original Genesis story—until we go back and look!

The power of the Genesis story, like all stories of "beginnings," is that it grounds us and tells us who we are. The Genesis story and Eve have long been the story of human condemnation—how we went wrong from the beginning, writing hopelessness and failure into the inevitable story of each of us. It's time for us to visit the garden anew with Eve as our tour guide, and find there a "beginnings" story of hope—that humans were launched as adults from the garden with the essential tool of knowledge of good and evil, to go into the world where they would, as part of everyday life, toil and give birth, nurture and replenish the earth. Adam and Eve went out *together* with a joint command to live as humans on God's good earth. God did *not* abandon them, but even as they went, made garments of skin to protect them on their way. In the first stories "outside the garden" God is close by, receiving the offerings of Cain and Abel and in conversation with them about life. How often we miss the repetition in the creation story—that God saw creation as good—very good—to concentrate on our own theology that everything went awry over an apple! Look again. There is no statement in the garden about the whole world becoming defective or everything being lost, unless we want to read it into the story.

The message of the Genesis story can be that God is with us, walking with us not just in the idyllic garden but in the harsh, dusty world of adulthood and responsibility. Eve is called Eve meaning "life," the mother of all living, and together Adam and Eve produce their first child, Cain. In the furor to find negative verses about Eve, her words as she gave birth are ignored:

> Now the man knew his wife Eve, and she conceived and bore Cain, saying, "I have produced a man with the help of the Lord." (Gen. 4:1)

This is the first act recorded after leaving the garden, and it is *Eve*, not Adam, whose comments are noted. Family life begins with her acknowledgment that God is with her. There is no sign of an evil, inferior, sinful woman who ruined the plans of God and made God furious with her, but of a woman recognizing the presence of God in her life. Where is the proud arrogance of wanting to be "like God" that has been read into the apple episode? The scene before us, conveniently ignored by the church fathers, resonates with the confidence of a woman understanding her responsibility as a cocreator with God, and acting on it. God's promise will be made real through this woman Eve—"I will be your God, and you will be my people."

EPILOGUE

Realizing Eve had been used for centuries to argue women's subordination to male rule in a "divine order of creation," Elizabeth Cady Stanton challenged theologians to take another look and free nineteenth-century women from the place supposedly assigned them by an old Jewish story of beginnings:

> The real difficulty in woman's case is that the whole foundation of the Christian religion rests on her [Eve's] temptation and man's fall, hence the necessity of a Redeemer and a plan of salvation. As the chief cause of this dire calamity, women's degradation and subordination were made a necessity. If however, we accept...that the story of the fall is a myth, we can exonerate the snake, emancipate the woman, and reconstruct a more rational religion for the Nineteenth Century, and thus escape all the perplexities of the Jewish mythology as of no more importance than those of the Greek, Persian, and Egyptian.[1]

One man, Karl Barth, took up her challenge, and from *his* perspective, saw *no* problem for women of the *twentieth* century with this "order of creation"!

> This order gives her her proper place, and in pride that it is hers, she may and should assume it as freely as man assumes his...the business of woman, her task and function, is to actualize the fellowship in which man can only precede her, stimulating, leading, and inspiring. How could she do this alone, without the precedence of man? How could she do it for herself and against him? How could she reject or envy his precedence, his task and function, as the one who stimulates, leads and inspires? To wish to replace him in this, or to do it with him, would be to wish not to be a woman...Why should not woman be second in sequence, but only in sequence? What other choice has she, seeing she can be nothing at all apart from this sequence and her place within it? And why should she desire anything else, seeing this function and her share in the common service has its own special honor and greatness, an honor and greatness which man in his place and within the limits of his function cannot have?[2]

But Elizabeth's challenge has not been forgotten, and comes back to us as we enter the twenty-first century. Will women, through Eve, spend another century having to defend their equality, or can we forever put to rest the type of thinking that glorifies woman with "special honor and greatness" so long as she stays in her place in a "divine" order of man first and dominant, woman second and subordinate, in whatever subtle ways this is played out in society?

After nine chapters of detective work tracing Eve's story through Christian history, I offer the following verdict: that not only is there no justification for continuing the argument of women's subordination and inequality, but that it is *contrary* to the radical message of the freedom of the gospel. The evidence speaks for itself:

- The argument for women's subordination is based on an ancient wisdom story of "beginnings," not a rule book eternally defining how men and women should live.[3] If the latter was so, men should still be farmers, and everyone vegetarian (Gen. 3:17–19).

- If we *do* use the Genesis story as a guide, we find *two* stories, one describing man and woman created together as equals, and the other describing woman created *after* man, but with no hint of inferiority. We do *not* find a fall, nor eternal blame laid on Eve. The story can equally be read as a tale of how humans came to be "different" from God and were assigned human tasks in a patriarchal society.

- The Hebrew God *YHWH* resisted God-images, using the unqualified title "I AM WHAT I AM." God as spirit, breath, wind accompanied the traveling Israelites, and not until the monarchical period did male, ruling metaphors appear for God, later dominating as Christianity became a male-led institution within Roman society. But nongendered images of God as Spirit remain in the Bible and church history, reminding us that God is not limited by any gender.

- If the story of Adam and Eve was so crucial, why is it never referred to again in Hebrew scripture? If Jesus reversed the curse of sin on humanity from Adam and Eve, why did Jesus not think to mention this?

- In the life and teachings of Jesus, there is no hint of women's subordination or exclusion. Many of Jesus' closest friends were women, and many stories center on his interest and support of women. To argue superiority of men because Jesus chose *male* disciples ignores the many stories of women followers. What of the seventy sent out at one time—were they all men?

- Jesus attacked the Jewish purity system of inclusions and exclusions, based on heredity, ethnicity, occupation, physical soundness, and sex, which produced a world of sharp boundaries favoring the male elite. He also challenged the Greco-Roman societal system that positioned free, propertied males as heads of household and state over women, children, and slaves. His way was stunningly different, eating with women and "sinners."

- Paul's overarching theme, gleaned from Jesus' teachings, was freedom in Christ from all rules, distinctions and barriers of Jewish and Greco-Roman society—best expressed in the baptismal formula of Galatians 3:28. Even when Paul encouraged women to conform to minor *cultural* conventions so as not to offend, he never compromised their freedom to lead and prophesy, and never suggested "cultural convention" included subordination to men. The few ambivalent comments in Paul's undisputed letters must be read in light of his overwhelming belief in mutuality and equality, rather than extracted from their contexts as "proof texts" for women's submission.

- Paul did not blame Adam for *everyone's* sin, but talked only of the disobedience of the first human. He did not include Eve, nor condemn her in either of two references he makes to her in his letters.

- Women were obviously active in ministry in early Christianity as leaders and deacons, prophesying and praying in public, and "on the road" as apostles.[4] They were not excluded from the general distribution of spiritual gifts.[5] Their gradual silencing in public and subordination to their husbands evolved in the non-Pauline letters, as secular Greco-Roman household codes based on Aristotle's ideas of women as inferior and subordinate became codes for the Christian community as well, accommodating to Roman society. By the latest letters (Timothy and Titus, and 1 Cor. 14:34–36), women's subordination, in direct opposition to the freedom and equality advocated by Jesus and Paul, was justified *scripturally* by Eve's "subordination" under male rule in an "order of creation" (1 Tim. 2:11–15).

- Church fathers by the fourth century had linked this lone condemnation of Eve with Greco-Roman ideas of women's inferiority and subordination, Eve's blame for the "fall," and her "earned" punishment of subordination under man's rule, to create a theology of women's inequality and subordination in an eternal "order of creation."

- When Christianity became the official religion of the Roman Empire, the church adopted Greco-Roman models of male leadership. Women's equality was now interpreted in the "spiritual realm"—heaven—not in earthly society, and male priests represented a male God.

- This theology of women's subordination linked with Eve and an "order of creation" remained dominant into this century, despite many challenges to it over Christian history. Such domination was accompanied by the exclusion of women from leadership and theology and a hatred of women by male celibate church fathers.

- Feminist theologians, both men and women, have challenged this theological exclusion and subordination of women as *contrary* to the message of the gospel, reclaiming the "theology" of a discipleship of equals that described the radical communities of Jesus and Paul.

- Central to feminist theology is women's experience. When the "divinely ordered" superiority of the male species does not fit with life experience, we must investigate more closely where that "divine" statement originated. Women keep on displaying abilities they are not supposed to have! Given the example of three great British queens—Elizabeth I, Victoria, and Elizabeth II— Scottish Presbyterian reformer John Knox's "divine truth" about the "unnaturalness" of women rulers seems a trifle silly!

> It is more than a monster in nature that a woman shall reign and have empire over man...to promote a woman to bear rule, above any realm, nation, or city, is repugnant to nature, contumely to God...the subversion of good order, of all equity and justice...When a woman rules, the blind lead the sighted, the sick the robust, the foolish, mad, and frenetic, the discreet and sober...For their sight in civil regiment is but blindness, their counsel foolishness, and judgment frenzy...For that women reigneth above man, she hath obtained it by treason and conspiracy committed against God...[Men] must study to repress her inordinate pride and tyranny to the uttermost of their power.[6]

My case rests. To be Christian *is* to be feminist, and uphold the equality of men and women! As I said in the first chapter, feminism recovers the "gospel" message of Jesus, and if contemporary Christianity still calls itself the Way of Jesus Christ, feminism is not in opposition to it, but *central* to its message. A feminist is "someone who struggles for the full development and equality of both men and women, and accepts no particular barriers on the basis of sexual identity." Sounds like Galatians 3:28 to me! A feminist is "a person who seeks the full humanity of women, so that they be a contributing part of every conversation." Sounds like Galatians 3:28 to me! Feminism is not *against* anyone but *for* everyone, reaffirming the early baptismal promise to reject systems that disadvantage some by exclusion and deny abundant life to *all.* Those who attack feminism do so for the same reason *Jesus* was attacked in his day— ideas of shared power and radical equality threaten the status quo for those who benefit from a system of some "naturally" above others in a "divine" order.

When we see this incredible movement of "feminists" through history taking seriously the gospel message that all are created equal in the image of God, we will honor and cherish the title "Feminist," which has described such good women and men. "Feminism" is the thread for the disconnected beads of women's history, stringing them together, so Joan of Arc is not just a courageous, eccentric exception and Mother Teresa an aberrant galactic star.

Feminism as a string of beads attests to the glorious continuity of women's desire, not for occasional gratuities beyond the limits chosen for them, but for the right *to choose life,* like their male counterparts. Choice is key to "feminism," as it is to all fair systems and democracies, and also the way of Jesus, who came to offer *abundant* life to *all* who would accept it. Feminism does not advocate one particular choice—career over motherhood, independence over marriage—even though some caricature it thus. Feminism asks that *each* woman choose how to live her life as a participant in the radical way of Jesus.

Choices are rarely either/or, but a consideration of many options and the weighing of this interconnected jumble until some resolution moves us toward greater richness and transformation. I have not chosen *between* career and motherhood, but have chosen both, living abundantly within the possibilities and limits of my situation and the people around me for whom I care. This has meant a great marriage, raising wonderful children in a family I love, pursuing theological studies and several public careers, using my gifts as a volunteer, and now reveling in the circle of life as I enjoy my two grandchildren! When women put down other women for choices different from their own, and when men assume they choose for everyone, I murmur a prayer of gratitude for the rebellious "new Theclas," the women mystics, the suffragists, and the radical feminists, thankful I was not forced to make *their* difficult public choices in order to live my life abundantly; but even more thankful that they so chose, and struggled to maintain the right to choose. Because of them, my daughters can go to college, have a career, vote, raise healthy and justly treated children, or stay single, all the while having great role models of what it means to change the world after the radical example of Jesus.

QUESTIONS FOR REFLECTION
AND DISCUSSION

CHAPTER 1: I'm Not a Feminist But...

1. Do some brainstorming. What words or images come to mind when you hear the word "feminist"?
2. What experiences have you had with feminism or feminists? Would you call yourself a feminist? If yes, why? If no, why not?
3. Do you think it is possible to be a feminist and a Christian?
4. What experiences have you had where you, or someone you know, has been denied an opportunity or excluded from some pursuits because she was a woman?
5. Are there differences between what you think about feminism, and what your sons and daughters (or grandchildren) think about feminism?
6. What influence does the media have on your feelings about feminism?
7. How would you describe a "virtuous" man? How would you describe a "virtuous" woman? What is different, and why do you think there are differences?
8. What have you been taught as a Christian about being angry? Do you think there is a different message for men and women about getting angry?

CHAPTER 2: Ever Since Eve

1. When a father takes his daughter down the aisle to give her to her fiancé, and the mother who raised her sits in the pew, this is a marriage custom left over from a patriarchal society where the daughter belonged to the father until given into her husband's possession. Discuss this custom, and think of other customs we continue that come from patriarchal ideas. Should we be more conscious of the origins of such customs, and what they say about the equality of women, or is it okay to simply reinterpret them and leave them in place?
2. What images come to mind when you think of Eve—Old Masters paintings, poems, cartoons? Is she a good woman or a bad woman in these images? What was her "sin"? How is she described in our cultural history?

3. Why, if the story of Adam and Eve, the fall, and the beginning of original sin is so central to Christianity, did Jesus not even mention it, especially since his purpose was said to "reverse" Adam's sin?
4. Can you think of ways the negative link between sexual desire/sexuality and sin made by Augustine and others plays out in church teachings and in our psyche today? What effect has this had on (a) our ideas of sexuality as part of God's good creation, (b) our own personal ideas about sex and sin, and (c) Catholic opposition to contraception?

CHAPTER 3: The Plot Thickens

1. Discuss the story of Abelard and Heloise. What does it tell us about theological ideas of sex, sin, and women at that time? Can we see similar ideas at play today? If so, what do you think about them?
2. What do you think of Luther's interpretation of Eve? Do you think he improved women's lot or not? Are there things that make you comfortable or uncomfortable about Luther's ideas?
3. Why was it so important for the 1930 encyclical and Karl Barth to challenge the women's vote and the women's movement? Do you think they had a valid point?
4. What do you think about the arguments made against contraception in the 1930 encyclical? Why are they made? Do you think disallowing contraception is more important theologically than risk in pregnancy to a mother's life? Why or why not?
5. What do you think of Barth's instructions for a woman to stay submissive in a marriage because of the order of creation, even if the husband is a tyrant? Take a look at the creation stories in Genesis 1 and 2. Do you find an order of creation there to justify Barth's comments? How do you think Barth's ideas address the problem of sexual abuse and violence against women today?
6. What experiences have you had recently with theological arguments similar to the ones made by the encyclical and Barth? What do you think of such arguments?
7. What place has Mary in Christianity? In what ways can she be a role model for women today? What do we know about her abilities as a mother?

CHAPTER 4: Stepping Out of Their Place

1. Esther was a brave woman honored for her protection of Jews in exile. Have you heard her story before? If not, are you surprised it earns a book in the Hebrew Bible and yet is rarely told as an example of a good biblical woman? Why do you think this might be? (Read the story for yourself to see the extent of Esther's efforts to save her people.)

2. How do you react to the death of the unnamed girl, Jephthah's daughter? Why do you think the story is in the Bible? Whom does it favor? What use is it today as a story of women?
3. What period of history described in this chapter do you think was most difficult for women in the church? Why? What strategies for survival and resistance did rebellious women choose in that era? How do you think church authorities were able to maintain women's subordination for so long?
4. What do you think of Agrippa's arguments for the superiority of women? Which of his points are useful for feminists today? Why do you think his writings were ignored or lost?
5. Do you hear a recurring theme of resistance and rebellion in women through history? What do they use as their authority, and where do they get their "power"? Which woman or group of women most speaks to you of all the ones in this chapter? Why?

CHAPTER 5: A Feeling Finds a Name

1. What images do you have of the Victorian Era, and what ideas about women have you encountered that maintain the values of that era? What do you think was good/bad about the role of women in a Victorian household? Can you see what scriptural passages might have been used to maintain women's place?
2. What surprised you about Florence Nightingale? Did you have a different image of her? How do you think she was able to negotiate such a position of power, given her circumstances as a woman in genteel Victorian society?
3. What was so different between women advocating temperance, freedom of slaves, and justice for prostitutes, and women advocating for their own right to vote? What biblical arguments were made against the women's movement? What biblical arguments were made for the women's vote and women's equality? What do you think of these arguments?
4. Elizabeth Cady Stanton blamed the Bible for women's low self-esteem and subordination hindering the move toward their equality. What do you think of her arguments? Do you think the women's movement was right or wrong in disassociating itself from *The Women's Bible?*
5. What do you think of Elizabeth's description of Adam and Eve in the garden? Despite her tongue-in-cheek style, is there something new for you to consider in her interpretation of the Genesis story?

CHAPTER 6: In Our Own Voices

1. Discuss your memories of growing up, and how the boy–girl distinctions played out. What were your expectations of marriage and parenting? What

were the expectations for women in terms of career and marriage? What Bible arguments were made about women's and men's roles? How did you feel about them? Do you have different feelings looking back now?

2. How have you experienced any of the women's movements described? Describe your feelings about the feminist movement originating in the '60s, and where, if anywhere, you fit on the continuum of feminisms. What new thoughts have you had about feminism reading this chapter? How do you feel about radical feminism? Why?

3. Valerie Saiving described her discomfort when male colleagues began to describe God, humanity, salvation, and sin, and it did not fit her experiences as a woman. Share with the group any similar experiences you have had—as a woman or someone from a different race or class—where God, humanity, salvation and sin have been described in a way that did not fit your experience. What did you do or think about it?

4. Can you think of passages in the Bible that give commands or describe the world in ways that don't "fit" your experience of life? Think about Valerie Saiving's challenge, and ask if the discrepancy might be because things are being described from a perspective different from yours. How much do differences between the biblical context of the passage and today's context matter? Can you see another way to read the passage so it is helpful to your experience of life today?

5. Share some of your favorite Bible stories, telling them in words and symbols from your unique perspective and experience. Think about which points you would emphasize, and how that differs from the original way the story was told, and why. (Remember, many of the stories in the Bible were first handed down orally, and told with respect to the situation and needs of the listeners).

CHAPTER 7: Introducing Feminist Theology

1. Why do you think women in the Catholic Church were so ready to accept the rules made for them about a woman's role, as Mary Daly suggests? What do you think should happen in a church community so women can be involved in deciding the way their lives are described? Who has the "authority" to do this?

2. Given the different ways women scholars look at the texts of scripture for their meaning, which most appeals to you and why? If this is a change from what you thought before, what are the benefits of this new way of thinking? What kept you from thinking this way before? What are the hardest things to get used to in a "critical" approach to what the Bible says?

3. Discuss together biblical quotations or stories that have been used to exclude you from doing something you would like to do. Use some of the

ideas of feminist theology to go back to those stories and look for clues in the story's setting that allow a different reading. Be creative! Let your imagination soar! Does this tell you something new about God?

4. Women from different countries, contexts, and religious traditions have different issues of oppression and different paths to liberation. I have mentioned some in this chapter. From your experiences of a foreign culture, or a different cultural group in this country, discuss what might be priority issues for their feminist theologians, and see if you can think of liberating Bible concepts that might help address their situation.

5. What arguments do you think can be used for and against women's ordination? Why do you think it has succeeded in some churches and not others? Discuss your experiences of women ministers.

CHAPTER 8: "I Am Who I Am"

1. Describe your image of God. Did you find you were using metaphors? Were they male metaphors, or do you imagine God in female and nonpersonal metaphors as well? Do you think it matters whether God is described as male or female? Why?

2. Think of as many metaphors as you can that are used for God in the Bible. Examine each one, and identify exactly what characteristics of the metaphor reflect "God-ness." Take the metaphors "father," "lord," and "king," and discuss how some aspects of those roles do *not* describe your experience of God. How useful or universal, then, are these metaphors for God?

3. Which cluster of metaphors best describe God for you—the monarchical model or the spirit model? Why? Does the image of the great "I Am" expand your image of God?

4. How do you feel about calling God "Sophia"? Why?

5. How would you argue that God is not male to a group of women who have not been exposed to such a thought? What do you think would be the biggest hurdle to convincing them?

6. When God is described as Father, and human fathers assume authority as God's representatives in a family, what do you see as potential problems or advantages? Discuss examples you have come across to illustrate your concerns.

CHAPTER 9: Reclaiming Eve—and the Rest of Us

1. How do you react to the decision of the Southern Baptist Convention to require wives to submit willingly to the servant leadership of their husbands? What are the advantages/dangers? Why do you think women in the Southern Baptist Convention accept this stance?

2. Do you think Paul successfully "balanced" his arguments between women's freedom in Christ and the need to conform in certain cultural ways so as

not to offend? Can you think of similar circumstances today where women are asked to conform to subordinate roles for social or cultural reasons, even though they are theoretically equal?

3. What do you consider Christian "family values"? On what authority do you base this? Do you think "family values" change with time and culture, or are they eternal?

4. How would you respond to someone who argues against women taking a public part in worship on the basis of 1 Timothy 2:8–15?

5. What new insights appeal to you in this discussion of Adam and Eve and the fall? What new views do you have of Eve? Is this important to you or not? What advantages do you see, if any, in reclaiming Eve?

6. What do you think of the argument made by some people today that the biblical creation story should be taught in schools along with evolution? What conclusions do you think would be drawn for modern society from the story of Adam and Eve? Do you think there is a connection between wanting to teach the creation story in schools and the subordination of women?

APPENDIX
Women's Movements around the World

In this book, for reasons of space, I have focused mainly on the history of contemporary women's movements in *America*, painfully aware that this is just a fraction of the story of women's resistance, and perhaps not even the finest story. Such movements have occurred across the world, changing the lives of women in many instances, and influencing each other as they reach hands across the waters. They have worked for change in women's education, health care, literacy, political power, right to vote, right to a job and benefits, access to childcare, protection against sexual abuse and discrimination, right to control one's reproductive powers, and the right of access to God. The movements have taken different forms, depending on the pressing "problems" in each unique context. I will mention just a few of these movements to show the breadth of sisterhood, the strong women who promote the cause, and the diversity of issues that affect women—and their men.[1]

The women's movement in Britain goes back to the 1700s with Mary Wollstonecraft's 1792 book *A Vindication of the Rights of Women*, the first major writing arguing for increased educational opportunities for women and political equality with men. By the mid-1800s, militant groups were forming to win the vote and further the cause of women. Emily Davies (1830–1921) sought higher education for women, founding the London Schoolmistresses' Association, and opening a women's college in 1869 with five students. She also started the Northumberland and Durham branch of the Society for Promoting the Employment of Women and was editor of the English Woman's Journal. She helped organize the first petition of women's suffrage presented to John Stuart Mill in 1866. Mill, influenced by his friend Harriet Taylor, wrote his classic 1869 document of women's rights, *The Subjection of Women*, and, as Liberal MP for Westminster, introduced the first motion in Britain in 1867 to enfranchise women, arguing that taxpayers should have representation. The motion was defeated, although unmarried taxpayers could vote in local elections. Emmeline Pankhurst (1858–1928) attended her first suffrage meeting at fourteen. Together with her husband, she formed the Women's Franchise League in their London home in 1889. In 1903, assisted by her daughters and other women, the widowed Emmeline founded the Women's Social and Political Union. As their campaign escalated, she was imprisoned more than a dozen times and went on hunger strikes that damaged her health. When World War I broke out, she and her friends concentrated on war work, and, somewhat in recognition of that, voting rights were granted to women over thirty, and extended to all women over twenty-one by 1928. This impetus rubbed off on the colonies. New Zealand, greatly influenced by John Stuart Mill, was the first country in the world to grant women a vote in 1893, and Australia the second in 1902.

For some women, the road to women's suffrage ended in death. Emily Wilding Davison (1872–1913), a teacher with degrees from Oxford and London University, joined the Women's Social and Political Union in 1906. She was a "radical," and not all her actions were sanctioned by the WSPU. During a 1912 hunger strike at Holloway Prison, she tried to kill herself by leaping over a stairrail. In June 1913, she attended the Derby at Epsom with a WSPU flag sewn into her coat, planning to disrupt the race by waving the flag in front of the horses. Instead, she leapt onto the course in front of the King's horse and was run down, dying a few days later. Her death did not achieve the vote, but attracted public attention and sympathy. Two thousand uniformed suffragists escorted her coffin to St. George's Church, Bloomsbury, where Emmeline Pankhurst, pledging to "carry on our Holy War for the emancipation of our sex," was arrested.

In Argentina, women's groups formed soon after independence from Spain in 1816. Later, women found an ally in Dictator Juan Péron's second wife, Eva (Evita), who championed women's rights and advocated women's suffrage, leading to the women's vote in 1947. Eva also persuaded her husband to name thirty women to the legislature, begin divorce reform, and relax governmental opposition to contraception. After his death, feminist groups were forced underground, reappearing when he returned to power in 1973 with third wife Isabel. She became president on his death, the first woman president of a South American nation, but was ousted by a military coup that imposed terror through the country, with many activists "disappearing." The first public opposition to this terror was by women, *Madres de Plaza de Mayo,* who staged weekly vigils in the main square of Buenos Aires wearing white head scarves and carrying banners of their "missing children." Their courage inspired women all over Argentina, and, even after the regime ended in 1983, they continued to seek the fate of their children. This group have since helped with genetic testing of children born to "missing" pregnant women. A National Women's Council was established in 1992 for projects on women's rights and a Cabinet of Women Advisors named to the President in 1993.

In Bangladesh, one of the world's most crowded and impoverished nations, the birth of a daughter is a disappointment. However, women's groups focusing on women's education emerged in the mid-1940s amongst upper-class women. When Bangladesh split from Pakistan in 1971, these groups took up women's equality and antidiscrimination, since war had seen many women tortured, raped, and widowed. Since the 1980s, governmental and private groups have opposed the dowry practice, enforced laws against rape and acid throwing, created battered women shelters, increased education opportunities, opened up employment for women, and promoted family planning. Since women are subordinate to men in this society, violence is a major problem. Brides are killed for insufficient dowries and acid-throwing practiced as punishment for a woman rejecting or offending a man. Existing laws are rarely enforced, and religious courts holding sway in villages punish women found guilty of adultery with flogging or stoning to death.

When Islam was established as Bangladesh's state religion in 1988, many women feared repression, and a volatile women's protest movement emerged. Feminist author Taslima Nasreen challenged the rise of Muslim fundamentalism, and her death has been called for. A campaign of terror in which over a thousand girls' schools were burned or vandalized, and women attacked for not following strict Islamic laws about dress and behavior, followed. Nasreen's charge was violating a penal code against insulting another's religious beliefs. She fled to Sweden in 1994. On the other end of power, two women have been prime ministers of Bangladesh, Khaleda Zia (1991–96) and Hsina Wazed (1996–), both assuming control in the absence of a male heir in their ruling families.

The Egyptian feminist movement is the oldest in the Arab world, dating to the 1920s, when Britain declared Egypt independent. Upper-class women founded the Feminist Union, emphasizing social and economic reform for women. Shortly after Word War II similar organizations fought for women's political rights, storming Parliament in 1951 to protest women's exclusion. In 1954 women staged a hunger strike because they were not included in drafting the new constitution. Women received the right to vote and run for office in 1956, with the proviso they petition the government to register to vote. This did not stop middle-class women, but did deter many uneducated women. Nasser's government of 1952 banned political organizations, both Islamic fundamentalist groups and women's groups, but his other policies have benefited women. By 1970, the scene for women tightened, and gender equality was allowed only where it did not contradict Islamic Law. Women were caught between government and Islamic fundamentalist conflict. However, one of the most powerful women in Egypt, President Sadat's wife, Jehan Sadat, persuaded her husband in 1979 to reserve a number of seats for women in Parliament and on local councils. Today, while there are a growing number of women's groups calling for reform from Islamic fundamentalist practices regarding women, there is also an "Islamic feminist" organization supporting reforms of basic education, health, and welfare services provided by fundamentalism when the government would not. These Islamic feminists encourage Egyptian women to stay home, wear traditional Muslim head covering, and advocate a complete segregation of the sexes in society.

Women's groups appeared in Israel by the early 1900s with the "kibbutz," a commune where everyone labored equally. At first, women were assigned traditional female roles and excluded from decision-making, but activists protested in 1911, believing equality with men could happen if women were trained at the same jobs. To free themselves from childcare for training, women established collectives in the "kibbutz," rotating responsibility for the children. Women took part in the 1973 Yom Kippur War, further changing attitudes toward women's roles and rights. The feminist movement gained considerable influence, with its first national conference in 1978.

In Russia, the women's movement was unlike most others. The right to vote, bitterly fought for in England and America, was handed to Russian women after the 1918 Revolution, and the right to divorce and abortions in 1922. The earliest women's organizations were "zhenotdels," women's sections, established by the Communist Party in 1918 to spread party publicity and to encourage women to join the work force and participate in the labor movement. Women lost many rights under Stalin but received some back under Khrushchev. By the mid- '60s, women accounted for over half the labor force while still carrying out traditional roles of wives and mothers. In the late '70s, an independent women's group, "Maria," emerged in Leningrad, openly protesting the exploitation and degradation of women and exposing substandard hospital conditions where abortions were performed. Its members were deported or sent to prison. Under Gorbachev, the women's councils of the 1920s were reestablished but lacked political influence, and therefore enthusiasm, among participants. Since the 1990s, new women's groups have emerged focusing on environmental and social issues, while others address feminist causes such as equal rights for women, unemployment, and women's representation in government.

Notes

Chapter 1   I'm Not a Feminist But . . .

[1]Noah Webster, *Webster's New Universal Unabridged Dictionary*, deluxe second edition, revised by Jean L. McKechnie (New York: Simon & Schuster, 1983), p. 674.

[2]Lisa Tuttle, *Encyclopedia of Feminism* (New York: Facts on File Publications, 1986), p. 7.

[3]Ibid., p. 153.

[4]Throughout this book, I will use the term Hebrew Bible instead of Old Testament.

Chapter 2   Ever Since Eve

[1]Quoted in John P. Bradley, Leo F. Daniels, and Thomas C. Jones, *The International Dictionary of Thoughts* (Chicago: J. G. Ferguson, 1969), p. 776.

[2]I am indebted to Rosemary Radford Ruether's entry "Patriarchy," in Letty M. Russell & J. Shannon Clarkson, eds. *Dictionary of Feminist Theologies* (Louisville: Westminster John Knox Press, 1996), pp. 205–206, for a concise description of patriarchy.

[3]Karen Jo Torjesen, *When Women Were Priests: Women's Leadership in the Early Church and the Scandal of their Subordination in the Rise of Christianity* (San Francisco: HarperSanFrancisco, 1993) p. 63.

[4]I will use B.C.E. (before common era) instead of B.C. (before Christ), and C.E. (common era) instead of A.D. (after Christ).

[5]Elizabeth Clark and Herbert Richardson, eds., *Women and Religion: A Feminist Sourcebook of Christian Thought* (San Francisco: Harper & Row, 1977), p. 122.

[6]Ibid., p. 92.

[7]Uta Ranke-Heinemann, *Eunuchs for the Kingdom of Heaven: Women, Sexuality, and the Catholic Church* (New York: Doubleday, 1990), p. 11.

[8]Clark and Richardson, *Women and Religion*, pp. 59–60.

[9]Eleventh-century Jewish kabbalistic text *Alphabet of Ben Sira*, quoted in *Sacred Sexuality*, A. T. Mann & Jane Lyle (Dorset: Elements Books, 1995) p. 136.

[10]Muslim tradition said, "Accursed the man who maketh woman heaven and himself earth." Catholic Fathers said any sexual position other than the male-superior sexual position—the missionary position—was sinful. Barbara G. Walker, *The Women's Encyclopedia of Myths and Secrets* (San Francisco: HarperSanFrancisco, 1983), p. 541.

[11]Mann and Lyle, *Sacred Sexuality*, p. 136.

[12]The NRSV refers to "Lilith" in Isaiah 34:14, instead of its previous translation "Night Hag."

[13]Barbara G. Walker, *The Women's Encyclopedia of Myths and Secrets*, p. 542.

[14]The actual fruit described was probably not an apple, but I use it since it is the association most people have, thanks to our artists and poets!

[15]Elaine Pagels, *Adam, Eve and the Serpent* (New York: Vintage Books, 1988), pp. 12–14.

[16]Ibid., p. 27. There is a parallel story in a Mesopotamian creation myth that talks of the first man gaining "knowledge" as sexual knowledge, and entering sexual maturity.

[17]Ibid., p. 83.

[18]Ibid., p. 86.

[19]Ibid., p. 89.

[20]Jerome, *Adversus Jovinian*, quoted in ibid., p. 94.

[21]Ranke-Heinemann, *Eunuchs for the Kingdom of Heaven*, p. 90. Toward the end of his life, Augustine agreed sexual pleasure may have existed also in Paradise, but without lust, or under the control of man's will.

[22]Augustine, *City of God*, quoted in ibid., p. 185.

[23]Elaine Pagels, *Adam, Eve and the Serpent*, p. 114.

[24]Tertullian, "On the Apparel of Women," quoted in John A. Phillips, *Eve, the History of an Idea* (San Francisco: Harper & Row, 1984), p. 76.

[25]Augustine, *De genesi as litteram*, quoted in Ranke-Heinemann, p. 88.
[26]Ranke-Heinemann, *Eunuchs for the Kingdom of Heaven*, pp. 105–112.
[27]Ibid., p. 121.
[28]Ibid., p. 154.

Chapter 3   The Plot Thickens

[1]Alison Weber, *Theresa of Avila and the Rhetoric of Feminity* (Princeton, N.J.: Princeton University Press, 1990), p. 20. As the *Malleus Malleficarum* (The Hammer of Witches) pointed out: "femina" is derived from "fe" and "minus," which means lacking in faith.
[2]Peter Abelard, "Historia Calamitatum," in *The Letters of Abelard and Heloise*, trans. Betty Radice (London: Penguin, 1974), pp. 67–68.
[3]Ibid., p. 74.
[4]Ibid., p. 65.
[5]Ibid., p. 113.
[6]Ibid., p. 133.
[7]Ibid., pp. 27–28.
[8]*Malleus Malleficarum*, quoted in Elizabeth Clark and Herbert Richardson, *Women and Religion, a Feminist Sourcebook of Christian Thought* (San Francisco: Harper & Row, 1977), p. 122.
[9]Ibid., pp. 126–27.
[10]Ibid., p. 129.
[11]Ibid., p. 130.
[12]Uta Ranke-Heinemann, *Eunuchs for the Kingdom of Heaven: Women, Sexuality and the Catholic Church* (New York: Doubleday, 1990), p. 238–39.
[13]Luther on Genesis 2:18, quoted in Clark and Richardson, *Women and Religion*, p. 145.
[14]Luther, "Lectures on Genesis," quoted in *Eve, the Story of an Idea*, by J. A. Phillips (San Francisco: Harper & Row, 1984), p. 58.
[15]Luther on Genesis 2:18, quoted in Clark and Richardson, *Women and Religion*, p. 144.
[16]Luther on Genesis 2:23, quoted in ibid., p. 147.
[17]Ibid., p. 148.
[18]Luther on Genesis 3:20, quoted in ibid., p. 148.
[19]Jane Dempsey Douglass, *Women, Freedom and Calvin* (Philadelphia: The Westminster Press, 1985), pp. 78–82.
[20]In quoting women, I have gone against convention, and used *first* names since in many instances this is the only name married women have retained since birth.
[21]Elizabeth Cady Stanton, *The Women's Bible* (Seattle: Coalition Task Force on Women and Religion, 1974), pp. 26–27.
[22]For further discussion, see Joel Schwartz, *The Sexual Politics of Jean Jacques Rousseau* (Chicago: University of Chicago Press, 1984).
[23]Pius XI, *Casti Connubii*, quoted in Clark and Richardson, *Women and Religion*, p. 230.
[24]Ibid., p. 231. Uta Ranke-Heinemann examines conflicting messages about the rhythm method at this time. It was ruled as "impoverishing conjugal love" in 1937, but "enriching it" in 1981. Uta Ranke-Heinemann, p. 294.
[25]Pius XI, *Casti Connubii*, quoted in Clark and Richardson, *Women and Religion*, p. 231.
[26]Ibid., p. 232.
[27]Genesis 3:16. Ranke-Heinemann, *Eunuchs for the Kingdom of Heaven*, p. 296.
[28]Pius XI, *Casti Connubii*, quoted in Clark and Richardson, *Women and Religion*, p. 235.
[29]Karl Barth, "The Doctrine of Creation," quoted in ibid., p. 253.
[30]Ibid., p. 254.
[31]Ibid., p. 255.
[32]Ibid., p. 255–56.
[33]Ibid., p. 257.
[34]Ibid.
[35]Jaroslav Pelikan, *Mary through the Centuries*, quoted in "The Mystery of Mary," Robert Sullivan, *Life* (December 1966), pp. 45–60.
[36]Ibid., p. 45.
[37]Ibid., p. 46.
[38]Justin Martyr, "Dialogue with Trypho," quoted in J. A. Phillips, *Eve, the Story of an Idea*, p. 133.

[39] Jerome claimed it was "godless, apocryphal day-dreaming" to say they were Joseph's children by a first marriage, since only a virginal Joseph would be suitable for a virginal Mary. Ranke-Heinemann, *Eunuchs for the Kingdom of Heaven*, p. 31.

[40]Ibid., p. 342.

[41]Robert Sullivan, "The Mystery of Mary," *Life* (December 1966), p. 54.

Chapter 4   Stepping Out of Their Place

[1]Nuttall, Fisher, and Dixon, *The Female Instructor: or The Young Woman's Companion: being a guide to all the accomplishments which adorn the female character* (Liverpool: Nuttall, Fisher, and Dixon, 1815), pp. 182–83.

[2]*Acts of Paul and Thecla* is part of a second-century writing about Paul's achievements as an apostle. It was circulated in the early centuries of the church, but not selected for the collection of writings that became the New Testament in the late fourth century.

[3]*Acts of Paul and Thecla*, quoted in Elaine Pagels, *Adam, Eve, and the Serpent* (New York: Vintage Books, 1988), p. 19.

[4]Ibid., p. 19.

[5]Daniel Bornstein and Roberto Rusconi, eds., *Women and Religion in Medieval and Renaissance Italy* (Chicago: University of Chicago Press, 1996), p. 246.

[6]E. M. Wilmot-Buxton, *The Story of Jeanne d'Arc* (London: George G. Harrap & Co, 1914, 1930), p. 162.

[7]Alison Weber, *Theresa of Avila and the Rhetoric of Feminity* (Princeton, N. J.: Princeton University Press, 1990), p. 32.

[8]Ibid.

[9]Ibid., p. 36.

[10]Ibid., p. 41.

[11]Ibid., p. 18.

[12]Ibid., p. 36, footnote.

[13]Castiglione, *The Courtier*, quoted in Margaret King, *Women and the Renaissance* (Chicago: University of Chicago Press, 1991), p. 164.

[14]Henricus Cornelius Agrippa, *Declamation on the Nobility and Preeminence of the Female Sex*, trans. & ed. Albert Rabil (Chicago: University of Chicago Press, 1996).

[15]Ibid., p. 47.

[16]Ibid., pp. 22–23.

[17]Albert Rabil's summary of Agrippa's argument in ibid., p. 15. The student of Aristotle will recognize these arguments as a rebuttal of Aristotle's claims for the superiority of the male!

[18]Ibid., p. 95.

[19]Ibid.

[20]Ibid., p. 96. The texts Agrippa is citing are Genesis 3:16; 1 Peter 3:1; Colossians 3:18; and Ephesians 5:22.

[21]Ibid.

[22]Quoted in William Wilson, *Heroines of the Household* (London: James Hogg & Sons, 1864), p. 58.

Chapter 5   A Feeling Finds a Name

[1]Anthony Trollope, *Barchester Towers*, quoted in Katharine Moore, *Victorian Wives* (London: Allison and Busby, 1985), p. xiii.

[2]Cecil Woodham-Smith, *Florence Nightingale 1820–1910* (London: The Reprint Society, 1950), p. 71.

[3]Katharine Moore, *Victorian Wives*, p. xvii.

[4]Bram Dijkstra, *Idols of Perversity: Fantasies of Feminine Evil in Fin-de-Siecle Culture* (New York: Oxford University Press, 1986), p. 20.

[5]Katharine Moore, *Victorian Wives*, p. 205.

[6]Bram Dijkstra, *Idols of Perversity*, p. 11.

[7]Betty Friedan, *The Feminine Mystique* (New York: Dell, 1963), p. 75.

[8]Bram Dijkstra, *Idols of Perversity*, p. 26.

[9]Cecil Woodham-Smith, *Florence Nightingale 1820–1910*, p. 48.

[10]Ibid., p. 60.

[11]Ibid., p. 67.

[12]Ibid., p. 72.

[13]Lisa Tuttle, *Encyclopedia of Feminism* (New York: Facts on File Publications, 1986), pp. 10–11.

[14]Bram Dijkstra, *Idols of Perversity,* p. 11.

[15]*The Advocate,* quoted in *"You Have Stept Out of Your Place": A History of Women and Religion in America,* Susan Hill Lindley (Louisville: Westminster John Knox Press, 1996), p. 95.

[16]Ibid., p. 101.

[17]Bordin,*Women and Temperance,* quoted in ibid., p. 102.

[18]Ibid., p.116.

[19]*Advocate,* quoted in ibid., p. 96.

[20]Ibid., p. 108.

[21]Elizabeth Clark and Herbert Richardson,*Women and Religion: A Feminist Sourcebook of Christian Thought* (San Francisco: Harper & Row, 1977), p. 210.

[22]Susan Hill Lindley, *"You Have Stept Out of Your Place,"* p. 109.

[23]Clark and Richardson, *Women and Religion,* p. 211.

[24]Elizabeth Cady Stanton, *The Women's Bible* (Seattle: Coalition Task Force on Women and Religion), p. vi.

[25]Lisa Tuttle, *Encyclopedia of Feminism,* p. 369.

[26]Betty Friedan, *The Feminine Mystique,* p. 77.

[27]Ibid., p. 82.

[28]Ibid., p. 83.

[29]Lisa Tuttle, *Encyclopedia of Feminism,* p. 328.

[30]Jeanne Stevenson-Moessner, "Elizabeth Cady Stanton, Reformer to Revolutionary: A Theological Trajectory," *JAAR* 62:3 (1994), p. 677.

[31]Ibid., p. 680.

[32]Susan Hill Lindley, *"You Have Stept Out of Your Place,"* p. 290.

[33]Elizabeth Cady Stanton, *The Women's Bible,* p. vi.

[34]Clark and Richardson, *Women and Religion,* p. 219.

[35]Ibid., p. 125.

[36]Ibid., p. 7.

[37]Ibid., p. 15.

[38]Ibid., pp. 26–27.

[39]Ibid., p. 11.

[40]Ibid., p. 291.

[41]Ibid., pp. 216–17.

[42]Lisa Tuttle, *Encyclopedia of Feminism,* p. 312.

Chapter 6   In Our Own Voices

[1]"The Woman Question,"*The Catholic World* (1869), quoted in Mary Bader Papa, *Christian Feminism: Completing the Subtotal Woman* (Chicago: Fides/Claretian, 1981), p. 29.

[2]Diane Bell and Renate Klein, eds. *Radically Speaking: Feminism Reclaimed* (North Melbourne: Spinifex Press Pty., 1996), p. 35.

[3]Cover quotation, Betty Friedan, *The Feminine Mystique* (New York: Dell, 1963).

[4]Ibid., p. 12.

[5]Ibid., p. 133.

[6]Ibid.

[7]Ibid., p. 53.

[8]Brett Harvey, *The Fifties: a Women's Oral History* (New York: HarperPerennial, 1993), p. 73.

[9]Betty Friedan,*The Feminine Mystique,* p. 56.

[10]Brett Harvey, *The Fifties: a Women's Oral History,* p. 49.

[11]Ibid., p. 89.

[12]Lillian B. Rubin,*Women of a Certain Age: the Midlife Search for Self* (New York: Harper & Row, 1979), p. 1.

[13]Mary Jo Meadow, and Carole A. Rayburn, eds. *A Time to Weep, a Time to Sing: Faith Journeys of Women Scholars of Religion* (Minneapolis: Winston Press, 1985), p. 84.

[14]Ibid., p. 122.

[15]bell hooks, *Feminist Theory: From Margin To Center* (Boston: South End Press, 1984), p. 18.

[16]Bell and Klein, *Radically Speaking: Feminism Reclaimed*, p. 18.

[17]Rene Denfield, *The New Victorians: A Young Woman's Challenge to the Old Feminist Order* (New York: Warner Books, 1995), p. 2.

[18]Susan Faludi, *Backlash: The Undeclared War Against American Women* (New York: Crown, 1991).

[19]Naomi Wolf, *The Beauty Myth: How Images of Beauty Are Used against Women* (New York: Doubleday, 1992). Her second book, *Fire with Fire: The New Female Power and How it Will Change the Twenty-First Century* (1993), moved to a more empowering feminism where women find their own voices in a positive way.

[20]Katie Roiphe, *The Morning After: Sex, Fear and Feminism* (Boston: Little Brown, 1993); Rene Denfield, *The New Victorians: a Young Woman's Challenge to the Old Feminist Order;* Daphne Patai, and Noretta Koertge, *Professing Feminism* (New York: HarperCollins, 1994); Christina Hoff Sommers, *Who Stole Feminism: How Women Have Betrayed Women* (New York: Simon and Schuster, 1994).

[21]Bell and Klein, *Radically Speaking: Feminism Reclaimed,* p. xxv.

[22]Susan Faludi, *Backlash: The Undeclared War Against American Women,* p. xxiii.

[23]Valerie Saiving, "The Human Situation: A Feminine View," in Carol P. Christ and Judith Plaskow, eds. *Womanspirit Rising: A Feminist Reader in Religion* (New York: Harper & Row, 1979), p. 25.

[24]Ibid., p. 26

Chapter 7   Introducing Feminist Theology

[1]David M. Gunn and Danna Nolan Fewell, *Narrative in the Hebrew Bible* (Oxford: Oxford University Press, 1993), p. 189.

[2]Marcus J. Borg, *The God We Never Knew: Beyond Dogmatic Religion to a More Authentic Contemporary Faith* (San Francisco: HarperSanFrancisco, 1997).

[3]Mary Daly, *The Church and the Second Sex* (New York: Harper & Row, 1968).

[4]Mary Bader Papa, *Christian Feminism* (Chicago: Fides/Claretan, 1981), p. xi.

[5]Simone de Beauvoir, *The Second Sex,* trans. H. M. Parshley (New York: Alfred A. Knopf, 1971).

[6]Father Daniel and Father Oliver, *Woman is the Glory of Man* (Westminster, Md.: The Newman Press, 1966).

[7]Mary Daly, *The Church and the Second Sex,* p. 122.

[8]From a 1958 marriage manual written by a priest. Quoted in ibid., p. 134.

[9]Mary Daly, *Beyond God the Father* (Boston: Beacon Press, 1973).

[10]Ibid., p. 2.

[11]Many scholars agree with Mary Daly that this is the meaning of the creation story, and that a fall into sin is not actually found in the Genesis story.

[12]Rosemary Radford Ruether, *New Woman, New Earth: Sexist Ideologies & Human Liberation* (New York: The Seabury Press, 1975); *Religion and Sexism: Images of Woman in the Jewish and Christian Traditions* (New York: Simon & Schuster, 1974).

[13]Elisabeth Schüssler Fiorenza, *Discipleship of Equals: A Critical Feminist Ecclesiology of Liberation* (New York: Crossroads, 1993), p. 3.

[14]Elisabeth Schüssler Fiorenza, *In Memory of Her: A Feminist Theological Reconstruction of Christian Origins* (New York: Crossroads, 1989), p. 29.

Chapter 8   "I Am Who I Am"

[1]I am indebted to Marcus Borg for this summary of God metaphors. See Marcus J. Borg, *The God We Never Knew: Beyond Dogmatic Religion to a More Authentic Contemporary Faith* (San Francisco: HarperSanFrancisco, 1997), p. 58.

[2]If *maleness* was the message, "judge" would need to be omitted, since Deborah was an Israelite judge, prophet, and *woman* (Judges 4). Against the argument she was an "exception," the only one recorded in the Bible, we could ask whether, because women surgeons are under-represented in prestigious surgical societies today, good women surgeons are the exception!

[3]Elohim, occurring 2,500 times, is a different name for God.

[4]*Adonai* is actually the plural form of the word.

[5]Numbers 11:12; Deuteronomy 32:18; Psalms 22:9–10.

[6]Psalms 61:3; also Psalms 48:12; Psalms 122:7; Proverbs 18:10.

[7]Some scholars see Abraham not as a historical person, but as a name for this group of people chosen by their God, who migrated from Mesopotamia to the region bordering the Mediterranean Sea–Palestine. This dating is favored because of correspondences between biblical names and personal names in other texts of that period; because that period was a non-urban period, making Abraham's migration more plausible; and because customs from Abraham's story link with recorded customs of that time.

[8]For this discussion, I am indebted to Barbara Sproul, *Primal Myths: Creating the World* (San Francisco: Harper and Row, 1979), p. 93ff.; Rosemary Radford Ruether, *Gaia and God: An Ecofeminist Theology of Earth Healing* (San Francisco: HarperSanFrancisco, 1992), p. 16ff; Catherine Kellar, *From a Broken Web: Separation, Sexism and Self* (Boston: Beacon Press, 1986), p. 73ff.; Jonathan Z. Smith, ed. *The HarperCollins Dictionary of Religion* (San Francisco: HarperSanFrancisco, 1995), p. 340.

[9]A Judean source (J); a north Israelite source (E); the core of Deuteronomy (D); and P, a source dated somewhere around the sixth-century exile. See Edward L. Greenstein, "Sources of the Pentateuch," in *Harper Bible Dictionary*, Paul J. Achtemeier, gen ed. (San Francisco: HarperSanFrancisco, 1985), p. 985.

[10]Marcus J. Borg, *The God We Never Knew*, p. 61.

[11]Mary Hayter, *The New Eve in Christ* (Grand Rapids: Eerdmans, 1987), p. 34.

[12]This gospel was written by an unknown author much later than the disciple of Jesus, but I will use "John" for the author so as not to complicate the argument with "the writer of John" each time.

[13]Mark 14:36.

[14]John 14:18.

[15]Elisabeth Schüssler Fiorenza's scholarly book *Jesus: Miriam's Child, Sophia's Prophet* (New York: Continuum, 1994) explores the importance of understanding Jesus as the messenger of Divine Sophia as well as Son of the Father.

[16]Ibid., pp. 135–36. Schüssler Fiorenza uses G*d to distract us from thinking God is male, by destabilizing the traditional God image to remind us we need new metaphors.

[17]1 Corinthians 1:23–25; 2:6–8.

[18]Matthew 11:16–20.

Chapter 9   Reclaiming Eve—and the Rest of Us

[1]Rosemary Haughton, *The Recreation of Eve* (Springfield: Templegate Publishers, 1985), p. vi.

[2]18th Article, Baptist Faith and Message, quoted in *Rochester Post Bulletin*, Rochester, June 10, 1998.

[3]Ephesians 5:21–33; Colossians 3:18–25; 1 Peter 3:1–12; 1 Timothy 2:11–15; 1 Corinthians 14:34–37.

[4]Such decisions have been made using tools of biblical criticism which I have already discussed, and are held by the majority of biblical scholars. Of course, those who read the Bible in a strictly literal fashion will read these texts as Paul's original work despite the discrepancies.

[5]I am indebted for this discussion to Paul Morris and Deborah Sawyer, eds., *A Walk in the Garden: Biblical, Iconographical and Literary Images of Eden* (Sheffield: Sheffield Academic Press, 1992), p. 105.

[6]Carol Meyers, *Discovering Eve: Ancient Israelite Women in Context* (New York: Oxford University Press, 1988), pp. 74–75. Eve was not blamed in Jewish literature until the second century B.C.E. in Ecclesiasticus (Wisdom of Ben Sirach), which said sin came from woman, but this was probably a minority position, because Adam was still held responsible.

[7]Note on Romans 5:12 in Wayne Meeks, gen. ed., *The HarperCollins Study Bible* (New York: HarperCollins, 1989), p. 2122.

[8]Jeremiah 31:33.

[9]Colossians 3:10.

[10]Galatians 3:28, 1 Corinthians 12:13; Colossians 3:11.

[11]Elisabeth Schüssler Fiorenza, *In Memory of Her: A Feminist Theological Reconstruction of Christian Origins* (New York: Crossroads, 1989), pp. 255–56.

[12]Philo, *Hypothetica*, quoted in ibid., p. 257.

[13]Josephus, *Against Apion*, quoted in ibid., p. 258. It is also worth remembering that a free Jewish male in his morning prayers thanked God he was not a Gentile, a slave, or a woman, the three major divisions in Jewish society at the time.

[14]1 Corinthians 10:23–24, 32.

[15]1 Corinthians 10:33.

[16]Elisabeth Schüssler Fiorenza, *In Memory of Her*, pp. 227–30.

[17]The only other reference to Eve in the genuine letters of Paul uses her as an example of an innocent soul being deceived (seduced) by false teachers (the serpent), thus a warning to the Corinthians about their false teachers (2 Corinthians 11:1–3). This will be used later by church fathers to argue Eve was weak, gullible, sexually promiscuous, and thus deceived, but there is nothing here to support that. To read it thus, we would also have to argue the inferiority of many biblical heroes who were also deceived–Isaac by his son Esau, Samson by Delilah, etc.

[18]Paul is arguing a *cultural* convention, the "headship" pairing linking with the hierarchical pairs of Aristotle's household code. The most obscure verse of all (v. 10) even suggests women's head-covering is a symbol of women's *authority* when prophesying!

[19]Karen Jo Torjesen, *When Women Were Priests: Women's Leadership in the Early Church and the Scandal of Their Subordination in the Rise of Christianity* (San Francisco: HarperSanFrancisco, 1993), p. 137.

[20]Ibid., p. 119.

[21]The "household code" formula appears in Ephesians 5:21–6:9; Colossians 3:18–4:1; 1 Corinthians 14:34–35; Titus 2:3–5; and 1 Peter 3:1–6; scholars place the 1 Corinthians 14:34–35 insert with these later non-Pauline letters.

[22]Dennis Ronald MacDonald, *The Legend and the Apostle* (Philadelphia: Westminster Press, 1983), p. 54.

[23]Ephesians 5:21; cf. 1 Corinthians 7:1–16; Colossians 3:18–25.

[24]The players are "Paul" and "Timothy," but biblical scholars date this writing long after Paul. The literary genre of a conversation between two historical church leaders is used to transmit the church's position.

[25]1 Peter 3:3–5.

[26]1 Timothy 5:11–14; 6:1–2.

[27]This also makes sense of the long discussion of the proper behavior for widows in 1 Timothy 5.

[28]See Karen Jo Torjesen, *When Women Were Priests*, p. 146.

[29]1 Timothy 5:11–16.

[30]Romans 5:12–21.

[31]Henricus Cornelius Agrippa, *Declamation on the Nobility and Preeminence of the Female Sex*, trans. & ed. Albert Rabil (Chicago: University of Chicago Press, 1996), p. 96.

[32]The Canon is the selection of books chosen in the late fourth century as the New Testament.

[33]Creationists argue that the story is a literal account of the creation of the universe; thus they reject any contrary theories proposed by science. They are afraid that anything less takes creation from God's doing. This, of course, goes along with a literal reading of the Bible where every word is taken at face value as a guide for life. I have already shown the many problems with that.

[34]J. Barr, *The Garden of Eden and the Hope of Immortality* (Minneapolis: Fortress, 1993); Walter Brueggemann, *Genesis* (Altanta: John Knox, 1982); Westermann, *Genesis 1–11: A Commentary* (Minneapolis: Augsburg, 1984); Terence E. Fretheim, "Is Genesis 3 a Fall Story?" *Word and World* 14:2 (Spring 1994), pp. 144–53; Marjorie Suchocki, *The End of Evil* (Albany: State University of New York, 1988), etc.

[35]Morris and Sawyer, *A Walk in the Garden*, pp. 248–50.

[36]Phyllis Trible, "Depatriarchalizing the Biblical Interpretation," *JAAR* 41 (1973), pp. 30–48.

[37]Exodus 18:4; Deuteronomy 33:7; Psalms 33:20; 115:9; 124:8.

[38]Proverbs 30:18–19; Matthew 10:16.

[39]The Babylonian creation story *Gilgamesh* also has a story of primal man encountering woman and "falling" into adulthood–life as we know it–from childhood (sexual) innocence. There is also a tree, a snake, and a flood. See Conrad E. L'Heureux, *In and Out of Paradise* (New York: Paulist Press, 1983), pp. 50–51.

[40]Isaiah 65:23–25; Revelation 2:7.

[41]Morris and Sawyer, *A Walk in the Garden*, p. 275.

[42]Carol Meyers, *Discovering Eve*, p. 91.

[43]Ibid., pp. 101–19.

[44]Elizabeth Cady Stanton, *The Women's Bible* (Seattle: Coalition on Women and Religion, 1974), p. 10.

Epilogue

[1]Elizabeth Clark and Herbert Richardson, *Women and Religion: A Feminist Sourcebook of Christian Thought* (San Francisco: Harper & Row, 1977), p. 224.

[2]Ibid., p. 256.

[3]If we want to argue some eternal rules about women's place from Genesis, what do we do about polygamy—more than one wife? By Genesis 4:19, we have Lamech taking two wives, which became a legitimate "family value" blessed by God in Hebrew society, as with Jacob and many other fathers of the faith. How does this fit with arguments for the Adam and Eve story as the eternal model for male-female unions and family values?

[4]Acts 1:14; 9:36; 12:12; 21:9; Romans 16; 1 Corinthians 11–12; Colossians 4:15; Philippians 4:2–3; 2 Thessalonians 1:3–4.

[5]Romans 12:4–8; 1 Corinthians 12.

[6]John Knox, *First Blast of the Trumpet Against the Monstrous Regiment of Women* (1558). Quoted in Margaret King, *Women and the Renaissance* (Chicago: University of Chicago Press, 1991), p. 159

Appendix: Women's Movements around the World

[1]For these summaries I am indebted to Naomi Neft and Ann D. Levine, eds., *Where Women Stand: An International Report on the Status of Women in 140 Countries, 1997-8* (New York: Random House, 1997); and Lisa Tuttle, *Encyclopedia of Feminism* (New York: Facts on File Publications, 1986). For further reading in the variety of feminist theologies emerging around the world, see "Feminist Theologies," Letty M. Russell and J. Shannon Clarkson, eds., *Dictionary of Feminist Theologies* (Louisville: Westminster John Knox Press, 1996); Ofelia Ortega, ed., *Women's Visions: Theological Reflection, Celebration, Action* (Geneva: WCC Publications, 1995); M. A. Oduyoye, *Daughters of Anowa: African Women and Patriarchy* (New York: Orbis Books, 1995); Delores S. Williams, *Sisters in the Wilderness: The Challenge of Womanist God-Talk* (New York: Orbis Books, 1993); M. P. Aquino, *Our Cry for Life: Feminist Theology from Latin America*, trans. Dinah Livingstone (New York: Orbis Books, 1993); Chung Hyun Kyung, *Struggle to be the Sun Again: Introducing Asian Women's Theology* (New York: Orbis Books, 1992); V. Fabella and S. A. L. Park, eds., *We Dare to Dream: Doing Theology as Asian Women* (New York: Orbis Books, 1989); Jacquelyn Grant, *White Women's Christ and Black Women's Jesus* (Atlanta: Scholars Press, 1989); and E. Tamez, ed., *Through Her Eyes: Women's Theology from Latin America* (New York: Orbis, 1989).

Rave Reviews for Val Webb's *In Defense of Doubt* (Chalice Press, 1995)

"...Webb's celebration of freedom to doubt and explore the 'adventure' of faith is an excellent work. It rings with the authenticity and passion of a hard-won freedom and maturity, and this alone is inspiring and will be for many people a great liberation."

Frank D. Rees, *The Beacon Hill Books Review*

"...Val Webb writes with insight and enthusiasm about faith...her call for communities which are more open and less fearful of doubt is a welcome note. This is a fine book which shows how profoundly doubt is integrated into the process of the deepening of faith."

William A. Beardslee, *Creative Transformation*

"...In a time when churches confront a post-modern world, voices such as Webb's encourage the creation of new faith paradigms...Webb has come to consider religious doubts as 'the grains of sand that irritate the oyster until the itching produces a beautiful pearl.'"

Nancy Victorin-Vangerud, *Daughters of Sarah*

"...Val Webb's journey parallels in many ways the great thinkers whose lives she has chronicled in her book. She has taken the next step by extending her hand to the rest of us to follow her into an adventure of exploration."

Cheryl Finnegan, *Focus*

"...*In Defense of Doubt* has a convincing ring. Openness to true dialogue rather than manipulative assertion of propositional beliefs is surely the way ahead. Permission to doubt is a necessary and a very freeing experience, as Webb testifies."

Don Saines, *Uniting Church Studies*

"...Val Webb does a fine job of blending religious and scientific paradigms for understanding God in our time...every congregation ought to secure several copies of this book and circulate them among the membership—but only if those in 'authority' are willing to allow members to doubt, question, and challenge the status quo of beliefs found in most churches."

William McDermet III, *The Disciple*

"[This book] deals with many of the permanent questions of the Christian faith and does this in a way that leads the mind and inspires the heart."

Winfield S. Haycock, *United Methodist Reporter*